International Human Rights

International Human Rights

Dr. Lalita Sharma

RANDOM

RANDOM PUBLICATIONS
NEW DELHI (INDIA)

International Human Rights

ISBN 978-81-89922-37-5

Published in 2014 in India by

RANDOM PUBLICATIONS
4376-A/4B, Gali Murari Lal, Ansari Road
New Delhi-110002
Phone : +9111-43580356, 011-23289044, 011-43142548
e-mail: sales@randompublications.com,
info@randompublications.com, randomexports@gmail.com

Reprinted 2025

Type Setting by : Keystoneprintads, Delhi-110051
Digitally Printed at: Replika Press Pvt. Ltd.

Preface

Human rights are rights inherent to all human beings, whatever our nationality, place of residence, sex, national or ethnic origin, colour, religion, language, or any other status. We are all equally entitled to our human rights without discrimination. These rights are all interrelated, interdependent, and indivisible. Universal human rights are often expressed and guaranteed by law, in the forms of treaties, customary international law, general principles, and other sources of international law. International human rights law lays down obligations of Governments to act in certain ways or to refrain from certain acts, in order to promote and protect human rights and fundamental freedoms of individuals or groups.

The principle of universality of human rights is the cornerstone of international human rights law. This principle, as first emphasized in the Universal Declaration on Human Rights in 1948, has been reiterated in numerous international human rights conventions, declarations, and resolutions. The 1993 Vienna World Conference on Human Rights, for example, noted that it is the duty of States to promote and protect all human rights and fundamental freedoms, regardless of their political, economic, and cultural systems. All States have ratified at least one, and 80% of States have ratified four or more, of the core human rights treaties, reflecting consent of States which creates legal obligations for them and giving concrete expression to universality. Some fundamental human rights norms enjoy universal protection by customary international law across all boundaries and civilizations. Human rights are inalienable. They should not be taken away, except in specific situations and according to due process. For example, the right to liberty may be restricted if a person is found guilty of a crime by a court of law.

All human rights are indivisible, whether they are civil and political rights, such as the right to life, equality before the law and freedom of expression; economic, social and cultural rights, such as the rights to work, social security and education , or collective rights, such as the rights to development and self-determination, are indivisible, interrelated and interdependent. The improvement of one right facilitates advancement of the others. Likewise, the deprivation of one right adversely affects the others.

Non-discrimination is a cross-cutting principle in international human rights law. The principle is present in all the major human rights treaties and provides the central theme of some of international human rights conventions such as the International Convention on the Elimination of All Forms of Racial Discrimination and the Convention on the Elimination of All Forms of Discrimination against Women. The principle applies to everyone in relation to all human rights and freedoms and it prohibits discrimination on the basis of a list of non-exhaustive categories such as sex, race, colour and so on. The principle of non-discrimination is complemented by the principle of equality, as stated in Article 1 of the Universal Declaration of Human Rights: "All human beings are born free and equal in dignity and rights."

Human rights entail both rights and obligations. States assume obligations and duties under international law to respect, to protect and to fulfil human rights. The obligation to respect means that States must refrain from interfering with or curtailing the enjoyment of human rights. The obligation to protect requires States to protect individuals and groups against human rights abuses. The obligation to fulfil means that States must take positive action to facilitate the enjoyment of basic human rights. At the individual level, while we are entitled our human rights, we should also respect the human rights of others.

This book presents the vital multilateral, regional and international human rights instruments that influence the individual and national behaviors. The book would be very useful for decision makers in the wings of the government, law enforcement officials, law professors, and research scholars, national and international NGOs, among others.

I thank all members of my team who have helped in the preparation of the book. My special thanks go to "Venus Books" who have published the book.

– Dr. Lalita Sharma

Contents

1

Introduction

Human rights are almost a form of religion in today's world. They are the great ethical yardstick that is used to measure a government's treatment of its people. A broad consensus has emerged in the twentieth century on rhetoric that frames judgment of nations against an international moral code prescribing certain benefits and treatment for all humans simply because they are human.

Within many nations political debates rage over the denial or abuse of human rights. Even in prosperous, democratic countries like Canada much public discourse is phrased in the rhetoric of rights. Legal documents to protect human rights have proliferated in Canada, culminating in the 1982 entrenchment of the Charter of Rights in the Constitution. Especially since the advent of the Charter, many Canadians have claimed that particular benefits they desire are a matter of human rights and must be provided.

Indeed, the claim that the desired benefit is a human right is often meant to undercut any opposition as unprincipled or even immoral. Lost in much of the discussion is any justification for the high moral grounded occupied by human rights. Most political activists and commentators are content just to look at the United Nations' ever-growing body of human rights agreements as proof that these rights exist universally and therefore have to be respected by everyone. Domestic human rights legislation represents the local implementation of internationally-recognized rights that are universal and inalienable. Unfortunately, human rights are far more complicated phenomena than that. Any inquiry into the origin, nature, and content of human rights reveals tremendous conceptual hurdles that need to be overcome before one can accept their pre-eminent authority. Indeed, many argue that the problems encountered in this analysis demonstrate that human "rights" are a misnomer, and that the rhetoric of human rights is really a description of ideals - and a controversial set of ideals at that.

THE HISTORICAL ORIGINS OF HUMAN RIGHTS

Human rights are a product of a philosophical debate that has raged for over two thousand years within the European societies and their colonial descendants. This argument has focused on a search for moral standards of political organization and behaviour that is independent of the contemporary society. In other words, many people have been unsatisfied with the notion that what is right or good is simply what a particular society or ruling elite feels is right or good at any given time. This unease has led to a quest for enduring moral imperatives that bind societies and their rulers over time and from place to place. Fierce debates raged among political philosophers as these issue were argued through.

While a path was paved by successive thinkers that lead to contemporary human rights, a second lane was laid down at the same time by those who resisted this direction. The emergence of human rights from the natural rights tradition did not come without opposition, as some argued that rights could only from the law of a particular society and could not come from any natural or inherent source. The essence of this debate continues today from seeds sown by previous generations of philosophers.

The earliest direct precursor to human rights might be found in the notions of 'natural right' developed by classical Greek philosophers, such as Aristotle, but this concept was more fully developed by Thomas Aquinas in his Summa Theologica. For several centuries Aquinas' conception held sway: there were goods or behaviours that were naturally right (or wrong) because God ordained it so. What was naturally right could be ascertained by humans by 'right reason' - thinking properly. Hugo Grotius further expanded on this notion in De jure belli et paci, where he propounded the immutability of what is naturally right and wrong:

Now the Law of Nature is so unalterable, that it cannot be changed even by God himself. For although the power of God is infinite, yet there are some things, to which it does not extend....Thus two and two must make four, nor is it possible otherwise; nor, again, can what is really evil not be evil. The moral authority of natural right was assured because it had divine authorship.

In effect, God decided what limits should be placed on the human political activity. But the long-term difficulty for this train of political thought lay precisely in its religious foundations. As the reformation caught on and ecclesiastical authority was shaken and challenged by rationalism, political philosophers argued for new bases of natural right. Thomas Hobbes posed the first major assault in 1651 on the divine basis of natural right by describing a State of Nature in which God did not seem to play any role.

Perhaps more importantly, however, Hobbes also made a crucial leap from 'natural right' to 'a natural right'. In other words, there was no longer just a list of behaviour that was naturally right or wrong; Hobbes added that there could be some claim or entitlement which was derived from nature. In Hobbes' view, this natural right was one of self-preservation. Further reinforcement of natural rights came with Immanuel Kant's writings later in the 17th century that reacted to Hobbes' work.

In his view, the congregation of humans into a state-structured society resulted from a rational need for protection from each other's violence that would be found in a state of nature. However, the fundamental requirements of morality required that each treat another according to universal principles. Kant's political doctrine was derived from his moral philosophy, and as such he argued that a state had to be organized through the imposition of, and obedience to, laws that applied universally; nevertheless, these laws should respect the equality, freedom, and autonomy of the citizens. In this way Kant, prescribed that basic rights were necessary for civil society:

A true system of politics cannot therefore take a single step without first paying tribute to morality....The rights of man must be held sacred, however great a sacrifice the ruling power must make. However, the divine basis of natural right was still pursued for more than a century after Hobbes published his Leviathan. John Locke wrote a strong defence of natural rights in the late 17th century with the publication of his Two Treatises on Government, but his arguments were filled with references to what God had ordained or given to mankind.

Locke had a lasting influence on political discourse that was reflected in both the American Declaration of Independence and France's Declaration of the Rights of Man and the Citizen, passed by the Republican Assembly after the revolution in 1789. The French declaration proclaimed 17 rights as "the natural, inalienable and sacred rights of man". The French Declaration of Rights immediately galvanized political writers in England and provoked two scathing attacks on its notion of natural rights. Jeremy Bentham's clause-by-clause critique of the Declaration, entitled Anarchical Fallacies, argued vehemently that there can be no natural rights, since rights are created by the law of a society:

Right, the substantive right, is the child of law: from real laws come real rights; but from laws of nature, fancied and invented by poets, rhetoriticians, and dealers in moral and intellectual poisons come imaginary rights, a bastard brood of monsters, 'gorgons and chimeras dire'. Natural rights is simple nonsense: natural and imprescriptible rights, rhetorical nonsense, - nonsense upon stilts. Edmund Burke also wrote a stinging attack on the French Declaration's assertion of natural rights, in which he argued that rights were those benefits won within each society. The rights held by the English and French were different, since they were the product of different political struggles through history. Soon after the attacks on the French Declaration, Thomas Paine wrote a defence of the conception of natural rights and their connection to the rights of a particular society.

In The Rights of Man, published in two parts in 1791 and 1792, Paine made a distinction between natural rights and civil rights, but he continued to see a necessary connection: Natural rights are those which appertain to man in right of his existence. Of this kind are all the intellectual rights, or rights of the mind, and also all those rights of acting as an individual for his own comfort and happiness, which are not injurious to the natural rights of others. Civil rights are those which appertain to man in right of being a member of society. Every civil right has for its foundation, some natural right pre-existing in the individual, but to the enjoyment of which his individual power is not, in all cases, sufficiently competent.

Of this kind are all those which relate to security and protection. This passage reflects another, earlier inspiration for human rights from the social contract views of writers such as Jean-Jacques Rousseau, who argued that people agree to live in common if society protects them. Indeed, the purpose of the state is to protect those rights that individuals cannot defend on their own.

Rousseau had set the ground for Paine decades earlier with his Social Contract, in which he not only lambasted attempts to tie religion to the foundations of political order but disentangled the rights of a society from natural rights. In Rousseau's view, the rights in a civil society are hallowed: "But the social order is a scared right which serves as a basis for other rights.

And as it is not a natural right, it must be one founded on covenants." Rousseau then eleaborated a number of rights of citizens and limits on the sovereign's power. The debate in the late eighteenth century has left telling traces. Controversy continues to swirl over the question whether rights are creations of particular societies or independent of them. Modern theorists have developed a notion of natural rights that does not draw its source or inspiration from a divine ordering.

The ground work for this secular natural rights trend was laid by Paine and even Rousseau. In its place has arisen a variety of theories that are humanist and rationalist; the 'natural' element is determined from the prerequisites of human society which are said to be rationally ascertainable. Thus there are constant criteria which can be identified for peaceful governance and the development of human society. But problems can develop for this school of thought when notions of a social contract are said to underlie the society from which rights are deduced.

Contemporary notions of human rights draw very deeply from this natural rights tradition. In a further extension of the natural rights tradition, human rights are now often viewed as arising essentially from the nature of humankind itself. The idea that all humans possess human rights simply by existing and that these rights cannot be taken away from them are direct descendants of natural rights.

However, a persistent opposition to this view builds on the criticisms of Burke and Bentham, and even from the contractarian views of Rousseau's image of civil society. In this perspective rights do not exist independently of human endeavour; they can only be created by human action. Rights are viewed as the product a particular society and its legal system. In this vein,

Karl Marx also left a legacy of opposition to rights that hindered socialist thinkers from accommodating rights within their theories of society.

Marx denounced rights as a fabrication of bourgeois society, in which the individual was divorced from his or her society; rights were needed in capitalist states in order to provide protection from the state. In the marxist view of society, an individual is essentially a product of society and, ideally, should not be seen in an antagonistic relationship where rights are needed. However, many socialists have come to accept certain conceptions of rights in the late twentieth century.

Thus, the history of political philosophy has been one of several centuries of debate. The child of natural rights philosophers, human rights, has come to hold a powerful place in contemporary political consciousness. However, neither preponderant belief in, nor even a consensus of support for human rights do not answer the concerns raised by the earlier thinkers - are rights truly the product of a particular vision and laws of a society? Or, are human rights so inherent in humanness that their origins and foundations are incontestable?

A further difficulty, with profound implications, that human rights theories have to overcome is their emergence from these Western political traditions. Not only are they a product of European natural rights, but the particular rights that are viewed as 'natural' have been profoundly shaped by the liberalism that emerged in the 19th and 20th centuries. With human rights, the rhetorical framework of the natural rights tradition has come to serve as a vehicle for the values of Western liberalism.

An easy and powerful criticism is that human rights cannot be universal. In their basic concept they are a Western creation, based on the European tradition that individuals are separable from their society. But one may question whether these rights can apply to collectivist or communitarian societies that view the individual as an indivisible element of the whole society. Westerners, and many others, have come to place a high value on each individual human, but this is not a value judgment that is universal.

There is substantive disagreement on the extent of, or even the need for, any protection of individuals against their society. In addition to this problem with the concept itself, there are strong objections to the manner in which human rights have been conceptualized. Many lists of human rights read like specifications for liberal democracy. A variety of traditional societies can be found in the world that operate harmoniously, but are not based on equality let alone universal suffrage. A question that will recur in later discussions is whether the 'human rights' advocated today are really civil rights that pertain to a particular - liberal - conception of society.

To a large extent, the resolution of this issue depends upon the ultimate goal of human rights. If human rights are really surrogate liberalism, then it will be next to impossible to argue their inherent authority over competing political values. In order for human rights to enjoy universal legitimacy they must have a basis that survives charges of ideological imperialism. Human rights must have a universally acceptable basis in order for there to be any substantial measure of compliance.

THE MOTIVATION FOR HUMAN RIGHTS

Some understanding about the nature of human rights can be gleaned from the various reasons that can be advanced for holding them. A prime concern is to offer protection from tyrannical and authoritarian calculations. Capricious or repressive measures of an autocratic government may be constrained with the recognition of supreme moral limits on any government's freedom of action.

But even among governments that are genuinely limited by moral considerations, there may still be a need to shield the populace from utilitarian decision-making. The greater good of the whole society may lead to sacrifice or exploitation of minority interests. Or, the provision of important benefits within the society may be limited by calculations that public resources should be spent on other enterprises.

The attraction of human rights is that they are often thought to exist beyond the determination of specific societies. Thus, they set a universal standard that can be used to judge any society. Human rights provide an acceptable bench mark with which individuals or governments from one part of the world may criticize the norms followed by other governments or cultures. With an acceptance of human rights, Moslems, Hindus, Christians, capitalists, socialists, democracies, or tribal oligarchies may all legitimately censure each other. This criticism across religious, political, and economic divides gains its legitimacy because human rights are said to enshrine universal moral standards.

Without fully universal human rights, one is left simply trying to assert that one's own way of thinking is better than somebody else's. The prime rhetorical benefit of human rights is that they are viewed as being so basic and so fundamental to human existence that they should trump any other consideration.

Just as Dworkin has argued that any conception of 'rights' trumps other claims within a society, human rights may be of a higher order that supersedes even other rights claims within a society. Other motivations for human rights may stem from a fear of the consequences of denying their existence.

Because of the currency given human rights in contemporary political debate, there is a danger that such a denial will provide support for brutal regimes who defend their repression on the grounds that international human rights norms are simply a fanciful creation that has no universal authority. The United Nations conference on human rights held in Vienna in 1993 saw some of the world's most repressive governments making precisely this argument, and few people would wish to provide further justification for this position. In addition, a great deal of political advocacy relies on human rights rhetoric to provide a legitimating moral force. Without the appeal to human rights, democratic champions would have to argue the desirability of values such as equality and freedom of speech across the often incomparable circumstances of the world's societies, rather than asserting that such benefits just inherently flow from human existence.

CHALLENGES TO THE UNIVERSALITY AND INALIENABILITY OF HUMAN RIGHTS

Unfortunately, the very motivations and benefits of human rights pose direct challenges to their existence. Human rights are universal since they are said to belong to all humans in every society. Human rights are also supposed to be inalienable; because they flow from and protect human existence, they cannot be taken away without endangering the value of that existence.

However, these universal and inalienable qualities of human rights are disputable in both their conception and operation. To some extent, the universality of human rights depends upon their genesis. Moral standards, such as human rights, can come into being in two manners. They may simply be invented by people, or they may only need to be revealed to, or discovered by, humans.

If human rights are simply an invention, then it is rather difficult to argue that every society and government should be bound by something they disagree with. If human rights have some existence independent of human creation, however, then it is easier to assert their universality. But such independent moral standards may arise in only two ways: if they are created by God, or if they are inherent in the nature of humankind or human society.

Unfortunately, both these routes pose substantive pitfalls. No divine origin for universal human rights would be acceptable, nor is it often advanced, since there is no one God that is recognized universally; just because Christians or Moslems claim that their divinity has ordained and proscribed certain treatment of humans does not provide the legitimacy needed for that moral code to bind devotees of another religion. The alternative origin that could justify universality would be the acceptance of human rights as natural rights that anyone could deduce from the nature of humankind or human society.

However, an atheistic critique of divine moral standards is just as telling when applied to rights derived from human nature. The God or human nature that is said to be the source of human rights may be nothing more than an invention of the human mind, an invention that may vary according to whoever is reflecting on the issue. A less astringent argument is still just as damning. Even if one accepts that there is a God or a core human nature, there is no definitive way to sort out differing visions that people have of God or human nature. The universal authority of any particular view is initially endorsed only by the adherents of that view. Nevertheless it is possible for human rights to have their genesis in religion or the prerequisites of human society.

Even if human rights start within a specific religious or societal tradition, they could acquire universality as other people come to agree. It is also possible for human rights to become globally recognized because several different approaches may reach the same cease. For instance, atheistic natural rights theorists, Christians, and Muslims, may all eventually agree for quite different reasons on a number of ways in which people should be treated; these then can form the basis of human rights standards.

However, the different paths to that agreement only lead to an agreement on the benefits, not necessarily on their origin, justification, or application. The differences become important when one moves from a focus on the benefits identified as "human rights" to their practical operation; there is a great difference between a duty-based and claim-based fulfillment of the benefits.

Another set of problems arise if human rights are creations, pure and simple, of the human intellect. Human rights standards could be created in a variety of ways. In one method, a gradual growth of consensus builds around norms of behaviour that eventually acquire an obligatory character. It may be difficult to trace the epistemological origins of this consensus, but the end result is a broad base of agreement that human beings should be treated in certain ways. In another method, there may be a conscious attempt to create binding rules of behaviour in a more contractarian manner. A certain group of individuals or state governments may lead the development of international agreements on human rights. And, as more states join in these agreements, the moral and legal force of the international accords become stronger and stronger. Essentially this is the course that has been followed in the development of the human rights documents created by the United Nations and other regional international organizations. In both these approaches to the creation of human rights, the motivation may be principled or consequentialist.

If principled, human rights are necessary because they reflect certain moral standards of how humans should be treated. If consequentialist, human rights are needed because they standards may prevent the awful repercussions of having no limits on the manner in which governments or groups may treat other human beings.

Beyond the genesis of human rights, wherever they come from, lies a fundamental challenge to their universality, regardless of their origin. With any inception of human rights, one is faced with having to acquire acceptance of their authority. There is a problem in that not everyone will share the same motivation or inspiration for human rights. Not everyone will agree that everything asserted as a human right is indeed one.

At a very basic level, the proclamation and acceptance of human rights norms inherently involves majoritarian morality. Human rights are agreed to exist because a majority says they do. Specific goods and benefits are treated as human rights because a majority says they do. But, what of the minorities who object to the concept of universal human rights, or disagree with the particular entitlements to be included in lists of human rights?

Why should they be bound by what others believe? What happens when a minority sincerely believe that some benefit being deliberately denied them by the majority is a matter that they view as a human right? In many specific human rights contexts, a problem of moral majoritarianism assumes central importance. With either an invented or natural genesis, human rights are meant to protect some aspect of humanity. Human rights may be those entitlements that we have by virtue of being human, but there are real difficulties in determining which attributes of human life require protection under human rights standards. Basic human traits are determined by both physical attributes and the activities undertaken by a human. The most obvious physical qualities encompass gender, race, size, shape, and health - including disabilities.

Among human activities, one can distinguish between those necessary for sustaining life and those which fill that life. The requirements for sustaining life include nourishment, shelter, clothing, and sleep. Proper health care is needed for human life to be sustained in the long term. And the human species can only survive with procreation.

But most humans do not merely exist, they fill their lives with myriad activities. Perhaps the most important activity is that which is usually referred to in order to distinguish humans from all other animals: humans have a creative imagination that provides higher forms of thought that lead to intellectual inquiry and spirituality.

Humans also communicate constantly the results of their thinking. Physical movement from one place to another is another continuous activity of all but the most disabled humans. Human beings are in essence very social animals and much of our activities take place through associating with other humans.

In some instances this association is the special intimacy of kinship or close friendships. In others, humans act gregariously with acquaintances and many perfect strangers. Most humans live within readily identifiable social units, such as family, tribal, or national groups, that fundamentally shape the manner in which an individual's most basic characteristics are manifested.

These social groupings determine what languages one learns to speak, the style of dress, acceptable foods, religion, form of communication and etiquette, sense of physical beauty and ugliness, the kind of shelter, and the notion of division of roles within one's social groupings. These are not simply superficial differences. While some individuals willingly adopt new life styles, many believe that their lives can only be satisfying by maintaining their traditional ways. For some, indeed, styles of dress, food, and behaviour are inextricably linked to deep religious beliefs. One group's delicacies or even staples may be quite unacceptable to others. There may be just disdain or revulsion, such as the reaction of many people to eating raw fish, or there may be a strong, religious offence taken to certain foods, such as offering pork to Moslems or beef to Hindus.

Thus, many profound differences emerge among human beings that are the product of where they were born and with whom they grew up. While one could identify various qualities of human life that are universal, there is tremendous variation in the manner in which those qualities are realised. These acquired societal values pose difficulties when they define, or even conflict with, the basic attributes of human life listed earlier. Individual societies develop particular conceptions of what constitutes a dignified life, the essential needs of humans, as well as the relationship between individuals and their community.

Particularly complex issues arise when there is a clash between conflicting spiritual and temporal values within or between societies. These difficulties come to the forefront when one tries to ascertain whether global standards can be set by human rights on the treatment that must be given to all human beings.

THE THEORETICAL FOUNDATION OF HUMAN RIGHTS

Several competing bases have been asserted for universal human rights. It is essential to understand these various foundations, since they can result in quite different understandings of the specific benefits protected by human rights. As well, each approach to human rights has different strengths and vulnerabilities in facing the challenges posed by relativism and utilitarianism. Many have argued that human rights exist in order to protect the basic dignity of human life. Indeed, the United Nations Declaration on Human Rights embodies this goal by declaring that human rights flow from "the inherent dignity of the human person". Strong arguments have been made, especially by western liberals, that human rights must be directed to protecting and promoting human dignity.

As Jack Donnelly has written, "We have human rights not to the requisites for health but to those things `needed' for a life of dignity, for a life worthy of a human being, a life that cannot be enjoyed without these rights" (original emphasis). This view is perhaps the most pervasively held, especially among human rights activists; the rhetoric of human-rights disputes most frequently invokes this notion of striving for the dignity that makes human life worth living. The idea of promoting human dignity has considerable appeal, since human life is given a distinctive weight over other animals in most societies precisely because we are capable of cultivating the quality of our lives. Unfortunately, the promotion of dignity may well provide an unstable foundation for the construction of universal moral standards. The inherent weakness of this approach lies in trying to identify the nature of this dignity. Donnelly unwittingly reveals this shortcoming in expanding upon the deliberate human action that creates human rights.

"Human rights represent a social choice of a particular moral vision of human potentiality, which rests on a particular substantive account of the minimum requirements of a life of dignity". Dignity is a very elastic concept and the substance given to it is very much a moral choice, and a particular conception of dignity becomes paramount. But, who makes this choice and why should one conception prevail over other views of dignity?

Even general rejection of outlandish assertions of dignity may not indicate agreement on a core substance. There might be widespread derision of my assertion that I can only lead a truly dignified life if I am surrounded by 100 doting love-slaves. But a disapproval of the lack of equality in my vision of dignity does not necessarily demonstrate that equality is a universal component of dignity. While one of the most basic liberal beliefs about human dignity is that all humans are equal, social division and hierarchy play important roles in aspects of Hindu, Confucian, Muslim, and Roman Catholic views of human life.

Indeed, 'dignity' is often achieved in these views by striving to fulfill one's particular vocation within an ordered set of roles. But, if human rights are meant to be universal standards, the inherent dignity that is supposed to be protected should be a common vision. Without sufficient commonality, dignity cannot suffice as the ultimate goal of human rights. An alternative basis for human rights draws from the requisites for human well-being. One advocate of this approach, Allan Gewirth, would agree with Donnelly that human rights are drawn in essence from humankind's moral nature, but Gewirth does not follow Donnelly's cease that human rights are a moral vision of human dignity. Rather, Gewirth argues that "agency or action is the common subject of all morality and practice".

Human rights are not just a product of morality but protect the basic freedom and well-being necessary for human agency. Gewirth distinguished between three types of rights that address different levels of well-being. Basic rights safeguard one's subsistence or basic well-being. Nonsubtractive rights maintain the capacity for fulfilling purposive agency, while additive rights provide the requisites for developing one's capabilities - such as education.

Gewirth differentiates between these rights because he accepts that humans vary tremendously in their capacity for purposive agency. Through what he calls the principle of proportionality, humans are entitled to those rights that are proportionate to their capacity for agency. Thus, individuals who are comatose only have basic rights to subsistence, since they are incapable of any purposive action. Gewirth's approach, however, has been strongly criticized by those who argue that human rights cannot be universal if they are derived from one's capacity for agency.

Indeed Douglas Husak has used Gewirth's theories to argue that there can be no rights that extend to all human beings. Husak makes the crucial distinction between humans and persons, and he points out that some humans may be considered non-persons because they are incapable of ever performing any purposive agency. Even if one accepts Gewirth's rebuttal that all humans are entitled to at least basic rights because they are either prospective or former purposive agents, there still remains in his theory the notion some will find unsettling: not all humans possess all human rights to the same degree.

Another basis for human rights has been put forward by John O'Manique that is based on evolution and human development. O'Manique was motivated by the desire to find a truly universal basis for human rights theories that are not as susceptible, as is dignity, to controversial interpretations or denial by others. Thus, human rights should be founded upon something inherent to humans rather than some moral vision that is created by human action.

O'Manique argues that a satisfactory basis may lie in the following set of propositions:

- P1 I ought to survive
- P2 X is necessary for my survival
- P3 Therefore, I ought to do/have X.

The real hurdle in this set of propositions lies in finding agreement in P1. The requisites for survival are fairly easily ascertained by scientific inquiry.

Thus if there is concordance on the notion I ought to survive, then the logical construction of this model produces the cease that one ought to have X if it is necessary to survival. O'Manique is on fairly firm ground when he asserts that, "The belief that survival is good is virtually universal". He does concede that there are religious beliefs that hold that a person's life can be sacrificed, but usually this sacrifice is done to further the survival of others. So O'Manique determines, "The exceptions do not `prove' the rule, but they do point to the strong probability that the belief that survival is good is found, explicitly or implicitly, in almost all human beings". One might add that some value in human survival may be found in any society, since no culture comes to mind that has tolerated unrestricted, recreational homicide. O'Manique also draws from theories of evolution to establish that the goal of humans has to be the survival of the species. So, there would be universal agreement with the statement, "Humans ought to survive". But survival of the group, community, or human species is very different from the survival of each and every particular individual.

O'Manique develops his theory much beyond the notion of survival. Indeed, he explicitly dismisses the idea that the source of human rights lies in the needs for human subsistence. O'Manique wishes to propel human rights into a further plane, by basing human survival upon the full development of human potential. The initial proposition P1 in the model really becomes "I ought to develop". As O'Manique says, "Human aspirations are not to the maintenance of existence but to the fulfilment of life... If we believe that one ought to survive, it is because we believe that one ought to develop".

In O'Manique's vision, human rights would include rights to things needed for subsistence but also go on to cover all aspects of intellectual and emotional development. He tries to limit in some way the range by insisting that the needs for development can be ascertained through research. However, he also reveals the broad sweep of matters that could be included when he addresses this issue: "The existence of such needs for human development - the need for association with other human beings, for self expression, for some control over one's destiny, and even the need for love and for beauty - can be observed and even empirically confirmed within the social sciences and psychology".

O'Manique may well lose some support with this incredibly vast range of issues that he would include within the human rights rubric. A fundamental difficulty with using the fulfillment of human development as a basis for human rights is that it can have a meaning that is relative to each culture and individual. This relativism even creeps into O'Manique's discussion when he concludes, "A community and its members will develop to the extent that the members of the community support the development needs of others in the community, in ways that are appropriate to that community" (emphasis added). Just what is needed for fulfillment in expression, love, or autonomy will be given profoundly different interpretations in Bedouin, German, or Japanese societies.

O'Manique tries to address this aspect of his theory by conceding that the specific entitlements necessary to human development may vary over space and time, but the general grounds for those claims will remain constant. The final alternative basis for human rights would provide the needs for human existence. Human rights may be limited to providing all humans with the needs for their physical subsistence.

But, this subsistence would involve a certain degree of minimal comfort beyond merely keeping one's organs working, because human subsistence also consists of being able to function. Advocates of the other approaches to human rights have dismissed needs to subsistence as too narrow a foundation, but this criticism may not account for the ramifications that flow from the range of human needs. Human rights would guarantee the provision of the food, clothing, and shelter without which anyone would perish.

In addition, basic health care assures human survival; my grandmother died in 1924 from appendicitis, while I am alive today because an operation was available for my own attack of appendicitis in 1968. Since most households are not simply provided with the requisites to life but buy them with the wages of their labour, one can easily extend the range of human rights into other benefits relating to the work force. This extension is particularly true if the satisfaction of needs is accomplished not by directly supplying the specific goods needed, but in providing the capacity for individuals to provide for themselves. In a broad socialist view, work should be guaranteed to all that are capable. In a more restricted view, the education necessary to obtaining the work needed to sustain oneself is a human right. Thus, human rights can cover a large, and very expensive, array of social-welfare programmes. Quite a fundamental reformation of most political systems would occur if governments seriously addressed welfare programmes as essential human rights.

There are some distinct advantages in basing human rights on the needs of subsistence. The prime benefit lies in a universality possible with this foundation that eludes the other approaches to human rights. One might possibly find a similar consensus on the propositions "Humans should survive", "Humans should develop", "Humans should lead a life of dignity (or well being)". However, there will be much less disagreement over what is meant by, or needed for, `survival' than one will find for `dignity', `well-being', or `development'. Human rights based on subsistence can be much more readily applied as global standards.

Nevertheless, there is still some concern with variations that will result from different societies' views of the specific ways in which needs should be satisfied. As noted earlier, different cultures have quite diverse notions of what food, dress, or shelter are acceptable. There are even profound differences in approaches to health care, with some societies rejecting 'western' medicine in favour of spiritually-based theories of ailments and therapies.

There is also a concern that it is just not practical to translate the proposition that humans in general should survive into concrete action to ensure that each and every human being survives. There is a point at which no society can afford to devote the resources needed to keep every individual alive as long as possible.

These four approaches to human rights reflect quite different inspirations and ultimate goals, but there is common ground among them. Theories of human rights based on dignity, well-being, or development all are motivated by a desire to protect and cultivate some quality of life; because one is alive, one should lead a life filled with dignity, well-being, or continuing development. A view of human rights based on subsistence is ultimately concerned with simply preserving life itself. But this distinction should not ignore an overlap, as a common ground among all theories of human rights is the assumption that human rights include subsistence rights.

Approaches based on dignity, well-being, and development add protections for these qualities of life onto the right to existence, although subsistence rights often seem to be forgotten. However, the recognition of these common aspects of the four theories of human rights should not lead one to conclude that their differences are simply ones of emphasis.

The distinctive focus of each theory results in significant variations in their lists of specific human rights or the kind of activities humans may indulge in. Human rights based on subsistence would not include the range of democratic rights that most liberals argue are an essential element of human rights based on dignity.

Some liberals would argue that a life without dignity may not be a life worth living; so disenfranchised, repressed people - such as Iraqi Kurds - may be justified in an armed rebellion involving deaths but which ultimately brought liberty to the whole population. However, a human rights approach based on subsistence may require on a non-violent strategy for political change since the preservation of life is the ultimate goal.

In the end, the choice of foundation for human rights may depend upon what one wishes to protect. One may be alarmed that democratic rights or equality may not be included in a human rights approach based on subsistence, in which case a theory based on liberal dignity would be adopted. But consequentialist motivations will not serve as a firm basis upon which to promote human rights among those who do not share one's concerns. These discussions emphasize that the foundation for human rights may be neither self-evident nor universally accepted. One chooses, explicitly or implicitly a particular justification or basis for human rights, and that choice will have important consequences upon the range of benefits that fall within human rights. Choice pervades human rights from their conception to their delivery, and those choices may well undermine the very foundation of human rights' moral authority.

WHO HOLDS HUMAN RIGHTS

Even if there were agreement upon a foundation for human rights, there remains another fundamental question: who can possess human rights? One may simply assert that all humans hold all human rights; after all, human rights are said to be those benefits to which we are entitled simply by being human. But what is meant by being 'human' is vague since the life cycle of homo sapiens ranges from conception to death and decay.

There is profound controversy over how and when a human acquires and then loses human rights between those two periods. Even before conception, sperm and eggs exist that contain human genetic material. One may decide easily that these are human cells but not 'human beings', because they contain incomplete sets of human genes. After conception, however, controversies arise about the status of the developing foetus.

From a mass of undifferentiated cells, the embryo quickly grows into a recognizably human entity. Many distinguish foetuses from babies that have emerged from their mothers and say that separate human life only begins with 'birth'. This can be an arbitrary distinction since a very premature baby is at much the same stage of development whether inside or outside the womb; the differences centre on how a baby receives nutrition and oxygen.

One can specify an arbitrary point for the acquisition of rights, such as conception, neural development, viability, or emergence from the womb. But this approach is bound to erupt in controversy, because not everyone will agree on a given point. Abortion is such a divisive issue precisely because various groups hold different beliefs about when human life starts. Alternatively, one can argue that there is some special quality of human life that provides a basis for possessing rights; when that quality is acquired, so are rights. This approach is favoured by many, since it allows for the distinction between humans and other animals.

Human rights are rights particular to human beings, thus the basis of the claim to rights should be something that differentiates humans from other animals. With a sharing of an enormous proportion of genetic material between humans and primates, the distinction is usually drawn on the basis of some quality of human life not shared by other animals rather than physiological characteristics.

Specifically human qualities are usually identified from our capacity for intellectual, moral, or spiritual development. The difficulty with trying to assign rights on the basis of some quality of human life is that not all human beings may possess such an attribute. Douglas Husak has written a poignant critique of the notion of human rights based on his objection that some human beings merely exist.

Some mentally-ill patients lack any basis for purposive agency; they are seemingly unaware of their surroundings, incapable of rationale thought, or unable to distinguish right from wrong. But, his most telling arguments arise from comatose patients, notably those with no known chance for recovery. Husak distinguishes between humans and persons, and he points out that some humans, such as the comatose, are non-persons. Persons are human beings with capacities beyond mere existence that produce a quality of life.

Non-persons simply lack the qualities of life that one wishes either to protect or use as the key to acquiring rights. The distinction between humans and persons is often used to justify aborting foetuses, because the human foetus is not considered by many to be a person. In the end, Husak argues that the phenomena called human rights are really rights of persons: "There are no human rights".

This debate over the qualification of a human creature to possess human rights is fundamental to a number of topics. The rights of children and the mentally ill may depend greatly upon what foundation one adopts for the possession of rights. Similarly, the existence of rights to life in abortion, infanticide, and euthanasia are directly related to what status one accords to undeveloped foetuses, mutant newborns, or terminally-comatose adults. If human rights are justified on some characteristics of the human species, can those rights be held by individual humans who lack these species traits? Some answer this question by distinguishing between possessing rights and exercising them. Thus a healthy child may possess the full range of human rights, but be unable to exercise them, particularly rights of an intellectual nature. Others may find this distinction too convenient an answer and contest the very existence of rights that cannot by exercised by their holders.

Another controversy over the possession of human rights relates to whether they are benefits intended for individual humans, or whether they can also be collective benefits for groups of humans. Some, such as Donnelly, argue that human rights are properly held by only individuals. Others contend that human lives are lived within group settings and the full enjoyment of human life can only be realised when those groups are able to flourish.

Whether human rights can include collective rights is a particularly crucial issue in analysing whether the human rights regime protects a group's culture and language, or a group's right to self-determination.

WHAT ARE THE 'RIGHTS' IN HUMAN RIGHTS

The nature of human rights is complicated even beyond the controversy over their source or who may hold them. A critical debate continues over what is meant by human rights. The universality and inalienability of a human right depends to a large extent on the character of the 'right' involved. It is necessary first of all to distinguish between the adjectival use of the word 'right', which means good or proper, from the substantive 'a right', which is a special, possessable benefit. Not everything which is right (good) is a right, although many people mistakenly inflate the concept of a right by asserting benefits they believe are 'right' to be 'rights'.

This confusion has become evident in the assertion of what are known as 'second-generation human rights' - such as the right to economic development and prosperity - and 'third generation human rights' - which cover the rights to world peace and a clean environment. While some human rights advocates accept the inclusion of these benefits as rights, others argue that prosperity and peace are 'right' but not substantive rights. Even with the substantive term 'a right', however, there are several different meanings.

In 1919, Wesley Hohfeld laid down a useful set of four distinctive connotations that can be given to the phrase "A has a right to X". Perhaps the most common meaning given to this phrase conveys the notion of a claim-right. It is a claim that A has against a correlative duty of another, B; A has a right to X, and B has a duty to let A have or do X. The duty B has may be positive, in the sense that action is required on B's part to allow A to enjoy X; if A has a right to health care, B has a duty to provide it. There may also be a negative duty, in the sense of B having to refrain from interfering in A's possession of benefit X; if A has a right to privacy, B must refrain from prying in A's affairs. It is important to note that the duty may be owed by a particular person or official, or the duty may generally lie in the whole community.

The essential characteristic of a claim-right is the inherent connection between A's claim to a benefit and B's duty - A can make a claim that B must perform the duty. However, there are other connotations of the phrase 'A has a right to X' that do not involve a corresponding duty on another's part. The term may mean that A has a liberty with respect to X. In this view, A has no obligation not to do or have X, which may be different from the status of other people. Also, A can make no claim against another, because no-one else as a duty with respect to A's enjoyment of X. A liberty may be enjoyed by all, such as the right to wear what one pleases while doing household chores. A subset of liberty is privilege, because A may have no duty not to do X but others do. For instance, in some English colleges the dons have a right to walk across the grass in the quadrangle, although others must use the pathways instead. In any liberty there is no duty on anyone to provide the X involved; *i.e.*, no-one has a duty to provide the lawns simply for the dons to walk upon.

To say that 'A has a right to X' may also indicate that A has a power to effect changes in X. Thus an owner of a bicycle has the right to sell it, and a customs officer has the right to confiscate property or detain people at the border. Hohfeld's fourth interpretation of 'A has a right to X' conveys the notion that A has an immunity that B is unable to change. Thus, MP's have a right to free speech that protects them from prosecution for speeches given in the House of Commons, and it is a right which cannot be changed by the executive, police, or courts.

There are other uses of 'having a right' that should be added to those identified by Hohfeld, because these other uses refer to ideals, needs, or wants that are simply expressed as rights. The confusion between adjectival and substantive right has led to the frequent use of rights to describe ideals. Thus, the rights to prosperity and peace are ideals or goals to strive for that some express as rights.

Another confusion arises when people assert a right to a benefit because it fills a need. But, not all needs are rights; I may need a car to drive to work in, but few would agree that I have a right to a car. Finally, many confuse benefits they want with benefits they have a right to; free, post-secondary education and complete bursaries may be desirable, but are not viewed as rights by many. These uses of rights also involve a confusion between making a claim and having a right. One does not hold a right simply because one claims so, neither is it necessary to make claims in order to possess rights. It is not the act of claiming that creates rights. Thus, the claim to a right to prosperity or world peace does not establish that those benefits exist as rights. Neither does the fact that someone satisfies another's claim confirm a right's existence; a beggar may claim a right to $5 from a businessman, who may give the money, but that does not establish the beggar's right to it. It is important also to note that one may benefit from another's duty, without having a right to that benefit. Christians may believe that they have a duty to give money to charity, but that does not mean that charities have a right to Christians' money. These different notions of 'right' are important to bear in mind when discussing human rights. The most common interpretation given to the 'right' in human rights is that of claim-rights.

There is a defined benefit to which individuals are entitled, and there is a correlative duty on others in relation to that benefit. This tendency may be partly due to the increasing codification of human rights into legal documents. It is far more efficacious if human rights are conceived of as claim-rights, because those who are deprived of their rights may argue that others (usually their government) must be compelled to fulfill a duty to provide the benefit.

Since much human rights activism centres on the respect for rights contained in international agreements, it is natural for attention to centre on governments as duty-holders since they are the entities directly bound by the human rights documents. If human rights are claim-rights with a correlative duty on some body to provide or safeguard the benefit, however, a major problem arises in identifying that duty-holder. Most often it is assumed that if an individual is being denied some human right, the duty falls on their government to rectify the situation.

A serious difficulty emerges if the correlative duty lies only with an individual's government, however, because the abuse of human rights may occur by private individuals or corporations. For example, tremendous injustices result from the caste system in India because of the way people treat others who belong to a lower caste. In this instance, the actual infringement of human rights is largely perpetrated by individuals rather than the government. While the government has accepted a responsibility to try and end the practise, caste is so deeply entrenched in Indian society that it has so far proved impossible to stamp out. A further complication arises when a government either is incapable of providing a benefit protected by human rights - such as the Ethiopian government's inability to provide food during the worst of the famines - or when a government simply fails to respect human rights. If an individual's government is the central duty-holder, then the rest of the world can shake their heads saying 'tut-tut' without feeling any sense of duty to intervene.

Other governments may feel bound to act, but that feeling of obligation may simply come from their own sense of altruism rather than a belief that human rights bind all governments to help if the government most directly responsible fails to fulfill its duties. Another scenario may arise when government leaders believe that a duty to help lies directly with its citizens rather than the government. Former Premier Van der Zalm of British Columbia argued in the 1980s that it was not his government's responsibility to provide resources to food banks that were struggling with soaring numbers of impoverished individuals. His view was that such acts of charity are best left to private individuals. One could develop this notion by asserting that every individual owes a duty to help others in their community, and that the government would be eroding this private duty if it intervened; indeed a government should not support food banks, in order to foster a relief effort by the members of the community. Another difficulty arises in those parts of the world where the state structure has dissolved into anarchy, such as occurred in Somalia and Lebanon; where there are no governments, are there no duty-holders? There is also a strong feminist critique of the idea that governments are the sole duty holders; Gayle Binion argues that non-government actors may be absolved of responsibility or left unimpeded in their ill-treatment of women. Complex problems arise because there are many possible duty-holders. If human rights set moral standards for the treatment of all humans, those standards should bind anyone who is capable of infringing those rights - be they corporations, governments, or other human beings. Thus, the correlative duties involved in human rights as claim-rights are duties that do not necessarily reside solely with an individual's government. The violation of some human right may be perpetrated by one individual against others, such as an employer who discriminates against a racial group in hiring.

Or, a duty to respect human rights may be held by a group within society, such as a religious majority's obligation to tolerate other religious practices. There may be a general duty on the community to act collectively, as with the example of community efforts to run food banks. An individual's own government often has a direct duty, for example, to refrain from arbitrary detention and torture. On some occasions, many will argue that foreign governments have a duty to intervene; for instance, the Front Line States in southern Africa believed they had some duty to help liberate the black majority from apartheid in South Africa.

Finally, there may be a duty that lies with all humanity; such an obligation is often expressed in private, international relief movements to alleviate suffering among famine victims. Governments may only be intermediary duty-holders who should try and intervene to safeguard human rights from actions by their citizens, but those citizens bear the direct duty to respect the human rights of others.

With any form of rights, but particularly with claim-rights, there are problems that arise with their definition, exercise, and enforcement. There may be conflicting views even on the existence of a particular right. For example, some islamic governments have denied that there can be freedom of religion because the Koran proclaims that one of the greatest sins for a muslim is to forsake Islam for another religion. Even if there is agreement in principle on the existence of a particular right, there may be conflicts over what activities or goods are specifically protected by that right.

In Canada, for instance, judges have been divided over whether the freedom of expression includes communications between prostitutes and their clients. There can also be profound debate when two or more rights conflict in a given situation. A continuing problem is posed for women's rights by several religions that stipulate particular roles for women that are subservient to men; in these instances the right to equality conflicts with the freedom of religion. Another difficulty may arise over whether a benefit is really a claim-right, with correlative duties, or some other type of right or claim without corresponding obligations.

For instance, academic freedom may be viewed as either a privilege or a claim-right. If a claim-right is involved, there may still be many questions about who in particular holds a correlative duty, and what type of action is required to satisfy that duty. For example, if there is a right to health care, must it be provided by the government or charities; and, must the health care be provided free of charge?

A central dilemma revolves around how to settle these questions of enforcement. If human rights operate uniquely in a moral plane, then the definition, acceptance, and respect for rights can involve a controversial, tortuous route. In the end, fulfillment of human rights will depend upon a spirit of consensus and the effect of community opprobrium. Disputes that involve profoundly different value systems, however, may go unresolved. With the codification of human rights into legal documents, one may limit some of the range of debate, but only with institutional structures for adjudicating can there be authoritative resolutions.

Controversial interpre-tations of human rights are not eliminated with the creation of agencies to enforce human rights. The record of national courts reveal that judges within the same society can be deeply divided over the definition and enforcement of human rights; for example, almost 31 per cent of the Supreme Court of Canada's Charter of Rights decisions between 1983 and 1989 involved dissenting opinions, where one or more judges disagreed completely with their colleagues on the resolution of the rights issues at stake. Within many societies there are patterns of deference to the judiciary that allows their court's majority view to settle authoritatively most disputes over human rights. However, some societies are so divided that deference is not voluntarily given, such as enforced black acquiescence to the white judiciary in South Africa during the apartheid regime, and the discretionary choices made by judges will not be accepted as final resolutions of rights disputes.

There is an even deeper problem if international institutions are to adjudicate rights disputes that involve societies with very different cultural norms; losing parties may simply not recognize the adjudicators' authority to impose what are seen as alien values. In these circumstances, codified human rights will end up operating on much the same plane as purely moral standards.

HUMAN RIGHTS TREATIES

International treaties are contracts signed between states. They are legally binding and impose mutual obligations on the states that are party to any particular treaty (States Parties). Human rights treaties impose obligations on states about the manner in which they treat all individuals within their jurisdiction, whether or not citizens of that country.

In order to stress the fundamental nature of the obligations that states have towards individuals, some human rights treaties are called 'covenants' or 'pacts' whilst others are called 'conventions'. Human rights treaties have been adopted by states worldwide and represent a global consensus about how individuals should be treated in accordance with their inherent rights and dignity. One treaty, the Convention on the Rights of the Child, has been signed by every state except two, Somalia and the United States of America.

These treaties are 'hard law' and are legally binding. This distinguishes them from other international instruments, such as 'declarations' and the outcomes of political conferences, which are sometimes referred to as 'soft law'. Although these latter are not legally binding they reflect international consensus and represent politically binding agreements and/or obligations.

Declarations often provide the consensual basis for the latter development of binding legal instruments. The Universal Declaration of Human Rights, for example, has been given legal force in two covenants: The International Covenant on Economic, Social and Cultural Rights (ICESCR) and The International Covenant on Civil and Political Rights (ICCPR), both of which were adopted in 1966 and came into force in 1976. These are two of six core human rights treaties, which between them provide the bedrock of the international legal protection of human rights. In this way, the subject of human rights is both concrete – confirmed in international law – and dynamic – able to develop in accordance with recognition of the need.

The six core human rights treaties:

- The International Covenant on Civil and Political Rights, adopted in 1966 and which entered into force 23 March 1976
- The International Covenant on Economic, Social and Cultural Rights, adopted in 1966, entered into force 3 January 1976
- The International Convention on the Elimination of All Forms of Racial Discrimination, adopted in 1965, entered into force 4 January 4 1969
- The Convention on the Elimination of All Forms of Discrimination Against Women, adopted in 1979, entered into force 3 September 1981
- The Convention Against Torture and Other Cruel, Inhuman or Degrading Treatment or Punishment, adopted in 1984, entered into force 26 June 1987
- The Convention on the Rights of the Child, adopted in 1989, entered into force 2 September 1990

The United Nations has played a critical role in adopting global human rights instruments and many others that deal with specific human rights issues or the rights of particular groups of people. Other international bodies, such as the United Nations Educational, Scientific and Cultural Organisation (UNESCO), the United Nations International Children's Emergency Fund (UNICEF) and the International Labour Organisation (ILO) have also adopted human rights instruments. For example, the Member States of the ILO have adopted a series of treaties concerned with labour rights.

Regional groupings have also adopted human rights texts. The European Union, the African Union, the Organisation of American States and the League of Arab States have all adopted human rights treaties open to signature by their respective member states. In addition, many States Parties to these international and regional instruments have fulfilled their legal obligation to incorporate the rights enshrined within those instruments into national law, adopting national human rights laws or 'bills of rights' and mechanisms providing access to legal redress at the national or local level.

STRATEGIES AND RESPONSES

In this chapter, a listing of strategies and responses of state and non-state Actors is attempted. Those attempted by non-state actors is inevitably more exhaustive, since a large proportion of our respondents belong to this description of person.

ORGANISING PEOPLE

This may be for effective and informed protest, as has been done by the NBA, for instance. Or in getting people to re-capturing control over their resources, as in the Aruvari Sansad in Alwar District in Rajasthan. Or to form collectives, as with the Durbar Mahila Sammanvaya Committee.

WORKING ON THE RIGHT TO INFORMATION

Led by the MKSS in Rajasthan, it has caught the imagination of activists across states, and fields of activity. It has also resulted in bureaucratic and political acknowledgment of the right/freedom. One aspect of this right is explored by activists who gain access to 'top secret' documents and share them with grass root level workers as also with the rest of the interested community. This happened with the Land Acquisition (Amendment) Bill, for instance, exploding thereby the unsustainable position that proposed legislation of this kind may need to be kept secret from the people it is likely to affect. The use of information technology to gather facts about offending enterprises, for instance, and disseminating them is another facet of the interpretation of this right.

ICONISATION

The changing of a victim into a symbol, as in Mathura (custodial rape),

Bhanwari Devi (in defiance of rape and oppression), Dominic D'Souza (AIDS), Budhan (denotified tribes) are some instances. Some places where the violations occurred also lend their names to a construction beyond immediate incident: Muzaffarnagar - the scene of killing and molestation of the Uttarakhand agitators; to activists it appears to epitomize the struggle against odds, but also of an isolation of the struggle from the human rights communities in other parts of the country. Or the 'Stchundur' treatment in Andhra Pradesh, where landlord retaliation against dalit assertion, inadvertent in this case, took place amidst police protection; this is now referred to as a phenomenon.

'Broken People' researched and written by Smita Narula for Human Rights Watch is said to have catalysed dalits into forming a national organization. There were references to Masanabu Fukuoka's One Star Revolution having helped shape perspective.

BRINGING IN THE MEDIA

While press briefings are frequent, taking the press along to witness an event is not unknown, *e.g.*, the Disability Rights Group being accompanied by press persons while doing a disability audit of public buildings in Delhi in April 2001. The presence of empathetic persons within the press establishment was also said to make a difference, as when dalits were professional journalists.

FACT-FINDING, PEOPLE'S TRIBUNALS AND PEOPLE'S COMMISSIONS

This is a process by which a state tactic has been co-opted by non-state actors. Previously human rights activists would demand judicial enquiry into incidents of violations of human rights. The use of judicial inquiry sometimes in the form of Commissions of Inquiry, to diffuse situations, or the inconclusive, or, sometimes, unfairly exculpatory, nature of the findings where judicial enquiry culminated in a report, discredited this state response. There is also the capacity of the state to scuttle such inquiry once the immediate need to set them up is past. The Srikrishna Commission is a rare instance of a report which commanded credibility, and it too had to go through the vicissitudes of winding up and re-starting.

Peoples' Tribunals and Peoples' Commissions of Inquiry have made the shift from legality to legitimacy. With the state privileging retired judges in appointment to commissions of inquiry, People's Tribunals and People's Commissions too have on their panel retired judges, who, in addition, carry the aura of integrity and competence.

The panels may also have other public figures including among them journalists, lawyers, academics and activists. There were two instances of attempts to thwart the functioning of People's Tribunals/Commissions which we encountered. The first was when a panel was constituted to hold public hearings on disappearances in Punjab. In keeping with the demands of 'natural justice', notices were issued to policemen, among others. The state contested the right of the people's tribunal to hold hearings, contending that that is a judicial function which the Tribunal cannot usurp. The activists' position was that this was a process in which participation was voluntary, and this was not an alternative to the judicial process. The High Court, and later, the Supreme Court, upheld the state view, and the tribunal was not allowed to function. The enquiry into the Srikrishna Commission was similarly threatened by the judge who issued notices for contempt to the People's Tribunal. Extra-mural intervention led him to set aside the notices. The People's Tribunal also explained that their inquiry was intended to facilitate the official inquiry, and was not an act of defiance. Fact-finding missions, which generally follow soon after an episode of violation, are also increasingly used where human rights defenders are subjected to harassment. The issuing of a statement by persons with credibility in the activist universe and generally after a visit to the site, and after meeting with as many of the actors as is possible, is meant to provide an alternative to self-serving versions that may emerge from the state or its agencies.

It is also intended to highlight an event to prevent further violations. It is important to ensure that the accusation of prejudgment which discredits state reports do not taint such non-governmental fact-finding missions. The report of a lawyer who visited Coimbatore to investigate the anti-Sikh riots in 1984 was the basis of a significant petition in the Madras High Court. This constitutes a turning point when 'culpable inaction' by the state was recognised, where injury to person or property could have been anticipated, but the state did not act to prevent such injury.

VISITING ZONES OF CONFLICT AND VIOLENCE

The cutting off of a free flow of people between areas of conflict and violence and the rest of the country also cuts off the possibility of understanding what the people experience, of information being shared, of extending solidarity and support. The report of the Women's Initiative in 1994, 'Women's Testimonies from Kashmir: The Green of the Valley is Khaki' is testimony and photographic depiction of the women in Kashmir. Uma Chakravarthi and Nandita Haksar's `Delhi Riots' is a testimony collected even while curfew made it difficult to reach the victims and witnesses of the anti-Sikh riots in Delhi.

PEOPLE TO PEOPLE DIALOGUE

This has been held, for instance, in the North East to break the barriers of distance and incomprehension. This also helps in exploring, in areas where the issue is of self-determination or autonomy, after the conflict, what is to follow. The meeting of Naga women and Kashmiri women, both caught in situations of conflict, organised in Delhi in April 2001 is another instance.

NEGOTIATING CONFLICT

The efforts of the Committee of Concerned Citizens in Andhra Pradesh to reduce the violence practised by the state and the naxalites is documented in 'Report of the Committee of Concerned Citizens (1997-2000)'. Comprising persons with whom both the state and the PWG would not be unwilling to speak, the CCC started its correspondence with asking the state for a cessation of 'encounter' killings, and asking the PWG to desist from killing its adversaries.

While the state response has been more formal than substantive,66 the PWG has had the CCC recognise the fundamental nature of land reforms and land re-distribution before violence ceases. The openness of this process of talks and dialogue, and the establishing of credible persons as dialogists, is a significant aspect of this process.

TRUTH COMMISSION

This was organised in the context of deaths of young women in their matrimonial home in Karnataka. A panel heard the parents and relatives of the murdered woman, giving the victim's version a space that it is not able to find in the systems of the state.

DISSEMINATION

A group of disabled persons working among the disabled in Andhra Pradesh, and producing a newspaper and running a press, said they had printed and disseminated 3000 copies of the 1995 Disabilities Act. The response, they said, was excellent.

They also spoke of sending out 10,000 letters to motivate handicapped people. The CEDAW too has been widely discussed, disseminated and translated and training modules developed for understanding, and using, the CEDAW.

The widespread use of posters setting out the rights of the accused as ordered in D.*K. Basu's* case and in *JoginderKumar* has been taken into police stations too. This has also been translated into the local language in many states. Use of information technology, films, reports, magazines and newsletters, both to gather and to share information. Video films and documentaries which assert facts with a perspective–*e.g., An Unfinished War* on population policies and women's perception of their bodies, *Kaise Jeebo Re* on the Narmada struggle, *Hamara Shehar* ondemolitions in Bombay.

PEACE COMMITTEES

This was particularly spoken of where political violence is widespread and routine, especially in West Bengal and Kerala and was also found in Tamil Nadu in the context of caste violence. Human rights groups send out peace committees to bring warring groups to negotiate peace.

CENSUS

The use of 'census' on the practice of untouchability is seen as a way of squarely placing. Disability having been brought on board as a factor to record in the 2001 census, disability groups have been motivating persons with disability to enter their data in the Census as a step towards recognition of their rights in state policy.

SETTING THE NON-NEGOTIABLE

This establishes the base lines in an issue. For instance, regarding child labour, a non-governmental organization has set them out like this: All children must attend full-time formal day schools; Any child out of school is child labour; All work/labour is hazardous, and harms the overall growth and development of the child; Any justification perpetuating the existence of child labour must be condemned.

LEGISLATION

Monitoring changes proposed in law, and in policy, which may affect people's rights. This may also involve the critiquing of proposed drafts and preparing alternative drafts which would be people friendly. The forest laws and the laws relating to land acquisition, as well as the rehabilitation policy went through this process. The Bill on domestic violence was prepared by non-governmental effort and has found its way into parliament. The Women's Reservation Bill has survived disinterest and active antagonism in Parliament because of the activists who have battled to keep it on the agenda.

In the 1980s, the changes to criminal law which dealt with crimes against women were the result of demand from the women's movement.

Participating in state processes, as in presenting memoranda to the Committee to review the working of the Constitution, or intervening with the Law Commission is also practised.

CAMPAIGNS

The Campaign against Death Penalty is one instance. Campaigns often accompany other modes of intervention, legislation or recognition of rights (or wrongs), for instance. Campaigns may also take on issues such as opposition to the WTO, or to the manner of opening up of the Indian economy to multinational power companies, for instance.

RESISTANCE AND PROTEST

This may take the form of rallies, padayatras, cycle rallies, processions, dharna, bandh, hartal and roadblocks. Apart from the 23 conditions that the Madras High Court has imposed on processions, the Kerala High Court has declared that bandhs are unconstitutional since they deny freedom of movement and the right to carry on one's avocation.68 This stands affirmed by the Supreme Court. Bandh seems to have got devalued as a means of protest because of the indiscriminate use of protest because of the indiscriminate use to which it has been subjected by political parties. This is particularly true in Kerala, where activists broadly supported the court's decision. This appropriation of non-governmental methods by governments - in power or in the opposition– appears to have robbed it of its legitimacy and meaning.

- Land invasion.
- Seminars, workshops, lectures, preparing of manuals, holding state and national level consultations and conventions, training of activists and grass root workers and getting a dialogue going among them, pamphlets and posters are usually used.
- The formation of networks has become frequent, as has the induction of issues and the broadening of agenda to accommodate such issues. This has also helped to move towards an understanding of the indivisibility of rights.
- Signature campaigns.
- Alternative election manifesto.
- Participatory methods of decision-making and policy making. The 'Van Gujjars proposal for the Rajaji area' published in 1997 where, through an overtly consultative process among forest-dwelling Van Gujjars, a scheme for community forest management in Protected Areas was drawn up.
- Budget analysis from a range of perspectives, including analysis of what it does for women, children and health.
- Social Development Report.
- Use of PIL in the Supreme Court and the High Court, using the NHRC and the State HRCs and human rights courts. In some states, either the SHRC has not been established, 70 or the SHRC is not a credible institution, and the NHRC is more regularly approached. The National Commission for Women (NCW) has also been used and, in a certain period of its functioning, it was seen as an institution which provided solidarity, by the unqualified acknowledge-ment of the justness of women's claims.
- Training of judges and police personnel. This has been most commonly on gender sensitisation and or human rights.
- Advocacy on rights of people with the state and agencies of the state.

HELP LINES

This has been established for street children, lesbians and gays, and for women in distress. While the first and the last mentioned have endorsement in state policy and practice, help lines for lesbians and gays is denied legalized spaces for operation. Help lines have also existed for some years now for those with suicide on their minds.

TRIAL OBSERVERS

This appears to be an underused method of demanding accountability in judicial and quasi-judicial processes. Yet we did hear of its use in two situations: at the Justice Mohan Commission of Inquiry into the Manjolai tea estate incident where 17 people drowned in the Tamaraparani river - 6-7 persons attended the hearings each day of its sitting. And, the Kerala State Commission for women had two lawyers attending as trial observers in the Vidhura case.

The state has adopted strategies, and measures, dealing with human rights violations, and for pre-empting the occurrence of such violations. While some of these strategies and measures are perceived by activists as having supportive potential, others are seen as providing spaces for human rights violations with impunity; this is particularly so in the case of extra ordinary laws.

The establishing of 'Commissions' including: the NHRC (by Act of 1993), the NCW (by Act of 1990), the National Commission for Backward Classes (by Act of 1992), the National Commission for Safai Karamcharis (by Act of 1993). It is a widely held opinion that the NHRC was established in response to international pressure. Though the Protection of Human Rights Act says that there shall be 'two members having knowledge, or practical experience in, matters relating to human rights' there has been no person from the human rights community in the NHRC; nor does there seem to be enthusiasm among the members of the human rights community to be appointed to the NHRC.

The NHRC has standardised compensation as a response to human rights violations. It does recommend disciplinary action and prosecution of errant officers, but this is not invariable. There has been an acknowledgment of custody deaths, and there is a direction that all cases of custody deaths be reported to the NHRC within 24 hours of its occurrence. The numbers have been seen to be increasing each year; the NHRC puts it down to increased reporting.

There is a direction that post-mortem of persons who have died in custody be videotaped; it is not apparent that this has made a difference.

The NHRC was at one with the human rights community in demanding that TADA be not re-enacted. It also recommended ratification of the Torture Convention, but the government does not have to heed the NHRC, since its opinion is only recommendatory; and the Torture Convention remains not ratified.

The exclusion of the armed forces from the purview of the NHRC is identified by activists as a grave lacuna in the Act that establishes the institution. This is especially so since human rights violations by the armed forces is a matter of concern and contention in the conflict-torn regions of the country. It is also that this exclusion is viewed in the context of the NHRC's reach over 'terrorism', and, therefore, found anomalous.

In defending its human rights record before the Human Rights Committee, the state has used the NHRC, along with PIL, as reason to believe that all human rights violations have avenues for redressal within the state.

The Supreme Court, too, has passed on the burden of PIL cases which deal with human rights issues, included bonded labour, mentally ill in institutions and women in 'protective' homes, to the NHRC. This shift from a binding fundamental rights jurisdiction to an institution with recommendatory powers has been viewed with growing concern by activist lawyers.

The judge-heavy composition of the NHRC has influenced the procedure of 'hearing', setting out of a 'case', and even 'affidavits' and 'arguments'.

The Annual Report of the NHRC is to be placed before Parliament, making it a public document. The government is to give an Action Taken Report along with it. In the Annual Report of 1998-99, the NHRC refers to the nontabling of the report of the previous year; the more significant recommendations from the previous year have beenreiterated in 1998-99. There has been no challenge to this governmental neglect.

The soft approach, sometimes amounting to a clear negation of rights, as in the Punjab Disappearances case, has been castigated by activists. The impact of directives issuing from the NHRC, on custody deaths for instance, is unclear. Documentation of cases, and the reports of investigations, is not easy of access, and no system has been devised for ensuring such transparency.

State Human Rights Commissions (SHRCs) have been set up only in some states. Andhra Pradesh, with its escalating record of encounter killings, has not established a SHRC. In West Bengal, activists do approach the SHRC, but they explained that they were confronted with popular prejudices– such as judging a victim of custodial torture as not worthy of the energies of human rights activists; and their concern being 'misplaced'. An orientation to human rights was found missing when such poses were struck, they contended.

Activists in other states, such Tamil Nadu, seemed to prefer approaching the NHRC rather than the SHRC; a question of competence and demonstrated seriousness of purpose at the state level, they explained.

2

History of Human Rights

The history of human rights involves religious, cultural, philosophical and legal developments throughout recorded history. While the modern human rights movement hugely expanded in post-World War II era, the concept can be traced through all major religions, cultures and philosophies. Ancient Hindu law, Confucianism, the Qur'an and the Ten Commandments all outline some of the rights now included in the Universal Declaration of Human Rights.

The concept of natural law, guaranteeing natural rights despite varying human laws and customs, can be traced back to Ancient Greek philosophers, while Enlightenment philosophers suggest a social contract between the rulers and the ruled. The world's first Buddhist state in India, known as the Maurya Empire, established the world's first welfare system, including free hospitals and education. The African concept of ubuntu is a cultural view of what it is to be human. Modern human rights thinking is descended from these many traditions of human values and beliefs.

EARLY HISTORY OF HUMAN RIGHTS

HUMAN RIGHTS IN THE ANCIENT WORLD

While it is known that the reforms of Urukagina of Lagash, the earliest known legal code, must have addressed the concept of rights to some degree, the actual text of his decrees has not yet been found. The oldest legal codex extant today is the Neo-Sumerian Code of Ur-Nammu. Several other sets of laws were also issued in Mesopotamia, including the Code of Hammurabi one of the most famous examples of this type of document. It shows rules, and punishments if those rules are broken, on a variety of matters, including women's rights, men's rights, children's rights and slave rights.

The prefaces of these codes invoked the Mesopotamian gods for divine sanction. Societies have often derived the origins of human rights in religious documents. The Vedas, the Bible, the Qur'an and the Analects of Confucius are also among the early written sources that address questions of people's duties, rights, and responsibilities.

MAURYA EMPIRE

The Maurya Empire of ancient India established unprecedented principles of civil rights in the 3rd century BC under Ashoka the Great. After his brutal conquest of Kalinga in circa 265 BC, he felt remorse for what he had done, and as a result, adopted Buddhism. From then, Ashoka, who had been described as "the cruel Ashoka" eventually came to be known as "the pious Ashoka". During his reign, he pursued an official policy of nonviolence and the protection of human rights, as his chief concern was the happiness of his subjects. The unnecessary slaughter or mutilation of animals was immediately abolished, such as sport hunting and branding. The first welfare state was established.

Ashoka also showed mercy to those imprisoned, allowing them outside one day each year, and offered common citizens free education at universities. He treated his subjects as equals regardless of their religion, politics or caste, and constructed free hospitals for both humans and animals. Ashoka defined the main principles of nonviolence, tolerance of all sects and opinions, obedience to parents, respect for teachers and priests, being liberal towards friends, humane treatment of servants, and generosity towards all. These reforms are described in the Edicts of Ashoka. In the Maurya Empire, citizens of all religions and ethnic groups also had rights to freedom, tolerance, and equality. The need for tolerance on an egalitarian basis can be found in the Edicts of Ashoka, which emphasize the importance of tolerance in public policy by the government. The slaughter or capture of prisoners of war was also condemned by Ashoka. Some sources claim that slavery was also non-existent in ancient India. Other state, however, that slavery existed in ancient India, where it is recorded in the Sanskrit Laws of Manu of the 1st century BC.

EARLY ISLAMIC CALIPHATE

Many reforms in human rights took place under Islam between 610 and 661, including the period of Muhammad's mission and the rule of the four immediate successors who established the Rashidun Caliphate. Historians generally agree that Muhammad preached against what he saw as the social evils of his day, and that Islamic social reforms in areas such as social security, family structure, slavery, and the rights of women and ethnic minorities improved on what was present in existing Arab society at the time.

For example, according to Bernard Lewis, Islam "from the first denounced aristocratic privilege, rejected hierarchy, and adopted a formula of the career open to the talents." John Esposito sees Muhammad as a reformer who condemned practices of the pagan Arabs such as female infanticide, exploitation of the poor, usury, murder, false contracts, and theft. Bernard Lewis believes that the egalitarian nature of Islam "represented a very considerable advance on the practice of both the Greco-Roman and the ancient

Persian world." Muhammed also incorporated Arabic and Mosaic laws and customs of the time into his divine revelations.

The Constitution of Medina, also known as the Charter of Medina, was drafted by Muhammad in 622. It constituted a formal agreement between Muhammad and all of the significant tribes and families of Yathrib, including Muslims, Jews, and pagans. The document was drawn up with the explicit concern of bringing to an end the bitter inter tribal fighting between the clans of the Aws and Khazraj within Medina. To this effect it instituted a number of rights and responsibilities for the Muslim, Jewish and pagan communities of Medina bringing them within the fold of one community-the Ummah. The Constitution established the security of the community, freedom of religion, the role of Medina as a haram or sacred place, the security of women, stable tribal relations within Medina, a tax system for supporting the community in time of conflict, parametres for exogenous political alliances, a system for granting protection of individuals, a judicial system for resolving disputes, and also regulated the paying of blood-wite.

Muhammad made it the responsibility of the Islamic government to provide food and clothing, on a reasonable basis, to captives, regardless of their religion. If the prisoners were in the custody of a person, then the responsibility was on the individual. Lewis states that Islam brought two major changes to ancient slavery which were to have far-reaching consequences. "One of these was the presumption of freedom; the other, the ban on the enslavement of free persons except in strictly defined circumstances," Lewis continues.

The position of the Arabian slave was "enormously improved": the Arabian slave "was now no longer merely a chattel but was also a human being with a certain religious and hence a social status and with certain quasi-legal rights." Esposito states that reforms in women's rights affected marriage, divorce, and inheritance. Women were not accorded with such legal status in other cultures, including the West, until centuries later. The Oxford Dictionary of Islam states that the general improvement of the status of Arab women included prohibition of female infanticide and recognizing women's full personhood.

"The dowry, previously regarded as a bride-price paid to the father, became a nuptial gift retained by the wife as part of her personal property." Under Islamic law, marriage was no longer viewed as a "status" but rather as a "contract", in which the woman's consent was imperative. "Women were given inheritance rights in a patriarchal society that had previously restricted inheritance to male relatives." Annemarie Schimmel states that "compared to the pre-Islamic position of women, Islamic legislation meant an enormous progress; the woman has the right, at least according to the letter of the law, to administer the wealth she has brought into the family or has earned by her own work." William Montgomery Watt states that Muhammad, in the historical context of his time, can be seen as a figure who testified on behalf of women's rights and improved things considerably.

Watt explains: "At the time Islam began, the conditions of women were terrible - they had no right to own property, were supposed to be the property of the man, and if the man died everything went to his sons." Muhammad, however, by "instituting rights of property ownership, inheritance, education and divorce, gave women certain basic safeguards." Haddad and Esposito state that "Muhammad granted women rights and privileges in the sphere of family life, marriage, education, and economic endeavors, rights that help improve women's status in society." However, other writers have argued that women before Islam were more liberated drawing most often on the first marriage of Muhammad and that of Muhammad's parents, but also on other points such as worship of female idols at Mecca.

Sociologist Robert Bellah argues that Islam in its seventh-century origins was, for its time and place, "remarkably modern...in the high degree of commitment, involvement, and participation expected from the rank-and-file members of the community." This is because, he argues, that Islam emphasized the equality of all Muslims, where leadership positions were open to all. Dale Eickelman writes that Bellah suggests "the early Islamic community placed a particular value on individuals, as opposed to collective or group responsibility."

MAGNA CARTA

Magna Carta is an English charter originally issued in 1215. Magna Carta was the most significant early influence on the extensive historical process that led to the rule of constitutional law today. Magna Carta influenced the development of the common law and many constitutional documents, such as the United States Constitution and Bill of Rights. Magna Carta was originally written because of disagreements amongst Pope Innocent III, King John and the English barons about the rights of the King.

Magna Carta required the King to renounce certain rights, respect certain legal procedures and accept that his will could be bound by the law. It explicitly protected certain rights of the King's subjects, whether free or fettered — most notably the writ of habeas corpus, allowing appeal against unlawful imprisonment.

For modern times, the most enduring legacy of Magna Carta is considered the right of habeas corpus. This right arises from what are now known as clauses 36, 38, 39, and 40 of the 1215 Magna Carta.

The Magna Carta also included the right to due process:

- "No Freeman shall be taken or imprisoned, or be disseised of his Freehold, or Liberties, or free Customs, or be outlawed, or exiled, or any other wise destroyed; nor will We not pass upon him, nor condemn him, but by lawful judgment of his Peers, or by the Law of the Land. As suggested, sell to no man, as suggested, not deny or defer to any man either Justice or Right."

MODERN HUMAN RIGHTS MOVEMENT

The conquest of the Americas in the 16th century by the Spanish resulted in vigourous debate about human rights in Spain. The debate from 1550-51 between Las Casas and Juan Ginés de Sepúlveda at Valladolid was probably the first on the topic of human rights in European history. Several 17th and 18th century European philosophers, most notably John Locke, developed the concept of natural rights, the notion that people are naturally free and equal.

Though Locke believed natural rights were derived from divinity since humans were creations of God, his ideas were important in the development of the modern notion of rights. Lockean natural rights did not rely on citizenship nor any law of the state, nor were they necessarily limited to one particular ethnic, cultural or religious group. Two major revolutions occurred that century in the United States and in France. The Virginia Declaration of Rights of 1776 sets up a number of fundamental rights and freedoms. The later United States Declaration of Independence includes concepts of natural rights and famously states "that all men are created equal, that they are endowed by their Creator with certain unalienable rights, that among these are life, liberty and the pursuit of happiness."

Similarly, the French Declaration of the Rights of Man and Citizen defines a set of individual and collective rights of the people. These are, in the document, held to be universal - not only to French citizens but to all men without exception.

1800AD TO WORLD WAR I

Philosophers such as Thomas Paine, John Stuart Mill and Hegel expanded on the theme of universality during the 18th and 19th centuries. In 1831 William Lloyd Garrison wrote in a newspaper called The Liberator that he was trying to enlist his readers in "the great cause of human rights" so the term human rights probably came into use sometime between Paine's The Rights of Man and Garrison's publication. In 1849 a contemporary, Henry David Thoreau, wrote about human rights in his treatise On the Duty of Civil Disobedience which was later influential on human rights and civil rights thinkers. United States Supreme Court Justice David Davis, in his 1867 opinion for Ex Parte Milligan, wrote "By the protection of the law, human rights are secured; withdraw that protection and they are at the mercy of wicked rulers or the clamor of an excited people."

Many groups and movements have managed to achieve profound social changes over the course of the 20th century in the name of human rights. In Western Europe and North America, labour unions brought about laws granting workers the right to strike, establishing minimum work conditions and forbidding or regulating child labour. The women's rights movement succeeded in gaining for many women the right to vote. National liberation movements in many countries succeeded in driving out colonial powers. One of the most influential was Mahatma Gandhi's movement to free his native India from British rule. Movements by long-oppressed racial and religious minorities succeeded in many parts of the world, among them the civil rights movement, and more recent diverse identity politics movements, on behalf of women and minorities in the United States.

The foundation of the International Committee of the Red Cross, the 1864 Lieber Code and the first of the Geneva Conventions in 1864 laid the foundations of International humanitarian law, to be further developed following the two World Wars.

BETWEEN WORLD WAR I AND WORLD WAR II

The League of Nations was established in 1919 at the negotiations over the Treaty of Versailles following the end of World War I. The League's goals included disarmament, preventing war through collective security, settling disputes between countries through negotiation, diplomacy and improving global welfare.

Enshrined in its Charter was a mandate to promote many of the rights which were later included in the Universal Declaration of Human Rights. The League of Nations had mandates to support many of the former colonies of the Western European colonial powers during their transition from colony to independent state.

Established as an agency of the League of Nations, and now part of United Nations, the International Labour Organization also had a mandate to promote and safeguard certain of the rights later included in the UDHR: "the primary goal of the ILO today is to promote opportunities for women and men to obtain decent and productive work, in conditions of freedom, equity, security and human dignity".

AFTER WORLD WAR II

Rights in War and the Geneva Conventions

The Geneva Conventions came into being between 1864 and 1949 as a result of efforts by Henry Dunant, the founder of the International Committee of the Red Cross.

The conventions safeguard the human rights of individuals involved in conflict, and follow on from the 1899 and 1907 Hague Conventions, the international community's first attempt to define laws of war. Despite first being framed before World War II, the conventions were revised as a result of World War II and readopted by the international community in 1949.

The Geneva Conventions are:

- First Geneva Convention "for the Amelioration of the Condition of the Wounded and Sick in Armed Forces in the Field"
- Second Geneva Convention "for the Amelioration of the Condition of Wounded, Sick and Shipwrecked Members of Armed Forces at Sea"
- Third Geneva Convention "relative to the Treatment of Prisoners of War"
- Fourth Geneva Convention "relative to the Protection of Civilian Persons in Time of War"

In addition, there are three additional amendment protocols to the Geneva Convention:

1. *Protocol I*: Protocol Additional to the Geneva Conventions of 12 August 1949, and relating to the Protection of Victims of International Armed Conflicts. As of 12 January 2007 it had been ratified by 167 countries.
2. *Protocol II*: Protocol Additional to the Geneva Conventions of 12 August 1949, and relating to the Protection of Victims of Non-International Armed Conflicts. As of 12 January 2007 it had been ratified by 163 countries.
3. *Protocol III*: Protocol Additional to the Geneva Conventions of 12 August 1949, and relating to the Adoption of an Additional Distinctive Emblem. As of May 20, 2008, it had been ratified by 28 countries and signed but not yet ratified by an additional 59 countries

All four conventions were last revised and ratified in 1949, based on previous revisions and partly on some of the 1907 Hague Conventions. Later conferences have added provisions prohibiting certain methods of warfare and addressing issues of civil wars. Nearly all 200 countries of the world are "signatory" nations, in that they have ratified these conventions. The International Committee of the Red Cross is the controlling body of the Geneva conventions.

Universal Declaration of Human Rights

The Universal Declaration of Human Rights is a non-binding declaration adopted by the United Nations General Assembly in 1948, partly in response to the barbarism of World War II. The UDHR urges member nations to promote a number of human, civil, economic and social rights, asserting these rights are part of the "foundation of freedom, justice and peace in the world".

The declaration was the first international legal effort to limit the behaviour of states and press upon them duties to their citizens following the model of the rights-duty duality. "...recognition of the inherent dignity and of the equal and inalienable rights of all members of the human family is the foundation of freedom, justice and peace in the world". The UDHR was framed by members of the Human Rights Commission, with Eleanor Roosevelt as Chair, who began to discuss an International Bill of Rights in 1947.

The members of the Commission did not immediately agree on the form of such a bill of rights, and whether, or how, it should be enforced. The Commission proceeded to frame the UDHR and accompanying treaties, but the UDHR quickly became the priority. Canadian law John Humphrey and French lawyer Rene Cassin were responsible for much of the cross-national research and the structure of the document respectively, where the articles of the declaration were interpretative of the general principle of the preamble. The document was structured by Cassin to include the basic principles of dignity, liberty, equality and brotherhood in the first two articles, followed successively by rights pertaining to individuals; rights of individuals in relation to each other and to groups; spiritual, public and political rights; and economic, social and cultural rights.

The final three articles place, according to Cassin, rights in the context of limits, duties and the social and political order in which they are to be realised.. Humphrey and Cassin intended the rights in the UDHR to be legally enforceable through some means, as is reflected in the third clause of the preamble: "Whereas it is essential, if man is not to be compelled to have recourse, as a last resort, to rebellion against tyranny and oppression, that human rights should be protected by the rule of law".

Some of the UDHR was researched and written by a committee of international experts on human rights, including representatives from all continents and all major religions, and drawing on consultation with leaders such as Mahatma Gandhi.

The inclusion of both civil and political rights and economic, social and cultural rights was predicated on the assumption that basic human rights are indivisible and that the different types of rights listed are inextricably linked. Though this principle was not opposed by any member states at the time of adoption, this principle was later subject to significant challenges.

BILL OF RIGHTS 1689

The Bill of Rights is an act of the Parliament of England, whose title is An Act Declaring the Rights and Liberties of the Subject and Settling the Succession of the Crown. It is often called the English Bill of Rights. The Bill of Rights was passed by Parliament in December 1689. It was a re-statement in statutory form of the Declaration of Right presented by the Convention Parliament to William and Mary in March 1689, inviting them to become joint sovereigns of England. It enumerates certain rights to which subjects and permanent residents of a constitutional monarchy were thought to be entitled in the late 17th century, asserting subjects' right to petition the monarch, as well as to have arms in defence.

It also sets out—or, in the view of its drafters, restates—certain constitutional requirements of the Crown to seek the consent of the people, as represented in parliament. Along with the 1701 Act of Settlement the Bill of Rights is still in effect, one of the main constitutional laws governing the succession to the throne of the United Kingdom and—following British colonialism, the resultant doctrine of reception, and independence—to the thrones of those other Commonwealth realms, by willing deference to the act as a British statute or as a patriated part of the particular realm's constitution.

Since the implementation of the Statute of Westminster in each of the Commonwealth realms the Bill of Rights cannot be altered in any realm except by that realm's own parliament, and then, by convention, and as it touches on the succession to the shared throne, only with the consent of all the other realms. In the United Kingdom, the Bill of Rights is further accompanied by the Magna Carta, Habeas Corpus Act 1679 and Parliament Acts 1911 and 1949 as some of the basic documents of the uncodified British constitution. A separate but similar document, the Claim of Right Act, applies in Scotland. The English Bill of Rights 1689 inspired in large part the United States Bill of Rights.

PROVISIONS OF THE ACT

The Bill of Rights laid out certain basic rights for all Englishmen. These rights continue to apply today, not only in England, but in each of the jurisdictions of the Commonwealth realms as well.

The people, embodied in the parliament, are granted immutable civil and political rights through the act, including:

- Freedom from royal interference with the law. Though the sovereign remains the fount of justice, he or she cannot unilaterally establish new courts or act as a judge.
- Freedom from taxation by Royal Prerogative. The agreement of parliament became necessary for the implementation of any new taxes.
- Freedom to petition the monarch.
- Freedom from the standing army during a time of peace. The agreement of parliament became necessary before the army could be moved against the populace when not at war.
- Freedom for Protestants to have arms for their own defence, as suitable to their class and as allowed by law.
- Freedom to elect members of parliament without interference from the sovereign.
- Freedom of speech and debates; or proceedings in Parliament ought not to be impeached or questioned in any court or place out of Parliament.

Certain acts of James II were also specifically named and declared illegal by the Bill of Rights, while James' flight from England in the wake of the Glorious Revolution was also declared to be an abdication of the throne.

Also, in a prelude to the Act of Settlement to come twelve years later, the Bill of Rights barred Roman Catholics from the throne of England as "it hath been found by experience that it is inconsistent with the safety and welfare of this Protestant kingdom to be governed by a papist prince"; thus William III and Mary II were named as the successors of James VII and II and that the throne would pass from them first to Mary's heirs, then to her sister, Princess Anne of Denmark and her heirs and, further, to any heirs of William by a later marriage. The monarch was further required to swear a coronation oath to maintain the Protestant religion.

AUGMENTATION AND EFFECT

The Bill of Rights was later supplemented by the Act of Settlement in 1701. Both the Bill of Rights and the Claim of Right contributed a great deal to the establishment of the concept of parliamentary sovereignty and the curtailment of the powers of the monarch. Leading, ultimately, to the establishment of constitutional monarchy, while also along with the Penal Laws, settle the political and religious turmoil that had convulsed Scotland, England and Ireland in the 17th century.

It was a predecessor of the United States Bill of Rights, the Canadian Charter of Rights and Freedoms, the United Nations Universal Declaration of Human Rights and the European Convention on Human Rights. For example, as with the Bill of Rights, the US constitution requires jury trials and prohibits excessive bail and "cruel and unusual punishments." Similarly, "cruel, inhuman or degrading punishments" are banned under Article 5 of the Universal Declaration of Human Rights and Article 3 of the European Convention on Human Rights.

The bill continues to be cited in legal proceedings in the Commonwealth realms. For instance, on 21 July 1995 a libel case brought by Neil Hamilton against The Guardian was stopped after Justice May ruled that the Bill of Rights' prohibition on the courts' ability to question parliamentary proceedings would prevent The Guardian from obtaining a fair trial. Section 13 of the Defamation Act, 1996, was subsequently enacted to permit an MP to waive his parliamentary privilege.

The Bill of Rights was also invoked in New Zealand in the 1976 case of Fitzgerald v. Muldoon and Others, which centred on the purporting of newly appointed Prime Minister Robert Muldoon that he would advise the Governor-General to abolish a superannuation scheme established by the New Zealand Superannuation Act, 1974, without new legislation. Muldoon felt that the dissolution would be immediate and he would later introduce a bill in parliament to retroactively make the abolition legal. This claim was challenged in court and the Chief Justice declared that Muldoon's actions were illegal as they had violated Article 1 of the Bill of Rights, which provides "that the pretended power of dispensing with laws or the execution of laws by regal authority...is illegal."

Two special designs of the British commemorative two pound coins were issued in the United Kingdom in 1989 to celebrate the tercentenary of the Glorious Revolution. One referred to the Bill of Rights and the other to the Claim of Right. Both depict the Royal Cypher of William and Mary and the mace of the House of Commons; one also shows a representation of the St Edward's Crown and, another, the Crown of Scotland.

CAIRO DECLARATION ON HUMAN RIGHTS IN ISLAM

The Cairo Declaration of Human Rights in Islam is a declaration of the member states of the Organisation of the Islamic Conference adopted in Cairo in 1990, which provides an overview on the Islamic perspective on human rights, and affirms Islamic Shari'ah as its sole source. CDHRI declares its purpose to be "general guidance for Member States [of the OIC] in the Field of human rights".

This declaration is usually seen as an Islamic response to the post-World War II United Nations' Universal Declaration of Human Rights of 1948. Predominantly Muslim countries, such as Sudan, Iran, and Saudi Arabia, frequently criticized the Universal Declaration of Human Rights for its perceived failure to take into account the cultural and religious context of non-Western countries.

In 1981, the post-revolutionary Iranian representative to the United Nations Said Rajaie-Khorassani articulated the position of his country regarding the Universal Declaration of Human Rights, by saying that the UDHR was "a secular understanding of the Judeo-Christian tradition", which could not be implemented by Muslims without trespassing the Islamic law. The CDHRI was adopted on August 5, 1990 by 45 foreign ministers of the Organisation of the Islamic Conference to serve as a guidance for the member states in the matters of human rights. The Declaration starts by forbidding "any discrimination on the basis of race, colour, language, belief, sex, religion, political affiliation, social status or other considerations". It continues on to proclaim the sanctity of life, and declares the "preservation of human life" as "a duty prescribed by the Shariah". In addition the CDHRI guarantees "non-belligerents such as old men, women and children", "wounded and the sick" and "prisoners of war", the right to be fed, sheltered and access to safety and medical treatment in times of war.

The CDHRI gives men and women the "right to marriage" regardless of their race, colour or nationality, but not religion. In addition women are given "equal human dignity", "own rights to enjoy", "duties to perform", "own civil entity", "financial independence", and the "right to retain her name and lineage", though not equal rights in general. The Declaration makes the husband responsible for the social and financial protection of the family. The Declaration gives both parents the rights over their children, and makes it incumbent upon both of them to protect the child, before and after birth. The Declaration also entitles every family the "right to privacy". It also forbids the demolition, confiscation and eviction of any family from their residence. Furthermore, should the family get separated in times of war, it is the responsibility of the State to "arrange visits or reunions of families".

Article 10 of the Declaration states: "Islam is the religion of unspoiled nature. It is prohibited to exercise any form of compulsion on man or to exploit his poverty or ignorance in order to convert him to another religion or to atheism." The Declaration protects each individual from arbitrary arrest, torture, maltreatment and/or indignity. Furthermore, no individual is to be used for medical or scientific experiments. It also prohibits the taking of hostages of any individual "for any purpose" whatsoever. Moreover, the CDHRI guarantees the presumption of innocence; guilt is only to be proven through a trial in "which he [the defendant] shall be given all the guarantees of defence". The Declaration also forbids the promulgation of "emergency laws that would provide executive authority for such actions".

Art. 19 stipulates that there are no other crimes or punishments than those mentioned in the Sharia, which include corporal punishment and capital punishment. The right to hold public office can only be exercised in accordance with the Sharia, which forbids Muslims to submit to the rule of non-Muslims.

The Declaration also emphasizes the "full right to freedom and self-determination", and its opposition to enslavement, oppression, exploitation and colonialism. The CDHRI declares the rule of law, establishing equality and justice for all. The CDHRI also guarantees all individuals the "right to participate, directly or indirectly in the administration of his country's public affairs".

The CDHRI also forbids any abuse of authority 'subject to the Islamic Shari'ah.' Article 22(a) of the Declaration states that "Everyone shall have the right to express his opinion freely in such manner as would not be contrary to the principles of the Shari'ah." 22(b) states that "Everyone shall have the right to advocate what is right, and propagate what is good, and warn against what is wrong and evil according to the norms of Islamic Shari'ah." 22(c) states: "Information is a vital necessity to society.

It may not be exploited or misused in such a way as may violate sanctities and the dignity of Prophets, undermine moral and ethical values or disintegrate, corrupt or harm society or weaken its faith." 22(d) states "It is not permitted to arouse nationalistic or doctrinal hatred or to do anything that may be an incitement to any form of racial discrimination."

The CDHRI concludes in article 24 and 25 that all rights and freedoms mentioned are subject to the Islamic Shariah, which is the declaration's sole source. The CDHRI declares "true religion" to be the "guarantee for enhancing such dignity along the path to human integrity". It also places the responsibility for defending those rights upon the entire Ummah.

CRITICISM

The CDHRI could be criticized for falling short of international human rights standards by distinguishing different fundamental equality of men and women (Art 6) and for permitting killing according to Sharia law (Art 2A).

Whereas the Universal declaration states: 'Everyone is entitled to all the rights and freedoms set forth in this Declaration, without distinction of any kind, such as race, colour, sex, language, religion, political or other opinion, national or social origin, property, birth or other status.'

CDHRI does not guarantee equal rights, but merely equal dignity:

Article 6: Woman is equal to man in human dignity, and has rights to enjoy as well as duties to perform; she has her own civil entity and financial independence, and the right to retain her name and lineage.

The husband is responsible for the support and welfare of the family.

'All men are equal in terms of basic human dignity and basic obligations and responsibilities, without any discrimination on the basis of race, colour, language, belief, sex, religion, political affiliation, social status or other considerations.'

In particular, CDHRI has been criticised for failing to guarantee freedom of religion. In a joint written statement submitted by the International Humanist and Ethical Union, a non-governmental organization in special consultative status, the Association for World Education and the Association of World Citizens: a number of concerns were raised, that the CDHRI limits Human Rights, Religious Freedom and Freedom of Expression. It concludes: "The Cairo Declaration of Human Rights in Islam is clearly an attempt to limit the rights enshrined in the UDHR and the International Covenants. It can in no sense be seen as complementary to the Universal Declaration." The Centre for Inquiry in September 2008 in an article to the United Nations writes that the CDHRI: "undermines equality of persons and freedom of expression and religion by imposing restrictions on nearly every human right based on Islamic Sharia law." Article 5 prohibits imposing any restrictions on marriage stemming from "race, colour or nationality."

Similarly, CDHRI is criticized as not endorsing equality between men and women; moreover, it is accused of asserting the superiority of men. Adama Dieng, a member of the International Commission of Jurists, criticised the CDHRI. He argued that the declaration gravely threatens the inter-cultural consensus on which the international human rights instruments are based; that it introduces intolerable discrimination against non-Muslims and women.

He further argued that the CDHRI reveals a deliberately restrictive character in regard to certain fundamental rights and freedoms, to the point that certain essential provisions are below the legal standards in effect in a number of Muslim countries; it uses the cover of the "Islamic Shari'a " to justify the legitimacy of practices, such as corporal punishment, which attack the integrity and dignity of the human being.

CHARTER 08

Charter 08 is a manifesto initially signed by over 303 Chinese intellectuals and human rights activists to promote political reform and democratization in the People's Republic of China. It was published on 10 December 2008, the 60th anniversary of the Universal Declaration of Human Rights, named after Charter 77 issued by dissidents in Czechoslovakia. Since its release, more than 8,100 people inside and outside of China have signed the charter.

DEMANDS

Many of the original signatories were prominent citizens inside and outside the government, including lawyers; a Tibetan blogger, Woeser; and Bao Tong, a former senior Communist Party official, who all faced a risk of arrest and jail. The Charter calls for 19 changes to improve human rights in China, including an independent legal system, freedom of association and the elimination of one-party rule. "All kinds of social conflicts have constantly accumulated and feelings of discontent have risen consistently," it reads.

"The current system has become backward to the point that change cannot be avoided." China remains the only large world power to still retain an authoritarian system that so infringes on human rights, it states. "This situation must change! Political democratic reforms cannot be delayed any longer!"

Specific demands are:

- Amending the Constitution.
- Separation of powers.
- Legislative democracy.
- An independent judiciary.
- Public control of public servants.
- Guarantee of human rights.
- Election of public officials.
- Rural–urban equality.
- Freedom of association.
- Freedom of assembly.
- Freedom of expression.
- Freedom of religion.
- Civic education.
- Protection of private property.
- Financial and tax reform.
- Social security.
- Protection of the environment.
- A federated republic.
- Truth in reconciliation.

The opening paragraph of the charter states:

"This year is the 100th year of China's Constitution, the 60th anniversary of the Universal Declaration of Human Rights, the 30th anniversary of the birth of the Democracy Wall, and the 10th year since China signed the International Covenant on Civil and Political Rights. After experiencing a prolonged period of human rights disasters and a tortuous struggle and resistance, the awakening Chinese citizens are increasingly and more clearly recognizing that freedom, equality, and human rights are universal common values shared by all humankind, and that democracy, a republic, and constitutionalism constitute the basic structural framework of modern governance.

A "modernization" bereft of these universal values and this basic political framework is a disastrous process that deprives humans of their rights, corrodes human nature, and destroys human dignity. Where will China head in the 21st century? Continue a "modernization" under this kind of authoritarian rule? Or recognize universal values, assimilate into the mainstream civilization, and build a democratic political system? This is a major decision that cannot be avoided".

RESPONSE

China

The Chinese government has said little publicly on the Charter. On 8 December 2008, two days before the 60th anniversary of the United Nations General Assembly's adoption of the Universal Declaration of Human Rights, Liu Xiaobo was detained by police, hours before the online release of the Charter. He was detained and later arrested on June 23, 2009, on charges of "suspicion of inciting the subversion of state power."

Several Nobel Laureates have written a letter to President Hu Jintao asking for his release. In response, the Chinese government is trying to crush the dissidents: at least 70 of its 303 original signatories have been summoned or interrogated by police while domestic media have been forbidden to interview anyone who has signed the document. Police have also searched for or questioned a journalist, Li Datong, and two lawyers, though none have been arrested. State media has been banned from reporting on the manifesto. A blogging website popular with activists, bullog.cn, which may have had ties to the Charter, has been shut down. On 25 December 2009 Liu Xiaobo was sentenced to 11 years in prison for "inciting subversion of state power" activities by the court.

International Response

A number of foreign governments, including the United States, Germany, and Taiwan have condemned the harassment of supporters of Charter 08 as well as hailed the Charter. International press has generally covered the Charter positively, and international NGOs have supported its message. Other international figures, including the Dalai Lama, have also voiced their support and admiration of the Charter. Artist ShawNshawN depicted a 90 x 30 inch painting of the 19 demands of the Charter.

CYRUS CYLINDER

The Cyrus Cylinder is a Babylonian document of the 6th century BC, discovered in the ruins of Babylon in 1879 and now in the British Museum. It is a clay cylinder, broken into several fragments, on which is written a declaration in Akkadian cuneiform script. The text is in the name of the Achaemenid Persian king Cyrus the Great.

The cylinder was created following the Persian conquest of Babylon in 539 BC, when the Persian army under Cyrus invaded the Neo-Babylonian Empire and incorporated it into the Persian Empire. The Babylonian king Nabonidus was defeated in battle by the Persians and was deposed by Cyrus, who replaced him as ruler of Babylonia.

The text on the cylinder commemorates the Persian victory and praises Cyrus's kingly virtues, listing his genealogy as a king from a line of kings, in contrast with the low-born Nabonidus. The deposed king is denounced as an impious oppressor of the people of Babylonia. The victorious Cyrus is portrayed as having been chosen by the chief Babylonian god Marduk to restore peace and order to the Babylonians. The text says that Cyrus was welcomed by the people of Babylon as their new ruler and entered the city in peace. It appeals to Marduk to protect and to help Cyrus and his son Cambyses. It exalts Cyrus's efforts as a benefactor of the citizens of Babylonia who improved their lives, repatriated displaced peoples and restored temples and cult sanctuaries across Mesopotamia. It concludes with a description of the work of Cyrus in repairing the city wall of Babylon, in which he found a similar inscription by an earlier Babylonian king.

The Assyro-British archaeologist Hormuzd Rassam discovered the cylinder during an excavation carried out for the British Museum. It had been placed as a foundation deposit in the foundations of the Esagila, the city's main temple. The British Museum, the cylinder reflects a long tradition in Mesopotamia where, from as early as the third millennium BC, kings began their reigns with declarations of reforms. Cyrus's declaration shows how he sought to obtain the loyalty of his new Babylonian subjects by stressing his legitimacy as king, and showing his respect for the religious and political traditions of Babylonia.

It has widely been regarded as an instrument of ancient Mesopotamian propaganda, most likely created by the Babylonian priests of Marduk working at the behest of Cyrus. The tradition of royal propaganda represented by the cylinder was revived in the late 1960s when the last Shah of Iran called it "the world's first charter of human rights". That interpretation has been disputed by many historians and has been characterised as anachronistic and tendentious, reflecting a misunderstanding of the cylinder's status as a generic foundation deposit. Nonetheless it became a key symbol of the Shah's political ideology and has since come to be regarded as part of Iran's cultural identity. The cylinder has also been linked to the repatriation of the Jews following their Babylonian captivity, a deed which the Book of Ezra attributes to Cyrus. A passage referring to the restoration of cult sanctuaries and repatriation of deported peoples has been widely interpreted as evidence of a general policy under which the Jews were allowed to return home, although it identifies only Mesopotamian sanctuaries, and makes no mention of Jews, Jerusalem or Judea.

HUMAN RIGHTS

Iranian Governmental View

The Cyrus Cylinder was dubbed the "first declaration of human rights" by the pre-1979 Iranian government, a reading first advanced by its Shah, Mohammed Reza Pahlavi, in 1967, The White Revolution of Iran. Pahlavi made Cyrus the Great a key figure in government ideology and associated himself personally with the Achaemenids. He wrote that "the history of our empire began with the famous declaration of Cyrus, which, for its advocacy of humane principles, justice and liberty, must be considered one of the most remarkable documents in the history of mankind."

The Shah described Cyrus as the first ruler in history to give his subjects "freedom of opinion and other basic rights" – although the text of the cylinder itself says nothing about citizens' rights. In 1968, the Shah opened the first United Nations Conference on Human Rights in Tehran by saying that the Cyrus Cylinder was the precursor to the modern Universal Declaration of Human Rights.

In his 1971 Nowruz speech, the Shah declared that 1971 would be Cyrus the Great Year, during which a grand commemoration would be held to celebrate 2,500 years of Persian monarchy. It would serve as a showcase for a modern Iran in which the contributions that Iran had made to world civilization would be recognized.

The main theme of the commemoration was the centrality of the monarchy within Iran's political system, identifying the Shah with the famous monarchs of Persia's past, and with Cyrus the Great in particular. The Shah looked to the Achaemenid period as "a moment from the national past that could best serve as a model and a slogan for the imperial society he hoped to create." The Cyrus Cylinder was adopted as the symbol for the commemoration. The British Museum loaned the original cylinder to the Iranian government for the duration of the festivities; it was put on display at the Shahyad Monument in Tehran, where a replica of the cylinder is still on display. The 2,500 year celebrations commenced on October 12, 1971 and culminated a week later with a spectacular parade at the tomb of Cyrus in Pasargadae.

On October 14, the shah's sister, Princess Ashraf Pahlavi, presented the United Nations Secretary General U Thant with a replica of the cylinder. The princess asserted that "the heritage of Cyrus was the heritage of human understanding, tolerance, courage, compassion and human liberty".

The Secretary General accepted the gift, linking the cylinder with the efforts of the United Nations General Assembly to address "the question of Respect for Human Rights in Armed Conflict". Since then the replica cylinder has been kept at the United Nations Headquarters in New York City on the second floor hallway, and the text has been translated into all six official U.N. languages.

Scholarly Views

The interpretation of the cylinder as a "charter of human rights" has been criticized by many scholars and characterized as political propaganda on the part of the Pahlavi regime. The German historian Josef Wiesehöfer comments that the image of "Cyrus as a champion of the UN human rights policy... is just as much a phantom as the humane and enlightened Shah of Persia."

Neil MacGregor, the Director of the British Museum, wrote that the cylinder was used by the Shah as "a mantra of his newly constructed national identity" that "must have startled many who had tried to assert their human rights under his regime." Writing in the immediate aftermath of the Shah's commemorations, the British Museum's C.B.F. Walker comments that the "essential character of the Cyrus Cylinder [is not] a general declaration of human rights or religious toleration but simply a building inscription, in the Babylonian and Assyrian tradition, commemorating Cyrus's restoration of the city of Babylon and the worship of Marduk previously neglected by Nabonidus." Two linguists of the ancient Near East, Bill T. Arnold and Piotr Michalowski, comment: "Generically, it belongs with other foundation deposit inscriptions; it is not an edict of any kind, nor does it provide any unusual human rights proclamation as is sometimes claimed."

Cyrus's policies towards subjugated nations have been contrasted to those of the Assyrians and Babylonians, who had treated subject peoples harshly; he permitted the resettling of those who had been previously deported and sponsored the reconstruction of religious buildings. While the Shah cited this as evidence of respect for human rights, the Iranologist Elton L. Daniel has described such an interpretation as "rather anachronistic" and tendentious.

T.C. Mitchell, a former Keeper of Western Asiatic Antiquities at the British Museum, takes the view that interpreting the cylinder as the first charter of human rights "reflects a misunderstanding." Curtis, Tallis, and Salvini note that despite the cylinder's reference to a just and peaceful rule, and repatriation of deported peoples, the modern concept of human rights would have been quite alien to Cyrus's contemporaries and is not mentioned by the cylinder. Neil MacGregor, the British Museum's Director, comments:

Comparison by scholars in the British Museum with other similar texts, however, showed that rulers in ancient Iraq had been making comparable declarations upon succeeding to the [Babylonian] throne for two millennia before Cyrus it is one of the museum's tasks to resist the narrowing of the object's meaning and its appropriation to one political agenda. He cautions that while the cylinder is "clearly linked with the history of Iran", it is "in no real sense an Iranian document: it is part of a much larger history of the ancient Near East, of Mesopotamian kingship, and of the Jewish diaspora." Cyrus has often been depicted as a particularly humane ruler, based on his characterization by ancient sources such as Persian texts, the Old Testament of the Bible and Herodotus. M.A. Dandamaev, the leading Russian scholar of the neo-Babylonian and Persian periods, has written that "almost all the texts... which praise Cyrus have the character of propagandistic writings and demand a very critical approach... by accepting everything said in the texts which were composed by Babylonian priests, we ourselves become the victims of Cyrus's propaganda."

Nonetheless, some scholars have supported the Shah's interpretation of the cylinder as a human rights charter. Neil MacGregor has written "the Cylinder may indeed be a document of human rights". The Iranian lawyer Hirad Abtahi argues that viewing the cylinder as merely "an instrument of legitimizing royal rule" is unjustified, as Cyrus issued the document and granted those rights when he was at the height of his power, with neither popular opposition nor visible external threat to force his hand. The former Iranian prime minister Hassan Pirnia describes the cylinder as "discuss human rights in a way unique for the era, dealing with ways to protect the honour, prestige, and religious beliefs of all the nations dependent to Iran in those days."

DECLARATION OF THE RIGHTS OF MAN AND CITIZEN OF 1793

The Declaration of the Rights of Man and Citizen of 1793 is a French political document. It was written by the commission that included Louis Antoine Léon de Saint-Just and Marie-Jean Hérault de Séchelles during the period of the French Revolution.

The main distinction between the Declaration of 1793 and the Declaration of the Rights of Man and of the Citizen of 1789 is its egalitarian tendency: equality is the prevailing right in this declaration. The text is often said to have been mainly written by Hérault de Séchelle, whose style and writing can be found on most of the documents of the commission that also wrote the French Constitution of 1793 that was never applied, but whose application was steadfastly demanded by the French left until the beginning of the 20th century. The first project of the Constitution of the French Fourth Republic also referred to this version of the Declaration of the Rights of Man and Citizen.

EQUALITY AS THE FIRST NATURAL RIGHT OF MAN

Equality is the most important aspect of the Declaration of 1793. Equality is the first right mentioned. "All men are equal by nature and before the law". As such, for the authors of this declaration equality is not only before the law but it is also a natural right, that is to say, a fact of nature. There was already at that time a school of thought that stated that liberty and equality can quickly become contradictory: indeed liberty doesn't solve social inequalities since there exist some natural inequalities. That school of thought considered that the government had only to protect liberty and to only proclaim natural equality, and eventually liberty would prevail over social equality since all people have different talents and abilities and are free to exercise them. The question raised by this declaration is how to solve social inequalities.

Article 21 states that every citizen has a right to public help, that society is indebted to each citizen and therefore has the duty to help them. Citizens have there a right to work and society has a duty to provide relief to those who cannot work. Article 22 declares a right to education. These rights are considered "2nd generation rights of Man", economical and social rights. These rights entail a greater government intervention in order to reach society's goal, stated in article 1: common welfare.

THE PROTECTIONS OF LIBERTY

Individual liberty is still a primary right and some aspects are more precisely defined than in Declaration of 1789. The declaration explicitly states the freedom of religion, of assembly and of the press, of commerce, of petition. It also prohibits slavery "Every man can contract his services and his time, but he cannot sell himself nor be sold: his person is not an alienable property."

THE PROTECTIONS OF THE CITIZENS AGAINST THEIR OWN GOVERNMENT

If in a way, this declaration has a more liberal bend in the modern American sense since it states that there ought to be public policies for the general welfare, it also contains some very strong libertarian aspects.

Article 7 states "The necessity of enunciating these rights supposes either the presence or the fresh recollection of despotism." Article 9: "The law ought to protect public and personal liberty against the oppression of those who govern." Article 33 states that resisting tyranny is a logical consequence of the rights of man: "Resistance to oppression is the consequence of the other rights of man.

Article 34 states that if one is oppressed, everyone is. Article 27 states "Let any person who may usurp the sovereignty be instantly put to death by free men." Though the usurpation of sovereignty is not detailed, sovereignty is explained in article 25 as residing "in the people". There is no doubt that this way of thinking deeply influenced the revolutionary government during the Terror. Finally, article 35 states "When the government violates the rights of the people, insurrection is for the people and for each portion of the people the most sacred of rights and the most indispensable of duties." Though this declaration was never enforced, History has shown that the French people has followed this advice with many successful and unsuccessful revolutions throughout the 19th century.

DRAFTING OF THE UNIVERSAL DECLARATION OF HUMAN RIGHTS

The Universal Declaration of Human Rights was drafted from early 1947 to late 1948 by Canadian John Peters Humphrey of the United Nations Secretariat and representatives of countries which were members of the first United Nations Commission on Human Rights, which was until 2006, when it was replaced by the United Nations Human Rights Council, a standing body of the United Nations.

Well known members of the Commission who contributed significantly to the creation of the Declaration included Eleanor Roosevelt of the United States, who was Chairman, Jacques Maritain and René Cassin of France, Charles Malik of Lebanon, and P. C. Chang of China, among others.

MEMBERSHIP OF THE COMMISSION

The membership of the Commission was designed to be broadly representative of the global community with representatives of the following countries serving: Australia, Belgium, Byelorussian Soviet Socialist Republic, Chile, China, Egypt, France, India, Iran, Lebanon, Panama, Philippines, United Kingdom, United States, Union of Soviet Socialist Republics, Uruguay and Yugoslavia.

THE HUMPHREY DRAFT

Humphrey was newly appointed as Director of the Division of Human Rights within the United Nations Secretariat. In this role he produced the first draft of a list of rights that were to form the basis of the Declaration.

THE CASSIN DRAFT

The underlying structure of the Universal Declaration was introduced in its second draft which was prepared by Rene Cassin. Cassin worked from a first draft prepared by John Peters Humphrey. The structure was influenced by the Code Napoleon, including a preamble and introductory general principles.

Cassin compared the Declaration to the portico of a Greek temple, with a foundation, steps, four columns and a pediment. Articles 1 and 2 are the foundation blocks, with their principles of dignity, liberty, equality and brotherhood. The seven paragraphs of the preamble, setting out the reasons for the Declaration, are represented by the steps. The main body of the Declaration forms the four columns. The first column constitutes rights of the individual, such as the right to life and the prohibition of slavery. The second column constitutes the rights of the individual in civil and political society.

The third column is concerned with spiritual, public and political freedoms such as freedom of religion and freedom of association. The fourth column sets out social, economic and cultural rights. In Cassin's model, the last three articles of the Declaration provide the pediment which binds the structure together. These articles are concerned with the duty of the individual to society and the prohibition of use of rights in contravention of the purposes of the United Nations.

SUBSEQUENT DRAFTING

The Cassin draft was submitted to the Commission on Human Rights and was to undergo editing in the Commission, then in further drafts considered by the Third Committee of the United Nations, and finally in a draft before the General Assembly of the United Nations, which ultimately adopted the Declaration on 10 December 1948.

UDHR CHRONOLOGY

1945:

- United Nations Conference on International Organization, San Francisco.

1946:

- 15 February, Establishment of "Nuclear Committee" of Commission on Human Rights.
- 29 April - 20 May 1946 - First Meeting of the Nuclear Committee.
- 21 June 1946 - ECOSOC adopts terms of reference of permanent Commission on Human Rights

1947:

- 27 January - 10 February - First Meeting of the Commission on Human Rights, Lake Success, New York. Drafting Committee established.
- 9 June - 25 June - First Meeting of the Drafting Committee, Lake Success, New York. Draft outline of an International Bill of Human Rights prepared by the UN Secretariat. Drafting Committee splits work into two documents: preparation of a declaration of human rights and a working paper on a draft international convention on human rights.
- 2 December - 17 December - Second Session of the Commission on Human Rights, Geneva. Commission begins to consider work on three projects: a declaration on human rights, and international convention on human rights and measures for implementation and enforcement

1948:

- 3 May - 21 May, Second Session of the Drafting Committee, Lake Success, New York.
- 24 May - 18 June, Third Session of the Commission on Human Rights, Lake Success, New York. Commission adopts a draft Declaration and transmits it to the Economic and Social Council.
- 26 August, Economic and Social Council transmits draft to the General Assembly.
- 30 September - 7 December, Third Committee of General Assembly spends 81 meetings considering the Declaration. 168 resolutions for amendments to the draft, submitted and considered.
- 1-4 December, Sub-committee of Third Committee charged with cross checking 5 official language versions.
- 10 December, Universal Declaration of Human Rights adopted by the United Nations General Assembly

EX OFFICIO OATH

The ex-officio oath was an English ecclesiastical and judicial weapon developed in the first half of the 17th century, and used as a form of coercion, persecution, and forcible self-incrimination in the religious trials of that era. The format was a religious oath imposed upon the accused prior to questioning, to answer truthfully all questions that might be asked. It gave rise to what became known as the "cruel trilemma" where the accused would find themselves trapped between a breach of religious oath, contempt of court for silence, or self-incrimination. The name derives from the questioner putting the accused on oath ex officio, meaning by virtue of his office or position. Outcry against this practice led to the establishment of the right to not incriminate oneself in common-law.

This was the direct precursor of similar rights in modern law, including the right to silence and non-self-incrimination in the Fifth Amendment to the United States Constitution. The right itself appears as item 16 in the Levellers Agreement of the Free People of England and first appeared in US law in the Massachusetts Body of Liberties and the Connecticut Code of the same era.

The Star Chamber itself, as a judicial body, was abolished by Parliament as part of the Habeas Corpus Act 1640. Early examples of a codified right appears in the Levellers manifesto Agreement of the Free People of England: "t shall not be in the power of any Representative, to punish, or cause to be punished, any person or persons for refusing to answer questions against themselves in Criminall cases", The right first appeared in US law in the Massachusetts Body of Liberties and the Connecticut Code of the same era.

The United States Supreme Court summarized the events of the time as part of the historical background in the landmark case Miranda v. Arizona:

- Perhaps the critical historical event shedding light on its [ie, the privilege against self-incrimination] origins and evolution was the trial of one John Lilburn, a vocal anti-Stuart Leveller, who was made to take the Star Chamber Oath in 1637. The oath would have bound him to answer to all questions posed to him on any subject. He resisted the oath and declaimed the proceedings, stating: "Another fundamental right I then contended for, was, that no man's conscience ought to be racked by oaths imposed, to answer to questions concerning himself in matters criminal, or pretended to be so." On account of the Lilburn Trial, Parliament abolished the inquisitorial Court of Star Chamber and went further in giving him generous reparation. The lofty principles to which Lilburn had appealed during his trial gained popular acceptance in England. These sentiments worked their way over to the Colonies and were implanted after great struggle into the Bill of Rights.

FOUR FREEDOMS

The Four Freedoms were goals articulated by US President Franklin D. Roosevelt on January 6, 1941. In an address known as the Four Freedoms speech, he proposed four fundamental freedoms that people "everywhere in the world" ought to enjoy:

1. Freedom of speech and expression
2. Freedom of religion
3. Freedom from want
4. Freedom from fear

His inclusion of the latter two freedoms went beyond the traditional US Constitutional values protected by its First Amendment, and endorsed a right to economic security and an internationalist view of foreign policy that have come to be central tenets of modern American liberalism. They also anticipated what would become known decades later as the "human security" paradigm in social science and economic development.

THE DECLARATIONS

The speech delivered by President Roosevelt incorporated the following. "In the future days, which we seek to make secure, we look forward to a world founded upon four essential human freedoms.

- The first is freedom of speech and expression—everywhere in the world.
- The second is freedom of every person to worship God in his own way—everywhere in the world.
- The third is freedom from want—which, translated into world terms, means economic understandings which will secure to every nation a healthy peacetime life for its inhabitants—everywhere in the world.
- The fourth is freedom from fear—which, translated into world terms, means a world-wide reduction of armaments to such a point

> and in such a thorough fashion that no nation will be in a position to commit an act of physical aggression against any neighbour—anywhere in the world.

That is no vision of a distant millennium. It is a definite basis for a kind of world attainable in our own time and generation. That kind of world is the very antithesis of the so-called new order of tyranny which the dictators seek to create with the crash of a bomb".

FOUR FREEDOMS MONUMENT

The Four Freedoms Monument was commissioned by President Franklin D. Roosevelt following his articulation of the "Four Freedoms" in his 1941 State of the Union Address. Roosevelt felt that, through the medium of the arts, a far greater number of people could be inspired to appreciate the concept of the Four Freedoms.

The statue was created by sculptor Walter Russell later that year, and was dedicated in 1943 before a crowd of 60,000 people at Madison Square Garden in New York City. It was dedicated to Colin P. Kelly, the first recognized American hero of World War II. On June 14, 1944 the monument was re-dedicated in Kelly's hometown of Madison, Florida, with a speech by Governor Spessard Holland. Another American artist, Norman Rockwell, was inspired by Roosevelt's vision to create his own visual depiction of the Four Freedoms — in his case, through a series of four paintings completed in early 1943. In Evansville, Indiana there is another Four Freedoms monument designed by Rupert Condict built in 1976, four Indiana Limestone columns. It has become the defacto photo image of the city. Another monument to the Four Freedoms stands in the Tremont neighbourhood of Cleveland, Ohio. It is a single column, with one of the Freedoms printed on each side. On top of the column is a sculpture of two hands holding a globe of the Earth.

MAGNA CARTA

Magna Carta is an English charter, originally issued in the year 1215, and reissued later in the 13th century in modified versions which omit certain temporary provisions, including the most direct challenges to the monarch's authority. The charter first passed into law in 1225. The 1297 version, described as The Great Charter of the Liberties of England, and of the Liberties of the Forest, still remains on the statute books of England and Wales.

The 1215 Charter required King John of England to proclaim certain liberties, and accept that his will was not arbitrary, for example by explicitly accepting that no "freeman" could be punished except through the law of the land, a right which is still in existence today. Magna Carta was the first document forced onto an English King by a group of his subjects in an attempt to limit his powers by law and protect their privileges. It was preceded and directly influenced by the 1100 Charter of Liberties, when King Henry I had specified particular areas where his powers would be limited. Despite its recognised importance, by the second half of the 19th century nearly all of its clauses had been repealed in their original form. Three clauses remain part of the law of England and Wales, however, and it is generally considered part of the uncodified constitution. In a recent ruling Lord Laws used Magna Carta as an example of a constitutional statute, one which could only be repealed by a later statute with that clear intention. The charter was an important part of the extensive historical process that led to the rule of constitutional law in the English speaking world, although it was "far from unique, either in content or form". In practice, Magna Carta in the medieval period did not in general limit the power of kings, but by the time of the English Civil War it had become an important symbol for those who wished to show that the King was bound by the law. It influenced the early settlers in New England and inspired later constitutional documents, including the United States Constitution.

HUMAN RIGHTS

Magna Carta was originally written in Latin. A large part of Magna Carta was copied, nearly word for word, from the Charter of Liberties of Henry I, issued when Henry became king in 1100, in which he said he would respect certain rights of the Church and the barons, for example not forcing heirs to pay a fee when they inherited.

Rights Still in Force Today

Magna Carta supports the right which became known as habeas corpus through clauses 36, 38, 39, and 40 of the 1215 Charter. Similar rights had existed before Magna Carta, and writs with the same effect had been issued as early as the 12th century, but Magna Carta was the first recording in writing of royal recognition of these rights. As the most recent version, it is the 1297 Charter which remains in legal force in England and Wales. In the 1297 charter: Clause 1 guarantees the freedom of the English Church. Although this originally meant freedom from the King, later in history it was interpreted differently. Clause 9 guarantees the "ancient liberties" of the City of London. Clause 29 guarantees a right to due process.

Feudal Rights Still in Place in 1225

Several clauses were present in the 1225 charter but are no longer in force and would have no real place in the post-feudal world. Clauses 2 to 7 refer to feudal death duties, defining their amounts and the provisions that applied if an heir to a fiefdom was under age or was a widow.

Clause 23 provides that no town or person should be forced to build a bridge across a river. Clause 33 requires the removal of all fish weirs. Clause 43 gives special provision for tax on reverted estates and Clause 44 states that forest law should only apply to those in the king's forest.

Feudal Rights Not in the 1225 Charter

Some provisions have no bearing in the world today, since they are feudal rights and were not even included in the 1225 charter. Clauses 9 to 12, 14 to 16, and 25 to 26 deal with debt and taxes and Clause 27 with intestacy.

The other clauses state that no one may seize land in debt except as a last resort; that under age heirs and widows should not pay interest on inherited loans; that county rents will stay at their ancient amounts; and that the crown may only seize the value owed in payment of a debt, that aid must be reasonable, and that scutage may only be sought with the consent of the kingdom.

Clause 14 states that the common consent of the kingdom was to be sought from a council of the archbishops, bishops, earls and greater Barons. This later became the great council, which led to the first parliament.

Judicial Rights

Clauses 17 to 22 allows for a fixed law court, which became the chancellery, and defines the scope and frequency of county assizes. They also state that fines should be proportionate to the offence, that they should not be influenced by ecclesiastical property in clergy trials, and that people should be tried by their peers.

Many think that this gave rise to jury and magistrate trial, but its only manifestation in the modern world was the right of a lord to a criminal trial in the House of Lords at first instance. Clause 24 states that crown officials may not try a crime in place of a judge. Clause 34 forbids repossession without a writ precipe. Clauses 36 to 38 state that writs for loss of life or limb are to be free, that one may use reasonable force to secure one's own land, and that no one can be tried on their own testimony alone. Clauses 36, 38, 39 and 40 collectively define the right of Habeas Corpus. Clause 36 requires courts to make inquiries as to the whereabouts of a prisoner, and to do so without charging any fee. Clause 38 provides that a person could not be put on trial by the mere word of an official. Clause 39 gives the courts exclusive rights to punish anyone. Clause 40 disallows the selling of or delay to justice. Clauses 36 and 38 were removed from the 1225 version, but were reinstated in later versions. The right of Habeas Corpus as such was first invoked in court in the year 1305. Clause 54 says that no man may be imprisoned on the testimony of a woman except on the death of her husband.

Anti-corruption and Fair Trade

Clauses 28 to 32 state that no royal officer may take any commodity such as grain, wood or transport without payment or consent or force a knight to pay for something the knight could do himself, and that the king must return any lands confiscated from a felon within a year and a day. Clause 35 sets out a list of standard measures, and Clauses 41 and 42 guarantee the safety and right of entry and exit of foreign merchants. Clause 45 says that the King should only appoint royal officers suitable for the post. In the United States, the Supreme Court of California interpreted clause 45 in 1974 as establishing a requirement at common law that a defendant faced with the potential of incarceration is entitled to a trial overseen by a legally trained judge. Clause 46 provides for the guardianship of monasteries.

Temporary Provisions

Some provisions were for immediate effect and were not in any later charter. Clauses 47 and 48 abolish most of Forest Law. Clauses 49, 52 to 53 and 55 to 59 provide for the return of hostages, land and fines taken in John's reign. Article 50 states that no member of the d'Athée family may be a royal officer. Article 51 calls for all foreign knights and mercenaries to leave the realm.

Articles 60, 62 and 63 provide for the application and observation of the Charter and say that the Charter is binding on the King and his heirs forever, but this was soon deemed dependent on each succeeding king reaffirming the Charter under his own seal.

Jews in England

Magna Carta contained two articles related to money lending and Jews in England. Jewish involvement with money lending caused Christian resentment, because the Church forbade usury; it was seen as vice and was punishable by excommunication, although Jews, as non-Christians, could not be excommunicated and were thus in a legal grey area. Secular leaders, unlike the Church, tolerated the practice of Jewish usury because it gave the leaders an opportunity for personal enrichment.

This resulted in a complicated legal situation: debtors were frequently trying to bring their Jewish creditors before Church courts, where debts would be absolved as illegal, while the Jews were trying to get their debtors tried in secular courts, where they would be able to collect both principal and interest. The relations between the debtors and creditors would often become very nasty.

There were many attempts over centuries to resolve this problem, and Magna Carta contains one example of the legal code of the time on this issue:

- If one who has borrowed from the Jews any sum, great or small, die before that loan be repaid, the debt shall not bear interest while the heir is under age, of whomsoever he may hold; and if the debt fall into our hands, as suggested, not take anything except the principal sum contained in the bond. And if anyone die indebted to the Jews, his wife shall have her dower and pay nothing of that debt; and if any children of the deceased are left under age, necessaries shall be provided for them in keeping with the holding

> of the deceased; and out of the residue the debt shall be paid, reserving, however, service due to feudal lords; in like manner let it be done touching debts due to others than Jews.

After the Pope annulled the 1215 Magna Carta, future versions contained no mention of Jews.

Great Council

The first long-term constitutional effect arose from Clauses 14 and 61, which permitted a council composed of the most powerful men in the country to exist for the benefit of the state rather than in allegiance to the monarch. Members of the council were also allowed to renounce their oath of allegiance to the King in pressing circumstances and to pledge allegiance to the council and not to the King in certain instances. The common council was responsible for taxation, and although it was not representative, its members were bound by decisions made in their absence.

The common council, later called the Great Council, was England's proto-parliament. The Great Council only existed to give input on the opinion of the kingdom as a whole, and it only had power to control scutage until 1258 when Henry III got into debt fighting in Sicily for the Pope. The barons agreed to a tax in exchange for reform, leading to the Provisions of Oxford. But Henry obtained a papal bull allowing him to set aside these provisions and in 1262 commanded royal officers to ignore the provisions and only to obey Magna Carta. The barons revolted and seized the Tower of London, the Cinque ports and Gloucester.

Initially the King surrendered, but when Louis IX of France arbitrated in favour of Henry, Henry crushed the rebellion. Later he made some concessions, passing the Statute of Marlborough in 1267, which allowed writs for breaches of Magna Carta to be free of charge, enabling anyone to have standing to apply the Charter. This secured the position of the Great Council forever, but its powers were still very limited. The council originally only met three times per year and so was subservient to the King's council, Curiae Regis, which, unlike the Great Council, followed the king wherever he went.

Still, in some ways the council was an early form of parliament. It had the power to meet outside the authority of the King and was not appointed by him. While executive government descends from the Curiae Regis, parliament descends from the Great Council, which was later called the parliamentum. However, the Great Council was very different from modern parliament. There were no knights, let alone commons, and it was composed of the most powerful men, rather than elected citizens.

Magna Carta had little effect on subsequent development of parliament until the Tudor period. Knights and county representatives attended the Great Council, and the council became far more representative under the model parliament of Edward I which included two knights from each county, two burgesses from each borough and two citizens from each city. The Commons separated from the Lords in 1341. The exclusive right of the Commons to sanction taxes was re-asserted in 1407, although it was not in force in this period. The power vested in the Great Council by, albeit withdrawn, Clause 14 of Magna Carta became vested in the House of Commons but Magna Carta was all but forgotten for about a century, until the Tudors.

UNDECLARATION ON SEXUAL ORIENTATION AND GENDER IDENTITY

The proposed United Nations declaration on sexual orientation and gender identity is a Dutch/French-initiated, European Union-backed statement presented to the United Nations General Assembly on 18 December 2008. The statement, originally intended to be adopted as resolution, prompted an Arab League-backed statement opposing it. Both statements remain open for signatures and none of them has been officially adopted by the United Nations General Assembly. The proposed declaration includes a condemnation of violence, harassment, discrimination, exclusion, stigmati-zation, and prejudice based on sexual orientation and gender identity. It also includes condemnation of killings and executions, torture, arbitrary arrest, and deprivation of economic, social, and cultural rights on those grounds.

The proposed declaration was praised as a breakthrough for human rights, breaking the taboo against speaking about LGBT rights in the United Nations. Opponents criticized it as an attempt to legitimize same-sex civil partnerships or marriage, adoption by same sex couples, pedophilia and other "deplorable acts" and curtail freedom of religious expression against homosexual behaviour.

As of December 2008, homosexuality is illegal in 77 countries and punishable by death in seven. In its 1994 decision in Toonen v. Australia, The UN Human Rights Committee, which is responsible for the International Covenant on Civil and Political Rights, declared that such laws are in violation of human rights law. In 2003 a number of predominantly European countries put forward the Brazilian Resolution at the UN Human Rights Commission stating the intention that lesbian and gay rights be considered as fundamental as the rights of all human beings. In 2006, with the effort of its founder, Louis George Tin, International Day Against Homophobia launched a worldwide campaign to end the criminalisation of same-sex relationships. The campaign was supported by dozens of international public figures including Nobel laureates, academics, clergy and celebrities.

In 2008, the 34 member countries of the Organization of American States unanimously approved a declaration affirming that human rights protections extend to sexual orientation and gender identity. Following meetings between Tin and French Minister of Human Rights and Foreign Affairs Rama Yade in early 2008, Yade announced that she would appeal at the UN for the universal decriminalization of homosexuality; the appeal was quickly taken up as an international concern.Co-sponsored by France, which then held the rotating presidency of the European Union, and The Netherlands on behalf of the European Union, the declaration had been intended as a resolution; it was decided to use the format of a declaration of a limited group of States because there was not enough support for the adoption of an official resolution by the General Assembly as a whole. The declaration was read out by Ambassador Jorge Argüello of Argentina on 18 December 2008, and was the first declaration concerning gay rights read in the General Assembly.

SUPPORT

Several speakers addressing a conference on the declaration noted that in many countries laws against homosexuality stemmed as much from the British colonial past as from religion or tradition.

Voicing France's support for the draft declaration, Rama Yade asked: "How can we tolerate the fact that people are stoned, hanged, decapitated and tortured only because of their sexual orientation?"

UK-based activist Peter Tatchell said of the declaration:

- "This was history in the making... Securing this statement at the UN is the result of an inspiring collective global effort by many LGBT and human rights organisations. Our collaboration, unity and solidarity have won us this success. As well as IDAHO, I pay tribute to the contribution and lobbying of Amnesty International; ARC International; Centre for Women's Global Leadership; COC Netherlands; Global Rights; Human Rights Watch; International Committee for IDAHO; International Gay and Lesbian Human Rights Commission; International Lesbian and Gay Association; International Service for Human Rights; Pan Africa ILGA; and Public Services International."

Signatories

67 of the United Nations' 192 member countries have sponsored the declaration, including every member of the European Union and most Western nations:

Africa:

- Cape Verde
- Central African Republic
- Gabon
- Guinea-Bissau
- Mauritius
- São Tomé and Príncipe

Americas:

- Argentina
- Bolivia
- Brazil

- Canada
- Chile
- Colombia
- Cuba
- Ecuador
- Mexico
- Nicaragua
- Paraguay
- United States
- Uruguay
- Venezuela

Asia:

- Israel
- Japan
- Nepal
- Timor-Leste

Europe:

- Albania
- Andorra
- Armenia
- Austria
- Belgium
- Bosnia and Herzegovina
- Bulgaria
- Croatia
- Cyprus
- Czech Republic
- Denmark
- Estonia
- Finland
- France initiative
- Georgia
- Germany
- Greece
- Hungary
- Iceland
- Ireland
- Italy
- Latvia
- Liechtenstein
- Lithuania
- Luxembourg
- Macedonia

- Malta
- Montenegro
- Netherlands initiative
- Norway
- Poland
- Portugal
- Romania
- San Marino
- Serbia
- Slovakia
- Slovenia
- Spain
- Sweden
- Switzerland
- United Kingdom

Oceania:

- Australia
- New Zealand

OPPOSITION

Among the first to voice opposition for the declaration, in early December, 2008, was the Holy See's Permanent Observer at the United Nations, Archbishop Celestino Migliore, who claimed that the declaration could be used to force countries to recognise same-sex marriage: "If adopted, they would create new and implacable discriminations. For example, states which do not recognise same-sex unions as 'matrimony' will be pilloried and made an object of pressure."

A key part of the Vatican opposition to the draft Declaration relates to the concept of gender identity. In a statement on 19 December, Archbishop Migliore noted: "In particular, the categories 'sexual orientation' and 'gender identity', used in the text, find no recognition or clear and agreed definition in international law.

If they had to be taken into consideration in the proclaiming and implementing of fundamental rights, these would create serious uncertainty in the law as well as undermine the ability of States to enter into and enforce new and existing human rights conventions and standards." However, Archbishop Migliore also made clear the Vatican's opposition to legal discrimination against homosexuals: "The Holy See continues to advocate that every sign of unjust discrimination towards homosexual persons should be avoided and urges States to do away with criminal penalties against them."

In an editorial response, Italy's La Stampa newspaper called the Vatican's reasoning "grotesque", claiming that the Vatican feared a "chain reaction in favour of legally recognised homosexual unions in countries, like Italy, where there is currently no legislation." The United States, citing conflicts with US law, originally opposed the adoption of the nonbinding measure, as did Russia, China, the Holy See, and members of the Organization of the Islamic Conference. The Holy See's Permanent Observer Mission issued a statement saying that the draft declaration "challenges existing human rights norms." The Obama administration changed the US position to support the measure in February 2009.

An alternative statement, supported by 57 member nations, was read by the Syrian representative in the General Assembly. The statement, led by the Organization of the Islamic Conference, rejected the idea that sexual orientation is a matter of genetic coding and claimed that the declaration threatened to undermine the international framework of human rights, adding that the statement "delves into matters which fall essentially within the domestic jurisdiction of states" and could lead to "the social normalization, and possibly the legitimization, of many deplorable acts including pedophilia." The Organization failed in a related attempt to delete the phrase "sexual orientation" from a Swedish-backed formal resolution condemning summary executions.

SIGNATORIES

57 UN member nations have co-sponsored the opposing statement:

Africa:

- Algeria
- Benin
- Cameroon
- Chad
- Comoros
- Côte d'Ivoire
- Djibouti
- Egypt
- Eritrea
- Ethiopia
- Gambia
- Guinea
- Kenya
- Libya
- Malawi
- Mali
- Mauritania
- Morocco
- Niger
- Nigeria
- Rwanda

- Senegal
- Sierra Leone
- Somalia
- Sudan
- Swaziland
- Tanzania
- Togo
- Tunisia
- Uganda
- Zimbabwe

Americas:

- Saint Lucia

Asia":

- Afghanistan
- Bahrain
- Bangladesh
- Brunei
- Indonesia
- Iran
- Iraq
- Jordan
- Kazakhstan
- Kuwait
- Lebanon
- Malaysia
- Maldives
- North Korea
- Oman
- Pakistan
- Qatar
- Saudi Arabia
- Syria initiative
- Tajikistan
- Turkmenistan
- United Arab Emirates
- Yemen

Oceania:

- Fiji
- Solomon Islands

VIRGINIA DECLARATION OF RIGHTS

The Virginia Declaration of Rights is a document drafted in 1776 to proclaim the inherent natural rights of men, including the right to rebel against "inadequate" government. It influenced a number of later documents, including the United States Declaration of Independence, the United States Bill of Rights, and the French Revolution's Declaration of the Rights of Man and of the Citizen.

The Declaration was adopted unanimously by the Virginia Convention of Delegates on June 12, 1776 as a separate document from the Constitution of Virginia adopted on June 29, 1776. It was later incorporated within the Virginia State Constitution as Article I, and a slightly updated version may still be seen in Virginia's Constitution, making it legally in effect to this day.

It was initially drafted by George Mason ca. March 22, 1765; James Madison assisted him with the section on religious freedom. It was later amended by Thomas Ludwell Lee and the Convention to add Section 14 on the Right to uniform government. Mason based his document on the rights of citizens described in earlier works such as the English Bill of Rights, and the Declaration can be considered the first modern Constitutional protection of individual rights for citizens of North America.

It rejected the notion of privileged political classes or hereditary offices such as the members of Parliament and House of Lords described in the English Bill of Rights. The Declaration consists of sixteen articles on the subject of which rights "pertain to [the people of Virginia]...as the basis and foundation of Government."

In addition to affirming the inherent nature of natural rights to life, liberty, and property, the Declaration both describes a view of Government as the servant of the people, and enumerates various restrictions on governmental power. Thus, the document is unusual in that it not only prescribes legal rights, but it also describes moral principles upon which a government should be run. Articles 1-3 address the subject of rights and the relationship between government and the governed.

Article 1 states that "all men are by nature equally free and independent, and have certain inherent rights of which...[they cannot divest;] namely, the enjoyment of life and liberty, with the means of acquiring and possessing property, and pursuing and obtaining happiness and safety," a statement later made internationally famous in the first paragraph of the U.S. Declaration of Independence, as "we hold these truths to be self-evident, that all men are created equal, and are endowed by their Creator with certain unalienable rights, that among these are life, liberty, and the pursuit of happiness." Articles 2 and 3 note the revolutionary concept that "all power is vested in, and consequently derived from, the people..." and that "whenever any government shall be found inadequate or contrary to these purposes, a majority of the community hath an indubitable, unalienable, and indefeasible right to reform, alter or abolish it, in such manner as shall be judged most conducive to the public weal." This latter concept effectively asserted the right of the people of Virginia to revolt against the British Empire.

Article 4 asserts the equality of all citizens, rejecting the notion of privileged political classes or hereditary offices - another criticism of British institutions such as the House of Lords and the privileges of the peerage: "no set of men, are entitled to exclusive or separate emoluments or privileges from the community, but in consideration of public services; which, not being descendible, neither ought the offices of magistrate, legislator, or judge be hereditary."

Articles 5 and 6 recommend the principles of separation of powers and free elections, "frequent, certain, and regular" of executives and legislators: "That the legislative and executive powers of the state should be separate and distinct from the judicative; and, that the members of the two first...should, at fixed periods, be reduced to a private station, return into that body from which they were originally taken...by frequent, certain, and regular elections."

Articles 7-16 propose restrictions on the powers of the government, declaring the government should not have the power of suspending or executing laws, "without consent of the representatives of the people,"; establishing the legal rights to be "confronted with the accusers and witnesses, to call for evidence in his favour, and to a speedy trial by an impartial jury of his vicinage," and to prevent a citizen from being "compelled to give evidence against himself." protections against "cruel and unusual punishments", baseless search and seizure, and the guarantees of a trial by jury, freedom of the press, freedom of religion "all men are equally entitled to the free exercise of religion,", and "the proper, natural, and safe defence of a free state" rested in a well regulated militia composed of the body of the people, trained to arms, that standing armies in time of peace, should be avoided as dangerous to liberty;

The following is the complete text of the Virginia Declaration of Rights:

- That all men are by nature equally free and independent, and have certain inherent rights, of which, when they enter into a state of society, they cannot, by any compact, deprive or divest their posterity; namely, the enjoyment of life and liberty, with the means of acquiring and possessing property, and pursuing and obtaining happiness and safety.
- That all power is vested in, and consequently derived from, the people; that magistrates are their trustees and servants, and at all times amenable to them.
- That government is, or ought to be, instituted for the common benefit, protection, and security of the people, nation or community; of all the various modes and forms of government that is best, which is capable of producing the greatest degree of happiness and safety and is most effectually secured against the danger of maladministration; and that, whenever any government shall be found inadequate or contrary to these purposes, a majority of the

community hath an indubitable, unalienable, and indefeasible right to reform, alter or abolish it, in such manner as shall be judged most conducive to the public weal.

- That no man, or set of men, are entitled to exclusive or separate emoluments or privileges from the community, but in consideration of public services; which, not being descendible, neither ought the offices of magistrate, legislator, or judge be hereditary.
- That the legislative and executive powers of the state should be separate and distinct from the judicative; and, that the members of the two first may be restrained from oppression by feeling and participating the burthens of the people, they should, at fixed periods, be reduced to a private station, return into that body from which they were originally taken, and the vacancies be supplied by frequent, certain, and regular elections in which all, or any part of the former members, to be again eligible, or ineligible, as the laws shall direct.
- That elections of members to serve as representatives of the people in assembly ought to be free; and that all men, having sufficient evidence of permanent common interest with, and attachment to, the community have the right of suffrage and cannot be taxed or deprived of their property for public uses without their own consent or that of their representatives so elected, nor bound by any law to which they have not, in like manner, assented, for the public good.
- That all power of suspending laws, or the execution of laws, by any authority without consent of the representatives of the people is injurious to their rights and ought not to be exercised.
- That in all capital or criminal prosecutions a man hath a right to demand the cause and nature of his accusation to be confronted with the accusers and witnesses, to call for evidence in his favour, and to a speedy trial by an impartial jury of his vicinage, without whose unanimous consent he cannot be found guilty, nor can he be compelled to give evidence against himself; that no man be deprived of his liberty except by the law of the land or the judgement of his peers.
- That excessive bail ought not to be required, nor excessive fines imposed; nor cruel and unusual punishments inflicted.
- That general warrants, whereby any officer or messenger may be commanded to search suspected places without evidence of a fact committed, or to seize any person or persons not named, or whose offense is not particularly described and supported by evidence, are grievous and oppressive and ought not to be granted.
- That in controversies respecting property and in suits between man and man, the ancient trial by jury is preferable to any other and ought to be held sacred.

- That the freedom of the press is one of the greatest bulwarks of liberty and can never be restrained but by despotic governments.
- That a well regulated militia, composed of the body of the people, trained to arms, is the proper, natural, and safe defence of a free state; that standing armies, in time of peace, should be avoided as dangerous to liberty; and that, in all cases, the military should be under strict subordination to, and be governed by, the civil power.
- That the people have a right to uniform government; and therefore, that no government separate from, or independent of, the government of Virginia, ought to be erected or established within the limits thereof.
- That no free government, or the blessings of liberty, can be preserved to any people but by a firm adherence to justice, moderation, temperance, frugality, and virtue and by frequent recurrence to fundamental principles.
- That religion, or the duty which we owe to our Creator and the manner of discharging it, can be directed by reason and conviction, not by force or violence; and therefore, all men are equally entitled to the free exercise of religion, according to the dictates of conscience; and that it is the mutual duty of all to practice Christian forbearance, love, and charity towards each other.

INFLUENCE

The Virginia Declaration of Rights heavily influenced later documents. Thomas Jefferson is thought to have drawn on it when he drafted the United States Declaration of Independence one month later. James Madison was also influenced by the Declaration while drafting the Bill of Rights as was the Marquis de Lafayette in voting the French Revolution's Declaration of the Rights of Man and of the Citizen. The importance of the Virginia Declaration of Rights is that it was the first constitutional protection of individual rights, rather than protecting just members of Parliament or consisting of simple laws that can be changed as easily as passed.

QUOTATIONS DERIVED FROM THE DECLARATION

- "We hold these truths to be self-evident, that all men are created equal, that they are endowed by their Creator with certain unalienable Rights, that among these are Life, Liberty and the pursuit of Happiness. —That to secure these rights, Governments are instituted among Men, deriving their just powers from the consent of the governed" — United States Declaration of Independence

"Men are born and remain free and equal in rights. Social distinctions can be founded only on the common utility." — Declaration of the Rights of Man and of the Citizen

YOGYAKARTA PRINCIPLES

The Yogyakarta Principles on the Application of International Human Rights Law in relation to Sexual Orientation and Gender Identity is a set of international principles relating to sexual orientation and gender identity, intended to address documented evidence of abuse of rights of lesbian, gay, bisexual, and transgender people, and further of intersexuality requested by Louise Arbour The International Human Rights Law. The outline of the Principles was drawn at a meeting of International Commission of Jurists and human rights experts from around the world at Gadjah Mada University on Java from 6 to 9 November in 2006. "It contains 29 Principles adopted unanimously by the experts, along with recommendations to governments, regional intergovernmental institutions, civil society, and the UN itself".

The principles are named after Yogyakarta, the smallest province of Indonesia located on the island of Java. Among 29 signatories of the principles, there are Mary Robinson, Manfred Nowak and Martin Scheinin. The principles are intended to be and have become a universal guide to human rights. In alignment with the movement towards establishing basic human rights for all people, the Principles specifically address sexual orientation and gender identity. The Principles were developed in response to patterns of abuse reported from around the world. These included examples of rape, torture, extrajudicial executions, medical abuse, denial of free speech and assembly as well as a range of discriminations in work, health, education, housing, access to justice and immigration. These are estimated to affect millions of people targeted on the basis of perceived or actual sexual orientation or gender identity.

It is noted on the website carrying the principles that concerns have been voiced about a trend of people's human rights being violated because of their sexual orientation or gender identity. Extrajudicial killing, torture and ill-treatment, sexual assault and rape, invasion of privacy, arbitrary arrest and imprisonment, denial of employment and education opportunities are cited. It is explained that the United Nations human rights instruments detail the obligations States are under to ensure people are protected from discrimination, which includes people's expression of sexual orientation or gender identity.

It is pointed out that implementation of these rights has been fragmented and inconsistent internationally. It is set out how the Principles provide a consistent understanding about application of international human rights law in relation to sexual orientation and gender identity.From 6 to 9 November 2006, an international seminar of legal experts on human rights took place at Yogyakarta, Indonesia.

The seminar clarified the nature, scope and implementation of States' human rights obligations under existing human rights treaties and law, in relation to sexual orientation and gender identity. The Principles that developed out of this meeting were adopted by human rights experts from around the world, and included judges, academics, a former UN High Commissioner for Human Rights, NGOs and others. Michael O'Flaherty was rapporteur responsible for drafting and development of the Yogyakarta Principles produced from the meeting. At the meeting, Vitit Muntarbhorn and Sonia Onufer Corrêa were the co-chairpersons. The compilers explain that the Principles detail how international human rights law can be applied to sexual orientation and gender identity issues, in a way that affirms international law and to which all States can be bound to. They suggest that the motivation is so that where ever people are recognised as being born free and equal in dignity and rights, this should include LGBT people as well. They argue that human rights standards also cover issues of sexual orientation and gender identity touch on issues of torture and violence, extrajudicial execution, access to justice, privacy, freedom from discrimination, freedom of expression and assembly, access to employment, health-care, education, and immigration and refugee issues.

The intention outlined is for the Principles to explain that States are obliged to ensure human rights, and each principle recommends how to achieve this, highlighting international agencies' responsibilities to promote and maintain human rights. The Principles are based on the recognition of the right against non-discrimination. The Committee on Economic, Social and Cultural Rights has dealt with the matter in its General Comments, the i nterpretative texts it issues to explicate the f ull meani ng of the provisions of the Covenant on Economic, Social and Cultural Rights.

In General Comments Nos 18 of Nos 18 of 2005, 15 of 2002 and 14 of 2000, it has indicated that the Covenant proscribes any discrimination on the basis of, inter-alia, sex and sexual orientation 'that has the intention or effect of null ifying or impairing the equal enjoyment or exercise of [the right at issue]'. The Committee on the Elimination of Discrimination against Women, notwithstanding that it has not addressed the matter in a General Comment or otherwise specified the applicable provisions of the Convention on the Elimination of All Forms of Discrimination Against Women, on a number of occasions has criticised States for discrimination on the basis of sexual orientation. For example, it also addressed the situation in Kyrgyzstan and recommended that, 'lesbianism be reconceptualised as a sexual orientation and that penalties for its practice be abolished'.

The finalised Yogyakarta Principles was launched as a global charter for gay rights on 26 March 2007 in Geneva. Michael O'Flaherty, spoke at the International Lesbian and Gay Association Conference in Lithuania on 27 October 2007; he explained that "All human rights belong to all of us. We have human rights because we exist – not because we are gay or straight and irrespective of our gender identities", but that in many situations these human rights are not respected or realised, and that "the Yogyakarta Principles is to redress that situation". The Yogyakarta Principles was presented at a United Nations event in New York on November 7, 2007, co-sponsored by Argentina, Brazil and Uruguay. Human Rights Watch explain that the first step towards this would be the de-criminalisation of homosexuality in 77 countries that still carry legal penalties for people in same-sex relationships, and repeal of the death penalty in the seven countries that still have the death penalty for such sexual practice.

Human and LGBT Rights groups took up the Principles, and discussion has featured in the gay press, as well as academic papers and text books. The Principles, while explaining the way existing Human Rights Statutes need to be applied in specific situations relevant to LGBT people's experience, influenced the proposed UN declaration on sexual orientation and gender identity in 2008.

Piero A. Tozzi, of the The Catholic Family and Human Rights Institute, issued a briefing paper 'Six Problems with the Yogyakarta Principles'. He argues that where Principle 24 seeks to recognize the diversity of family forms, this could devalue the concept of the family by including any grouping of two people. He also argues that Principles 20 and 21 could be used to restrict freedom of speech.

The Council of Europe states in "Human Rights and Gender Identity" that Principle 3 of the Yogyakarta Principles is of "of particular relevance": Because same sex marriage is possible only in five member states of the Council of Europe, transgender persons who are already married usually have to divorce prior to their new gender being officially recognised, although in many cases they would prefer to remain a legally recognised family unit, especially if they have children. Such enforced divorces may have a negative impact on the children of the marriage.

They recommend that member states "abolish sterilisation and other compulsory medical treatment as a necessary legal requirement to recognise a person's gender identity in laws regulating the process for name and sex change." As well as to "make gender reassignment procedures, such as hormone treatment, surgery and psycological support, accessible for transgender person, and ensure that they are reimbursed by public health insurance schemes."

3

Issues in Human Rights

ADEQUATE HOUSING

"The human right to adequate housing is the right of every woman, man, youth and child to gain and sustain a safe and secure home and community in which to live in peace and dignity". This definition is in line with the core elements of the right to adequate housing as defined by General Comment No. 4 of the United Nations Committee on Economic, Social and Cultural Rights. The Committee, while adequacy is determined in part by social, economic, cultural, climatic, ecological and other factors, it is nevertheless possible to identify certain aspects of the right that must be taken into account for this purpose in any particular context.

They include the following:

- Legal security of tenure;
- Availability of services, materials, facilities and infrastructure;
- Affordability;
- Habitability;
- Accessibility;
- Location; and
- Cultural adequacy.

THE OBLIGATIONS OF STATES

The legal obligations of Governments concerning the right to housing consist of:

- The duties found in article 2.1 of the Covenant; and
- The more specific obligations to recognize, respect, protect and fulfil this and other rights.

Three phrases in article 2.1 are particularly important for understanding the obligations of Governments to realise fully the rights recognized in the Covenant, including the right to adequate housing:

1. *"Undertakes to take steps... by all appropriate means"*: In addition to legislative measures, administrative, judicial, economic, social and educational steps must also be taken. States parties are also obliged to develop policies and set priorities consistent with the Covenant.

They are also required to evaluate the progress of such measures and to provide effective legal or other remedies for violations. With specific reference to the right to adequate housing, States parties are required to adopt a national housing strategy.

2. *"To the maximum of its available resources*: The obligation of States is to demonstrate that, in aggregate, the measures being taken are sufficient to realise the right to adequate housing for every individual in the shortest possible time using the maximum available resources.
3. *"To achieve progressively"*: This obligation "to achieve progressively" of the Covenant, in particular the reference to the right to the "continuous improvement of living conditions". The obligation of progressive realization, moreover, exists independently of any increase in resources.

The four additional obligations that Governments have to fulfill in order to implement the right to adequate housing are: The obligation to *recognize* the human right dimensions of housing and to ensure that no measures are taken with the intention of eroding the legal status of this right. The adoption of measures and appropriate policies geared towards progressive realization of housing rights form part of this obligation.

The obligation to *respect* the right to adequate housing means that Governments must abstain from carrying out or otherwise advocating the forced or arbitrary eviction of persons and groups. States must respect people's rights to build their own dwellings and order their environments in a manner which most effectively suits their culture, skills, needs and wishes.

The obligation to *protect* effectively the housing rights of a population means that Governments must ensure that any possible violations of these rights by "third parties" such as landlords or property developers are prevented. Where such infringements do occur, the relevant public authorities should act to prevent any further deprivations and guarantee to affected persons access to legal remedies of redress for any infringement caused. The obligation to *fulfil* the right to adequate housing is both positive and interventionary. The Committee on Economic, Social and Cultural Rights has asserted that identifiable governmental strategies aimed at securing the right of all persons to live in peace and dignity should be developed.

CHILDREN'S RIGHTS

Children's rights are the human rights of children with particular attention to the rights of special protection and care afforded to the young, including their right to association with both biological parents, human identity as well as the basic needs for food, universal state-paid education, health care and criminal laws appropriate for the age and development of the child. Interpretations of children's rights range from allowing children the capacity for autonomous action to the enforcement of children being physically, mentally and emotionally free from abuse, though what constitutes "abuse" is a matter of debate. Other definitions include the rights to care and nurturing. "A child is any human being below the age of eighteen years, unless under the law applicable to the child, majority is attained earlier." Cornell University, a child is a person, not a subperson, and the parent has absolute interest and possession of the child, but this is very much an American view. The term "child" does not necessarily mean minor but can include adult children as well as adult nondependent children.

There are no definitions of other terms used to describe young people such as "adolescents", "teenagers," or "youth" in international law, but the children's rights movement is considered distinct from the youth rights movement. The field of children's rights spans the fields of law, politics, religion, and morality.

RATIONALE

As minors by law children do not have autonomy or the right to make decisions on their own for themselves in any known jurisdiction of the world. Instead their adult caregivers, including parents, social workers, teachers, youth workers and others, are vested with that authority, depending on the circumstances. Some believe that this state of affairs gives children insufficient control over their own lives and causes them to be vulnerable. Louis Althusser has gone so far as describe this legal machinery, as it applies to children, as "repressive state apparatuses".

Structures such as government policy have been held by some commentators to mask the ways adults abuse and exploit children, resulting in child poverty, lack of educational opportunities, and child labour. On this view, children are to be regarded as a minority group towards whom society needs to reconsider the way it behaves. However, there is no evidence that such views are widely shared in society. Researchers have identified children as needing to be recognized as participants in society whose rights and responsibilities need to be recognized at all ages.

HISTORIC DEFINITIONS OF CHILDREN'S RIGHTS

Consensus on defining children's rights has become clearer in the last fifty years. A 1973 publication by Hillary Clinton stated that children's rights were a "slogan in need of a definition". Some researchers, the notion of children's rights is still not well defined, with at least one proposing that there is no singularly accepted definition or theory of the rights held by children.

Children's rights law is defined as the point where the law intersects with a child's life. That includes juvenile delinquency, due process for children involved in the criminal justice system, appropriate representation, and effective rehabilitative services; care and protection for children in state care;

ensuring education for all children regardless of their origin, race, gender, disabilities, or abilities, and; health care and advocacy.

TYPES OF RIGHTS

Children's rights are defined in numerous ways, including a wide spectrum of civil, cultural, economic, social and political rights. Rights tend to be of two general types: those advocating for children as autonomous persons under the law and those placing a claim on society for protection from harms perpetrated on children because of their dependency.

These have been labeled as the right of empowerment and as the right to protection.

One Canadian organization categorizes children's rights into three categories:

- *Provision*: Children have the right to an adequate standard of living, health care, education and services, and to play. These include a balanced diet, a warm bed to sleep in, and access to schooling.
- *Protection*: Children have the right to protection from abuse, neglect, exploitation and discrimination. This includes the right to safe places for children to play; constructive child rearing behaviour, and acknowledgment of the evolving capacities of children.
- *Participation*: Children have the right to participate in communities and have programmes and services for themselves. This includes children's involvement in libraries and community programmes, youth voice activities, and involving children as decision-makers.

In a similar fashion, the Child Rights Information Network, or CRIN for short, categorizes rights into two groups:

- Economic, social and cultural rights, related to the conditions necessary to meet basic human needs such as food, shelter, education, health care, and gainful employment. Included are rights to education, adequate housing, food, water, the highest attainable standard of health, the right to work and rights at work, as well as the cultural rights of minorities and indigenous peoples.
- Environmental, cultural and developmental rights, which are sometimes called "third generation rights," and including the right to live in safe and healthy environments and that groups of people have the right to cultural, political, and economic development.

Amnesty International openly advocates four particular children's rights, including the end to juvenile incarceration without parole, an end to the recruitment of military use of children, ending the death penalty for people under 21, and raising awareness of human rights in the classroom.

Human Rights Watch, an international advocacy organization, includes child labour, juvenile justice, orphans and abandoned children, refugees, street children and corporal punishment. Scholarly study generally focuses children's rights by identifying individual rights.

The following rights "allow children to grow up healthy and free":

- Freedom of speech
- Freedom of thought
- Freedom from fear
- Freedom of choice and the right to make decisions
- Ownership over one's body

Other issues affecting children's rights include the sale of children, child prostitution and child pornography.

Difference between Children's Rights and Youth Rights

"In the majority of jurisdictions, for instance, children are not allowed to vote, to marry, to buy alcohol, to have sex, or to engage in paid employment." Within the youth rights movement, it is believed that the key difference between children's rights and youth rights is that children's rights supporters generally advocate the establishment and enforcement of protection for children and youths, while youth rights generally advocates the expansion of freedom for children and/or youths and of rights such as suffrage. Also, many people who support youth rights, are concerned with adolescents and not children.

Parental Rights

Parents affect the lives of children in a unique way, and as such their role in children's rights has to be distinguished in a particular way. Particular issues in the child-parent relationship include child neglect, child abuse, freedom of choice, corporal punishment and child custody. There have been theories offered that provide parents with rights-based practices that resolve the tension between "commonsense parenting" and children's rights. The issue is particularly relevant in legal proceedings that affect the potential emancipation of minors, and in cases where children sue their parents. A child's rights to a relationship with both their parents is increasingly recognized as an important factor for determining the best interests of the child in divorce and child custody proceedings. Some governments have enacted laws creating a rebuttable presumption that shared parenting is in the best interests of children.

MOVEMENT

The Children's Rights Movement is a historical and modern movement committed to the acknowledgment, expansion, and/or regression of the rights of children around the world. While the historical definition of child has varied, the United Nations Convention on the Rights of the Child explains, "A child is any human being below the age of eighteen years, unless under the law applicable to the child, majority is attained earlier." There are no definitions of other terms used to describe young people such as "adolescents", "teenagers" or "youth" in international law. Thomas Spence's The Rights of Infants is an early English-language assertion of the natural rights of children. In the USA, the Children's Rights Movement was born in the 1800s with the orphan train. In the big cities, when a child's parents died or were extremely poor, the child frequently had to go to work to support himself and/or his family.

Boys generally became factory or coal workers, and girls became prostitutes or saloon girls, or else went to work in a sweat shop. All of these jobs paid only starvation wages. In 1852, Massachusetts required children to attend school. In 1853, Charles Brace founded the Children's Aid Society, which worked hard to take street children in. The following year, the children were placed on a train headed for the West, where they were adopted, and often given work. By 1929, the orphan train stopped running altogether, but its principles lived on. The National Child Labour Committee, an organization dedicated to the abolition of all child labour, was formed in the 1890s.

It managed to pass one law, which was struck down by the Supreme Court two years later for violating a child's right to contract his work. In 1924, Congress attempted to pass a constitutional amendment that would authorize a national child labour law. This measure was blocked, and the bill was eventually dropped. It took the Great Depression to end child labour nationwide; adults had become so desperate for jobs that they would work for the same wage as children. In 1938, President Franklin D. Roosevelt signed the Fair Labour Standards Act which, amongst other things, placed limits on many forms of child labour. Now that child labour had been effectively eradicated in parts of the world, the movement turned to other things, but it again stalled when World War II broke out and children and women began to enter the work force once more. With millions of adults at war, the children were needed to help keep the country running. In Europe, children served as couriers, intelligence collectors, and other underground resistance workers in opposition to Hitler's regime.

In the early twentieth century, moves began to promote the idea of children's rights as distinct from those of adults and as requiring explicit recognition. The Polish educationalist Janusz Korczak wrote of the rights of children in his book How to Love a Child; a later book was entitled The Child's Right to Respect. In 1917, following the Russian Revolution, the Moscow branch of the organization Proletkult produced a Declaration of Children's Rights.

However, the first effective attempt to promote children's rights was the Declaration of the Rights of the Child, drafted by Eglantyne Jebb in 1923 and adopted by the League of Nations in 1924. This was accepted by the United Nations on its formation and updated in 1959, and replaced with a more extensive UN Convention on the Rights of the Child in 1989. From the formation of the United Nations in the 1940s and extending to present day, the Children's Rights Movement has become global in focus. While the situation of children in the United States has become grave, children around the world have increasingly become engaged in illegal, forced child labour, genital mutilation, military service, and sex trafficking. Several international organizations have rallied to the assistance of children. They include Save the Children, Free the Children, and the Children's Defence Fund.

The Child Rights Information Network, or CRIN, formed in 1983, is the group of 1,600 non-governmental organizations from around the world which advocate for the implementation of the Convention on the Rights of the Child. Organization's report on their countries' progress towards implementation, as do governments that have ratified the Convention. Every 5 years reporting to the United Nations Committee on the Rights of the Child is required for governments.

While there is a long history of children's rights in the U.S., scholars contend that there is no "golden age". Many children's rights advocates in the U.S. today advocate for a smaller agenda than their international peers. Groups predominately focus on child abuse and neglect, child fatalities, foster care, youth aging out of foster care, preventing foster care placement, and adoption. A longstanding movement promoting youth rights in the United States has made substantial gains in the past.Anti-Children's Rights propagandists often raise the spectre of Rights without Responsibilities. The Children's Rights Movement assert that it is rather the case that children have rights which adults, states and government have a responsibility to uphold.

The UK maintains a position that UNCRC is not legally enforceable and is hence 'aspirational' only - albeit a 2003 ECHR ruling states: "The human rights of children and the standards to which all governments must aspire in realizing these rights for all children are set out in the Convention on the Rights of the Child.". 18 years after ratification, the four Children's Commissioners in the devolved administrations have united in calling for adoption of the Convention into domestic legislation, making children's rights legally enforceable.

Several countries have created an institute of children's rights ombudsman, most notably Sweden, Finland and Ukraine, which is first country worldwide to install children at that post. In Ukraine Ivan Cherevko and Julia Kruk became first children's rights ombudsmen in late 2005.The United Nations Convention on the Rights of the Child has outlined a standard premise for the children's rights movement and has been ratified by all but two nations - the United States and Somalia. Somalia's inability to sign the Convention is attributed to their lack of governmental structure. The US administration under Bush has opposed ratifying the Convention because of "serious political and legal concerns that it conflicts with U.S. policies on the central role of parents, sovereignty, and state and local law." However, the new administration may be taking another look at it.

INTERNATIONAL LAW

The Universal Declaration of Human Rights is seen as a basis for all international legal standards for children's rights today. There are several conventions and laws that address children's rights around the world.

A number of current and historical documents affect those rights, including the 1923 Declaration of the Rights of the Child, drafted by Eglantyne Jebb and her sister Dorothy Buxton in London, England in 1919, endorsed by the League of Nations and adopted by the United Nations in 1946. It later served as the basis for the Convention on the Rights of the Child.

Convention on the Rights of the Child

The United Nations' 1989 Convention on the Rights of the Child, or CRC, is the first legally binding international instrument to incorporate the full range of human rights—civil, cultural, economic, political and social rights. Its implementation is monitored by the Committee on the Rights of the Child.

National governments that ratify it commit themselves to protecting and ensuring children's rights, and agree to hold themselves accountable for this commitment before the international community.

The CRC is the most widely ratified human rights treaty with 190 ratifications. Somalia and USA are the only two countries which have not agreed to the CRC. The CRC is based on four core principles, namely the principle of non discrimination, the best interests of the child, the right to life, survival and development, and considering the views of the child in decisions which affect them. The CRC, along with international criminal accountability mechanisms such as the International Criminal Court, the Yugoslavia and Rwanda Tribunals, and the Special Court for Sierra Leone, is said to have significantly increased the profile of children's rights worldwide.

Enforcement

A variety of enforcement organizations and mechanisms exist to ensure children's rights and the successful implementation of the Union. They include the Child Rights Caucus for the United Nations General Assembly Special Session on Children. It was set up to promote full implementation and compliance with the Convention on the Rights of the Child, and to ensure that child rights were given priority during the UN General Assembly Special Session on Children and its Preparatory process.

The United Nations Human Rights Council was created "with the hope that it could be more objective, credible and efficient in denouncing human rights violations worldwide than the highly politicised Commission on Human Rights." The NGO Group for the Convention on the Rights of the Child is a coalition of international non-governmental organisations originally formed in 1983 to facilitate the implementation of the United Nations Convention on the Rights of the Child.

Many countries around the world have children's rights ombudspeople or children's commissioners whose official, governmental duty is to represent the interests of the public by investigating and addressing complaints reported by individual citizens regarding children's rights. Children's ombudspeople can also work for a corporation, a newspaper, an NGO, or even for the general public.

United States Law

Children are generally afforded the basic rights embodied by the Constitution, as enshrined by the Fourteenth Amendment to the United States Constitution. The Equal Protection Clause of that amendment is to apply to children, born within a marriage or not, but excludes children not yet born. This was reinforced by the landmark US Supreme Court decision of In re Gault. In this trial 15-year-old Gerald Gault of Arizona was taken into custody by local police after being accused of making an obscene telephone call.

He was detained and committed to the Arizona State Industrial School until he reached the age of 21 for making an obscene phone call to an adult neighbour. In an 8–1 decision, the Court ruled that in hearings which could result in commitment to an institution, people under the age of 18 have the right to notice and counsel, to question witnesses, and to protection against self-incrimination. The Court found that the procedures used in Gault's hearing met none of these requirements.

There are other concerns in the United States regarding children's rights. The American Academy of Adoption Attorneys is concerned with children's rights to a safe, supportive and stable family structure. Their position on children's rights in adoption cases states that, "children have a constitutionally based liberty interest in the protection of their established families, rights which are at least equal to, and we believe outweigh, the rights of others who would claim a 'possessory' interest in these children." Other issues raised in American children's rights advocacy include children's rights to inheritance in same-sex marriages and particular rights for youth.

CIVIL RIGHTS

In contemporary political thought, the term 'civil rights' is indissolubly linked to the struggle for equality of American blacks during the 1950s and 60s. The aim of that struggle was to secure the status of equal citizenship in a liberal democratic state.

Civil rights are the basic legal rights a person must possess in order to have such a status. They are the rights that constitute free and equal citizenship and include personal, political, and economic rights. No contemporary thinker of significance holds that such rights can be legitimately denied to a person on the basis of race, colour, sex, religion, national origin, or disability. Antidiscrimination principles are thus a common ground in contemporary political discussion. However, there is much disagreement in the scholarly literature over the basis and scope of these principles and the ways in which they ought to be implemented in law and policy.

In addition, debate exists over the legitimacy of including sexual orientation among the other categories traditionally protected by civil rights law, and there is an emerging literature examining issues of how best to understand discrimination based on disability.

RIGHTS

The Civil-Political Distinction

Until the middle of the 20th century, civil rights were usually distinguished from 'political rights'. The former included the rights to own property, make and enforce contracts, receive due process of law, and worship one's religion. Civil rights also covered freedom of speech and the press. But they did not include the right to hold public office, vote, or to testify in court. The latter were political rights, reserved to adult males.

The civil-political distinction was conceptually and morally unstable insofar as it was used to sort citizens into different categories. It was part of an ideology that classified women as citizens who were entitled to certain rights but not to the full panoply to which men were entitled. As that ideology broke down, the civil-political distinction began to unravel.

The idea that a certain segment of the adult citizenry could legitimately possess one bundle of rights, while another segment would have to make do with an inferior bundle, became increasingly implausible. In the end, the civil-political distinction could not survive the cogency of the principle that all citizens of a liberal democracy were entitled, in Rawls's words, to "a fully adequate scheme of equal basic liberties". It may be possible to retain the distinction strictly as one for sorting rights, rather than sorting citizens. But it is difficult to give a convincing account of the principles by which the sorting is done.

It seems neater and cleaner simply to think of civil rights as the general category of basic rights needed for free and equal citizenship. Yet, it remains a matter of contention which claims are properly conceived as belonging to the category of civil rights. Analysts have distinguished among "three generations" of civil rights claims and have argued over which claims ought to be treated as true matters of civil rights.

Three Generations of Rights

The claims for which the American civil rights movement initially fought belong to the first generation of civil rights claims. Those claims included the pre-20th century set of civil rights — such as the rights to receive due process and to make and enforce contracts — but covered political rights as well.

However, many thinkers and activists argued that these first-generation claims were too narrow to define the scope of free and equal citizenship.

They contended that such citizenship could be realised only by honouring an additional set of claims, including rights to food, shelter, medical care, and employment. This second generation of economic "welfare rights," the argument went, helped to ensure that the political, economic, and legal rights belonging to the first generation could be made effective in protecting the vital interests of citizens and were not simply paper guarantees.

Yet, some scholars have argued that these second-generation rights should not be subsumed under the category of civil rights. Thus, Cranston writes, "The traditional 'political and civil rights' can...be readily secured by legislation. Since the rights are for the most part rights against government interference...the legislation needed had to do no more than restrain the executive's own arm. This is no longer the case when we turn to the 'right to work', the 'right to social security' and so forth". However, Cranston fails to recognize that such first-generation rights as due process and the right to vote also require substantial government action and the investment of considerable public resources. Holmes and Sunstein have made the case that all of the first-generation civil rights require government to do more than simply "restrain the executive's own arm."

It seems problematic to think that a significant distinction can be drawn between first and second-generation rights on the ground that the former, but not the latter, simply require that government refrain from interfering with the actions of persons. Moreover, even if some viable distinction could be drawn along those lines, it would not follow that second-generation rights should be excluded from the category of civil rights.

The reason is that the relevant standard for inclusion as a civil right is whether a claim is part of the package of rights constitutive of free and equal citizenship. There is no reason to think that only those claims that can be "readily secured by legislation" belong to that package. And the increasingly dominant view is that welfare rights are essential to adequately satisfying the conditions of free and equal citizenship. In the United States, however, the law does not treat issues of economic well-being per se as civil rights matters. Only insofar as economic inequality or deprivation is linked to race, gender or some other traditional category of antidiscrimination law is it considered to be a question of civil rights.

In legal terms, poverty is not a "suspect classification." On the other hand, welfare rights are protected as a matter of constitutional principle in other democracies. For example, section 75 of the Danish Constitution provides that "any person unable to support himself or his dependents shall, where no other person is responsible for his or their maintenance, be entitled to receive public assistance." And the International Covenant on Economic, Social, and Cultural Rights provides that the state parties to the agreement "recognize the right of everyone to an adequate standard of living for himself and his family, including adequate food, clothing and housing, and to the continuous improvement of living conditions."

A third generation of claims has received considerable attention in recent years, what may be broadly termed "rights of cultural membership." These include language rights for members of cultural minorities and the rights of indigenous peoples to preserve their cultural institutions and practices and to exercise some measure of political autonomy. There is some overlap with the first-generation rights, such as that of religious liberty, but rights of cultural membership are broader and more controversial.

Article 27 of the International Covenant on Civil and Political Rights declares that third-generation rights ought to be protected: In those States in which ethnic, religious or linguistic minorities exist, persons belonging to such minorities shall not be denied the right, in community with the other members of their group, to enjoy their own culture, to profess and practice their own religion, or to use their own language.

Similarly, the Canadian Charter of Rights and Freedoms protects the language rights of minorities and section 27 provides that "This Charter shall be interpreted in a manner consistent with the preservation and enhancement of the multicultural heritage of Canadians." In the United States, there is no analogous protection of language rights or multiculturalism, although constitutional doctrine does recognize native Indian tribes as "domestic dependent nations" with some attributes of political self-rule, such as sovereign immunity.

There is substantial philosophical controversy over the legitimacy and scope of rights of cultural membership. Kymlicka has argued that the liberal commitment to protect the equal rights of individuals requires society to protect such rights. He argues that "granting special representational rights, land claims, or language rights to a minority....can be seen as putting the various groups on a more equal footing, by reducing the extent to which the smaller group is vulnerable to the larger". Such special rights do not amount to "group rights," in the sense of granting the group any power or priority over the individual. Rather, the rights "compensate for unequal circumstances which put the members of minority cultures at a systemic disadvantage in the cultural marketplace".

Waldron criticizes Kymlicka for exaggerating the importance for the individual of membership in her particular culture and for underestimating the mutability and interpenetration of cultures. Individual freedom requires some cultural context of choice, but it does not require the preservation of the particular context in which the individual finds herself. Liberal individuals must be free to evaluate their culture and to distance themselves from it.

Kukathas criticizes Kymlicka for implying that the liberal commitment to the protection of individual rights is insufficient to treat the interests of minorities with equal consideration. Kukathas contends that "we need to reassert the importance of individual liberty or individual rights and question the idea that cultural minorities have collective rights". But the system of uniform legal rules that he endorses would keep the state from intervening even when a minority culture inflicts significant harm on its more vulnerable members, e.g., when cultural norms strongly discourage females from seeking the same educational and career opportunities as males.

Barry asserts that "there are certain rights against oppression, exploitation, and injury, to which every single human being is entitled to lay claim, and...appeals to cultural diversity and pluralism under no circumstances trump the value of basic liberal rights". The legal system should protect those rights by impartially imposing the same rules on all persons, regardless of their cultural or religious membership. Barry allows for a few exceptions, such as the accommodation of a Sikh boy whose turban violated school dress regulations, but thinks that the conditions under which such exceptions will be justified "are rarely satisfied". Barry's position reflects and elaborates Gitlin's earlier condemnation of views advocating distinctive rights for cultural and ethnic minorities. Gitlin condemned such views on the ground that they represent a "swerve from civil rights, emphasizing a universal condition and universalizable rights, to cultural separatism, emphasizing difference and distinct needs".

At the other end of the spectrum, Taylor argues for a form of communitarianism that attaches intrinsic importance to the survival of cultures. In his view, differential treatment under the law for certain practices is sometimes justifiable on the ground that such treatment is important for keeping a culture alive. Taylor goes as far as to claim that cultural survival can sometimes trump basic individual rights, such as freedom of speech.

He defends legal restrictions on the use of English in Quebec, invoking the survival of Quebec's French culture. However, it is unclear why intrinsic value should attach to cultural survival as such. Following John Dewey, Kymlicka rightly emphasizes that liberty would have little or no value to the individual apart from the life-options and meaningful choices provided by culture. But both thinkers also reasonably contend that human interests are ultimately the interests of individual human beings.

In light of that contention, it would seem that a culture that could not gain the uncoerced and undeceived adherence of enough individuals to survive would have no moral claim to its continuation. Legal restrictions on basic liberties that are designed to perpetuate a given culture have the cart before the horse: persons should have their basic liberties protected first, as those protections serve the most important human interests.

Only when those interests are protected can we then say that a culture should survive, not because the culture is intrinsically valuable, but rather because it has the uncoerced adherence of a sufficient number of persons.

Blacks and Native Americans

The treatment of blacks under slavery and Jim Crow presents a history of injustice and cultural annihilation that is similar in some respects to the treatment of Native Americans. However, civil rights principles played a very different role in the struggle of Native Americans against the injustices perpetrated against them by whites. Civil rights principles demand inclusion of the individuals from a disadvantaged group in the major institutions of society on an equal basis with the individuals who are already treated as full citizens.

The principles do not require that the disadvantaged group be given a right to govern its own affairs. A right of political self-determination, in contrast, demands that a group have the freedom to order its affairs at it sees fit and, to that extent, political self-determination has a separatist aspect, even if something less than complete sovereignty is involved. The pursuit of civil rights by American blacks overshadowed the pursuit of political self-determination.

The fact that American blacks lacked any territory of their own on which they could rule themselves favoured the civil rights strategy. Moreover, the civil war amendments, and the civil rights laws that accompanied them, were meant to incorporate black Americans into the body politic as free and equal citizens.

Although this effort was defeated by Jim Crow, the principle of citizenship for blacks had been enshrined in law. And so, in their struggle to defeat Jim Crow, blacks could and did repeatedly demand that white Americans live up to their constitutional promise of equality. In contrast, for Native Americans, the pursuit of political-self-determination, in the form of tribal sovereignty, overshadowed the pursuit of civil rights.

Even after the coerced tribal removals and federal efforts to impose regimes of individual land ownership, tribes still retained some territorial basis on which a measure of self-rule was possible. Moreover, a line of Supreme Court decisions dating to the early 1800's held that Indian tribes possessed some — albeit very limited — inherent powers of sovereignty. Pursuit of political self-determination rather than civil-rights protections seemed, in the eyes of many Indians, to be the most reasonable strategy for counteracting white oppression.

During the civil rights movement of the 1950's and 60's, there was some tension between Native Americans and blacks due to their different attitudes towards self-determination and civil rights. Some Native Americans looked askance at the desire of blacks for inclusion and thought the desire hopelessly naïve.

And activists emerged from the black power movement who had a similar view of the effort at racial inclusion and who called for a form of political self-determination. Such a call was part of a tradition of black nationalism that can still be found today in the United States. Nonetheless, in the United States, unlike civil rights principles, black nationalist principles have not become part of the law. In 1968, Congress enacted an Indian Civil Rights Act. The act extended the reach of certain individual constitutional rights against government to intratribal affairs.

Tribal governments would for the first time be bound by constitutional principles concerning free speech, due process, cruel and unusual punishment, and equal protection, among others. Freedom of religion was omitted from the law as a result of the protests of the Pueblo, whose political arrangements were theocratic, but the law was a major incursion on tribal self-determination, nonetheless.

A married pueblo woman brought suit in federal court, claiming that the tribe's marriage ordinances constituted sex discrimination against her and other women of the tribe, thus violating the ICRA. The ordinances excluded from tribal membership the children of a Pueblo woman who married outside of the tribe, while the children of men who married outsiders were counted as members.

Martinez had initially sought relief in tribal forums, to no avail, before turning to the federal courts. The Supreme Court held that federal courts did not have jurisdiction to hear the case: the substantive provisions of the ICRA did apply to the Pueblo, but the inherent sovereign powers of the tribe meant that the tribal government had exclusive jurisdiction in the case. The ruling has been both questioned and defended by feminist legal scholars.

In contrast to the United States, the Canadian Indian Act provides that men and women are to be treated equally when it comes to the band membership of their children. This law and the Santa Clara case raise the general issue of whether and when it is justifiable for a liberal state to impose liberal principles on illiberal political communities that had been involuntary incorporated into the larger state. Addressing this issue, Kymlicka argues that "there is relatively little scope for legitimate coercive interference" because efforts to impose liberal principles tend to be counterproductive, provoking the charge that they amount to "paternalistic colonialism." Moreover, "liberal institutions can only really work if liberal beliefs have been internalized."

Kymlicka concludes, then, that liberals on the outside of an illiberal culture should support the efforts of those insiders who seek reform but should generally stop short of coercively imposing liberal principles. At the same time, Kymlicka acknowledges that there are cases in which a liberal state is clearly permitted to impose its laws, citing with approval the decision in a case that involved the application of Canadian law to a tribe that had kidnapped a member and forced him to undergo an initiation ceremony.

Applying Kymlicka's general line of thinking might prove contentious in many cases. Consider Santa Clara. His arguments could be used to support the decision in that case: the exercise of jurisdiction might be deemed "paternalistic colonialism." But one might argue, instead, that jurisdiction is needed to vindicate the basic liberal right of gender equality. However, it does seem that, if a wrong akin to kidnapping or worse is required before federal courts can legitimately step in, then the Santa Clara case falls short of meeting such a requirement. The argument might then shift to whether the requirement imposes an excessively high hurdle for the exercise of federal jurisdiction. Kymlicka's approach might not settle the disagreement over Santa Clara, but it does provide a very reasonable normative framework in terms of which liberal thought can address the difficult issues presented by the case and, more generally, by the problem of extending liberal principles to Native American tribes.

FREE AND EQUAL CITIZENSHIP

Civil rights are those rights that constitute free and equal citizenship in a liberal democracy. Such citizenship has two main dimensions, both tied to the idea of autonomy. Civil rights are essentially connected to securing the autonomy of the citizen.

Public and Private Autonomy

To be a free and equal citizen is, in part, to have those legal guarantees that are essential to fully adequate participation in public discussion and decisionmaking. A citizen has a right to an equal voice and an equal vote. In addition, she has the rights needed to protect her "moral independence," that is, her ability to decide for herself what gives meaning and value to her life and to take responsibility for living in conformity with her values.

Equal citizenship has two main dimensions: "public autonomy," *i.e.*, the individual's freedom to participate in the formation of public opinion and society's collective decisions; and "private autonomy," *i.e.*, the individual's freedom to decide what way of life is most worth pursuing.

The importance of these two dimensions of citizenship stem from what Rawls calls the "two moral powers" of personhood: the capacity for a sense of justice and the capacity for a conception of the good. A person stands as an equal citizen when society and its political system give equal and due weight to the interest each citizen has in the development and exercise of those capacities.

Ancient and Modern Citizenship

The idea of equal citizenship can be traced back to Aristotle's political philosophy and his claim that true citizens take turns ruling and being ruled. In modern society, the idea has been transformed, in part by the development of representative government and its system of elections. For modern liberal thought, by contrast, citizenship is no longer a matter of having a direct and equal share in governance, but rather consists in a legal status that confers a certain package of rights that guarantee to an individual a voice, a vote, and a zone of private autonomy. The other crucial differences between modern liberalism and earlier political theories concern the range of human beings who are regarded as having the capacity for citizenship and the scope of private autonomy to which each citizen is entitled as a matter of basic right. Modern liberal theory is more expansive on both counts than its ancient and medieval forerunners.

It is true that racist and sexist assumptions plagued liberal theory well into the twentieth-century. However, two crucial liberal ideas have made possible an internal critique of racism, sexism, and other illegitimate forms of hierarchy. The first is that society is constructed by humans, a product of human will, and not some preordained natural or God-given order. The second is that social arrangements need to be justified before the court of reason to each individual who lives under them and who is capable of reasoning.

The conjunction of these ideas made possible an egalitarianism that was not available to ancient and medieval political thought, although this liberal egalitarianism emerged slowly out of the racist and sexist presuppositions that infused much liberal thinking until recent decades. Many contemporary theorists have argued that taking liberal egalitarianism to its logical cease requires the liberal state to pursue a programme of deliberately reconstructing informal social norms and cultural meanings. They contend that social stigma and denigration still operate powerfully to deny equal citizenship to groups such as blacks, women, and gays. Kernohan has argued that "the egalitarian liberal state should play an activist role in cultural reform", and Koppelman has taken a similar position: "the antidiscrimination project seeks to reconstruct social reality to eliminate or marginalize the shared meanings, practices and institutions that unjustifiably single out certain groups of citizens for stigma and disadvantage".

This position is deeply at odds with at least some of the ideas that lie behind the advocacy of third-generation civil rights. Those rights ground claims of cultural survival, whether or not a culture's meanings, practices and institutions stigmatize and disadvantage the members of some ascriptively-defined group. The egalitarian proponents of cultural reconstruction can be understood as advocating a different kind of "third-generation" for the civil rights movement: one in which the state, having attacked legal, political and economic barriers to equal citizenship, now takes on cultural obstacles.

A cultural-reconstruction phase of the civil rights movement would run contrary to Kukathas's argument that it is too dangerous to license the state to intervene against cultures that engage in social tyranny. It also raises questions about whether state-supported cultural reconstruction would violate basic liberties, such as freedom of private association. The efforts of New Jersey to apply antidiscrimination law to the Boy Scouts, a group which discriminates against gays, emphasizes the potential problems. The Supreme Court invalidated those efforts on grounds of free association. Nonetheless, it may be necessary to reconceive the scope and limits of some basic liberties if the principle of free and equal citizenship is followed through to its logical ceases.

DISCRIMINATION

In liberal democracies, civil rights claims are typically conceptualized in terms of the idea of discrimination. Persons who make such claims assert that they are the victims of discrimination. In order to gain an understanding of current discussion and debate regarding civil rights, it is important to disentangle the various descriptive and normative senses of 'discrimination'.

The Idea of Discrimination

In one of its central descriptive senses, 'discrimination' means the differential treatment of persons, however justifiable or unjustifiable the treatment may be. In a distinct but still primarily descriptive sense, it means the disadvantageous treatment of some persons relative to others. This sense is not purely descriptive in that an evaluative judgment is involved in determining what counts as a disadvantage.

But the sense is descriptive insofar as no evaluative judgment is made regarding the justifiability of the disadvantageous treatment. In addition to its descriptive senses, there are two normative senses of 'discrimination'. In the first, it means any differential treatment of the individual that is morally objectionable. In the second sense, 'discrimination' means the wrongful denial or abridgement of the civil rights of some persons in a context where others enjoy their full set of rights.

The two normative senses are distinct because there can be morally objectionable forms of differential treatment that do not involve the wrongful denial or abridgement of civil rights. If I treat one waiter rudely and another nicely, because one is a New York Yankees fan and the other is a Boston Red Sox fan, then I have acted in a morally objectionable way but have not violated anyone's civil rights.

Discrimination that does deny civil rights is a double wrong against its victims. The denial of civil rights is by itself a wrong, whether or not others have such rights. When others do have such rights, the denial of civil rights to persons who are entitled to them involves the additional wrong of unjustified differential treatment. On the other hand, if everyone is denied his civil rights, then the idea of discrimination would be misapplied to the situation. A despot who oppresses everyone equally is not guilty of discrimination in any of its senses. In contrast, discrimination is a kind of wrong that is found in systems that are liberal democratic but imperfectly so: it is the characteristic injustice of liberal democracy.

The first civil rights law, enacted in 1866, embodied the idea of discrimination as wrongful denial of civil rights to some while others enjoyed their full set of rights. It declared that "all persons" in the United States were to have "the same right...to make and enforce contracts...and to the full and equal benefit of all laws...as is enjoyed by white citizens". The premise was that whites enjoyed a fully adequate scheme of civil rights and that everyone else who was entitled to citizenship was to be legally guaranteed that same set of rights. It is a notable feature of civil rights law that its prohibitions do not protect only citizens. Any person within a given jurisdiction, citizen or not, can claim the protection of the law, at least within certain limits.

Thus, noncitizens are protected by fair housing and equal employment statutes, among other antidiscrimination laws. Noncitizens can also claim the legal protections of due process if charged with a crime. Even illegal aliens have limited due process rights if they are within the legal jurisdiction of the country.

On the other hand, noncitizens cannot claim under U.S. law that the denial of political rights amounts to wrongful discrimination. Noncitizens can vote in local and regional elections in certain countries, but the denial of equal political rights would seem to be central to the very status of noncitizen. The application of much of civil rights law to noncitizens indicates that many of the rights in question are deeper than simply the rights that constitute citizenship.

They are genuine human rights to which every person is entitled, whether she is in a location where she has a right to citizenship or not. And civil rights issues are, for that reason, regarded as broader in scope than issues regarding the treatment of citizens.

Why Discrimination is Unjust

Given the principle of equal citizenship, discrimination in the sense of the denial of civil rights is an injustice that denies certain citizens the rights to which they are entitled. But it is not obvious that the principle entails that discrimination in the sense of differential treatment is unjust, even if the differential treatment disadvantages persons based on their race, sex, or another paradigmatic civil rights category. The common view is that such differential treatment is an injustice that violates the basic rights of the individual. In other words, the view is that it is a civil right to not be treated disadvantageously on account of one's race or sex.

An argument for the soundness of the common view cannot simply invoke existing laws that ban discrimination based on race, sex, and similar categories. The point of the common view is that the injustice of racial and gender discrimination explains why there ought to be those laws. What is required is an account that shows why such discrimination is an injustice.

There are two main approaches to providing an account of the injustice of discrimination based on race and sex. The first is "individualistic" in that it seeks to explain the injustice in a way that abstracts from the broader social and political context in which the differential treatment occurs. The second is "systemic" in that it seeks to explain the injustice in a way that links the differential treatment to social patterns that reduce, or threaten to reduce, the members of certain groups to second-class citizenship.

Individualistic Accounts

Kahlenberg asserts the popular view that race discrimination is unjust because it treats a person on the basis of a characteristic that is immutable or beyond her control. But Boxill rejects such a view, arguing that there are many instances in which it is justifiable to treat persons based on features that are beyond their control. Denying blind people a driver's license or persons with little athletic ability a place on the basketball team is not an injustice to such individuals. Moreover, Boxill notes that, if scientists developed a drug that could change a person's skin colour, it would still be unjust to discriminate against people because of their skin colour.

Flew argues that racism is unjust because it treats differently persons who "are *in all relevant respects* the same". The defining characteristics of a race "are strictly superficial and properly irrelevant to all, or almost all, questions of social status and employability". But if 'relevant' means 'rationally related', then it does not appear to be a requirement of justice that a person always treat others only on the basis of relevant characteristics.

The idea that it is such a requirement rests on the false premise that all morally bad treatment is a violation of justice and rights. If I give a waiter a poor tip because he is not a fan of my favourite sports team, then I have behaved badly but have not violated the waiter's rights or committed an injustice against him. And it is unclear, on Flew's account, why giving a poor tip because of a waiter's race is any different than doing so because of his preferences in sports.

Often people will insist that the injustice of racial or sex discrimination stems from the connection between those forms of discrimination and the reliance on stereotypes. It is not just that race is irrelevant but that those who act on race-based grounds are using inaccurate stereotypes instead of treating a person "as an individual," as the phrase goes. However, if "being treated as an individual" means that others must take into account all of the potentially relevant information about the person in their behaviour towards her, then there is no plausibility to the claim that anyone has a right to such treatment. Life's scarcity of time and resources undermines the idea that there is such a right.

Moreover, in some cases, stereotypical beliefs reflect reliable generalizations about a group. The term 'statistical discrimination' refers to the use of such reliable generalizations. Consider the case of a pregnant job applicant: as a statistical matter, there is a higher antecedent likelihood that she will take more sick days than a nonpregnant applicant during the first year of employment. Yet, an employer who relies on statistical discrimination in excluding the pregnant applicant is acting illegally under the Pregnancy Discrimination Act. The act was passed because many people quite reasonably thought that it was unjust for a pregnant applicant to be treated in that way. But if the treatment is unjust, then one cannot explain why that is so by invoking the unreliability of the generalization on which the treatment is based.

Garcia provides an account of racial discrimination that loosens the link between it and injustice, but still preserves some connection. On his account, such discrimination against others expresses a character defect, viz., the failure to care enough, or in the right way, for their interests. Such discrimination is a matter of what is "in the heart" of the racist individual: "racially focused ill-will or disregard. This echoes the claim made by Gunnar Myrdal in his classic work, *An American Dilemma,* that "the American Negro problem is a problem in the heart of Americans".

Garcia's account weakens the link between racial discrimination and injustice because not every act expressing racial ill-will or disregard will be an injustice. Garcia writes that racial discrimination against a person "will often offend against justice," but he does not argue that it always so offends. He points out that discrimination against a person based on race may amount to a failure of benevolence, rather than a violation of rights. For example, racial disregard may lead a person to refuse to contribute to a charity organization that works with inner-city youth. In such a case, the person has failed to show benevolence for morally discreditable reasons, and so has behaved badly. But no injustice has been committed.

On the other hand racial ill-will is often expressed in violations of the rights of persons: hate crimes that harm the property or person of an individual on account of race; efforts to prevent members of certain racial groups from voting; charging racial minorities higher prices for the same product than the prices charged to similarly situated whites; denying persons equality of opportunity in the job and housing markets on account of their race. Such actions would count as injustices, not simply failures of benevolence. Thus, Garcia's approach preserves some link between discrimination and injustice, but it is much more attenuated than the link posited by the popular view that disadvantageous treatment on the basis of race is *ipso facto* an injustice to the person so treated.

Systemic Accounts

Many thinkers reject the idea that the injustice of discrimination stems fundamentally from what is in the mind or heart of the individual. Crespi criticized Myrdal on the ground that the latter's individualistic understanding of racial discrimination entailed that "ethical exhortation" was the remedy for racial injustice.

Crespi argued that what really needed remedy were the social and economic structures that advantage whites. More recently, Steinberg and Bonilla-Silva, among others, have argued that racial discrimination should not be understood as a "moral problem," *i.e.,* as a problem with individual attitudes or actions, but rather as a problem of persistent structural inequality. And MacKinnon has made a parallel argument when it comes to sex discrimination. For example, she contends that pornography is "not a moral problem" but rather a political one, meaning that it does not pose a problem of the virtue and vice of individuals and their behaviour but rather one concerning relations of power that subordinate women to men.

On the systemic account of racial and sex discrimination, the injustice of discriminatory acts lies in their connection to broader patterns in society that reduce the members of certain groups to second-class citizenship, or worse. Considered in abstraction from these broader patterns, refusing employment to someone on account of her race might be morally objectionable insofar as it treated a person arbitrarily when some important interest of hers was at stake.

But the objectionable treatment amounts to an injustice because such acts are not sporadic but rather systemic and add up to a system in which persons have their entire lives substantially diminished on account of their race or sex. And such a system is what violates the right to equality — the basic civil right. Individual acts of racial or gender discrimination do so only derivatively, by reinforcing the systemic violation.

There are different ways in which a systemic account can be elaborated. For example, in MacKinnon's account of sex discrimination, the system of gender inequality revolves around the sexual subordination of women. Butler, Brown and other feminists provide accounts which do not share MacKinnon's focus on sexual subordination. On the matter of racial discrimination, Cox focuses on the ways in which racial conflict is rooted in class conflict, while Omi and Winant emphasize "the specificity of race as an autonomous field of social conflict, political organization, and cultural/ideological meaning".

All systemic accounts rest on the premise that women, racial minorities, and other groups are second-class citizens and that they are so because of their group membership. The advocates of systemic accounts typically represent their views as incompatible with individualistic ones. They do so by insisting that discrimination is "not a moral problem" of the individual's heart or mind, but one concerning group power relations and social patterns of disadvantage. But their insistence rests on a false dichotomy.

Discrimination based on race, sex and other categories can be a problem of the individual's heart and mind, as well as an issue that concerns systemic patterns of disadvantage in society. As Wasserstrom pointed out, discrimination can operate at both the individual and systemic levels. It is not necessary to deny the existence of patterns of discriminatory treatment that reduce, or threaten to reduce, some persons to second-class citizenship in order to affirm that it is an injustice to deny a person a job because of her sex. And it is not necessary to deny that, apart from social patterns of disadvantage, the individual who is denied a job for such reasons has been treated in an unjust way, in order to affirm that there are such patterns that reduce some to second-class status.

Justifying Antidiscrimination Law

Antidiscrimination laws typically pick out certain categories such as race and sex for legal protection, define certain spheres such as employment and public accommodations in which discrimination based on the protected categories is prohibited, and establish special government agencies, such as the Equal Employment Opportunity Commission, to assist in the laws' enforcement. There are many questions that can be raised concerning the justifiability of such laws.

Some of the central philosophical questions derive from the fact that the laws restrict freedom of association, including the liberty of employers to decide whom they will hire. Some have argued that the liberal commitment to free association requires the rejection of antidiscrimination laws, including those that ban employment discrimination such as the Civil Rights Act of 1964. Most liberals thinkers reject this view, but any liberal defence of antidiscrimination laws must cite considerations sufficiently strong to override the infringements on freedom of association that the laws involve.

There are two different approaches within liberal thought to the justification of antidiscrimination laws. Both approaches regard as very important the interests people have in the areas protected by the laws, such as employment and public accommodations. And both approaches agree that the disadvantageous treatment of a person in those areas on the basis of race, sex, and the other traditional civil rights categories is morally arbitrary. However, on the first approach, the key to the justification of antidiscrimination laws rests squarely on the fact that the conduct prohibited by the laws is morally arbitrary. In contrast, the second approach holds that it is not the morally arbitrary conduct as such that justifies the laws but rather the fact that conduct based on those categories has had systemic effects reducing the members of certain groups to second-class citizenship. Thus, the difference between the two approaches tracks the distinction between the individualistic and systemic accounts of why discrimination is wrong. Although many legal theorists endorse the systemic approach to the justification of antidiscrimination law, the U.S. Supreme Court seems to have adopted the individualistic one.

The Existence of Discrimination

Many debates over civil rights issues turn on assumptions about the scope and effects of existing discrimination against particular groups. For example, some thinkers hold that systemic discrimination based on race and gender is largely a thing of the past in contemporary liberal democracies and that the current situation allows persons to participate in society as free and equal citizens, regardless of race or gender. Many others reject that view, arguing that white skin privilege and patriarchy persist and operate to substantially and unjustifiably diminish the life-prospects of nonwhites and women. These differences drive debates over affirmative action, race-conscious electoral districting, and pornography, among other issues.

Questions about the scope and effects of discrimination are largely but not entirely empirical in character. Such questions concern the degree to which participation in society as a free and equal citizen is hampered by one's race or sex. And addressing that concern presupposes some normative criteria for determining what is needed to possess the status of such a citizen.

Moreover, there are subtle aspects of discrimination that are not captured by thinking strictly in terms of categories such as race, sex, religion, sexual orientation, and so on. Piper analyses "higher-order" forms of discrimination in which certain traits, such as speaking style, come to be arbitrarily disvalued on account of their association with a disvalued race or sex. Determining the presence and effects of such forms of discrimination in society at large would be a very complicated conceptual and empirical task. Additional complications stem from the fact that different categories of discrimination might intersect in ways that produce distinctive forms of unjust disadvantage.

Thus, some thinkers have asserted that the intersection of race and sex creates a form of discrimination against black women which has not been adequately recognized or addressed by judges or liberal legal theorists. And other thinkers have begun to argue that our understanding of discrimination must be expanded beyond the white-black paradigm to include the distinctive ways in which Asian-Americans and other minority groups are subjected to discriminatory attitudes and treatment.

Among the most careful empirical studies of discrimination have been those conducted by Ayers. He found evidence of "pervasive discrimination" in several types of markets, including retail car sales, bail-bonding, and kidney-transplantation. Yet, his assessment is that "we still do not know the current ambit of race and gender discrimination in America".

SEXUAL ORIENTATION

Some civil rights laws in the United States include the category of sexual orientation, but many people contest the legitimacy of the laws. The state of Colorado went so far as to ratify an amendment to its constitution that would prohibit any jurisdiction within the state from enacting a civil rights law that would protect homosexuals.

The amendment was eventually invalidated by the U.S. Supreme Court on the ground that it was the product of simple prejudice and served no legitimate state purpose, thus violating the Equal Protection Clause. But federal courts have upheld the military's "don't ask, don't tell" policy and the U.S. Congress enacted the Defence of Marriage Act, which prohibits courts from ruling that same-sex marriages must be recognized on equal protection grounds. On the other hand, same-sex marriages are legally recognized in Massachusetts, though there are efforts to rescind the recognition, and marriage laws have also been extended to same-sex couples in the Netherlands, Belgium, Canada and Spain. In addition, several jurisdictions have recognized same-sex partnerships with many, though not all, of the legal rights of marriage. Opponents of same-sex marriage have claimed that it would weaken the commitment of heterosexuals to marriage, but some advocates have presented empirical data that appears to undercut any such claim.

Much of the discussion of "gay rights" involves the question of whether sexual orientation is genetically determined, socially determined, or the product of individual choice. However, it is not clear why the question is relevant. The discussion appears to assume that genetic determination would vindicate the civil rights claims of gays, because sexual orientation would then be like race or sex insofar as it would be biologically fixed and immutable.

But it is a mistake to think that racial or sex discrimination is morally objectionable because of the biological fixity or unchosen nature of race and sex. It is objectionable because it expresses ill-will or indifference, and it is unjust because it treats an individual in a morally arbitrary manner and, under current conditions, reinforces social patterns of disadvantage that seriously diminish the life prospects of many persons. The view that sexual orientation is like race or sex in a morally relevant way should focus on the analogous features of discrimination based on sexual orientation.

Wintermute and Koppelman assert that discrimination based on sexual orientation is not just analogous to sex discrimination but that it is a form of sex discrimination. If it is legally permissible for Jane to have sex with John, then banning Joe's having sex with John would seem to amount to discrimination against Joe on grounds of his sex. If Joe were a woman, his having sex with John would be permitted, so he is being treated differently because of his sex. However, Koppelman contends that this formal argument should be supplemented by more substantive ones referring to the systemic patterns of social disadvantage from which gays and lesbians suffer. In fact, one can argue that the treatment of gays and lesbians is an injustice to them as individuals and amounts to a systemic pattern of unjust disadvantage. The individual injustice arises from the arbitrary nature of denying persons valuable life-opportunities, such as employment and marriage, on the basis of their sexual orientation. The systemic injustice arises from the repeated and widespread acts of individual injustice.

The most controversial civil rights issues regarding sexual orientation concern the principle of equal treatment for same-sex and heterosexual couples. Most scholars endorse such a principle and argue that equal treatment requires that same-sex marriages be legalized. Moreover, it is often argued in the literature that a person's choice of sex partner is central to her life and protected under a right of privacy. In Bowers v. Hardwick, the United States Supreme Court rejected this argument, upholding the criminalization of homosexual sodomy.

The decision was condemned by legal and political thinkers and was overturned by the Court in Lawrence v. Texas. The Court invoked the right of privacy in declaring the state's criminal ban on sodomy between same-sex partners. Nonetheless, some scholars who argue for the equal legal treatment of same-sex relations contend that privacy-based arguments are inadequate. They point out that one can hold the view that adults have a right to engage in same-sex intimacies even as one contends that such intimacies are morally abominable and ought not to receive any encouragement from government.

Such a view would reject equal legal treatment for those in intimate same-sex relationships. Finnis takes such a view, arguing that same-sex relations are "manifestly unworthy of the human being and immoral" and should not be encouraged by the state, but finding that criminalizing same-sex relations violates rights of individual privacy. Lee and George also find such relations to be morally defective and unworthy of equal treatment by the state; though George does not think that any sound *a priori* principle prohibits criminalization. Finnis, Lee and George argue for their condemnation of same-sex relations on the ground of natural law theory.

However, unlike traditional versions of natural law theory, their version does not rest on any explicit theological or metaphysical claims. Rather, it invokes independent principles of practical reasoning that articulate the basic reasons for action. Such reasons are the fundamental goods that action is capable of realizing and, for Finnis, Lee and George, include "marriage, the *conjuntio* of man and woman". Homosexual conduct, masturbation, and all extra-marital sex aim strictly at "individual gratification" and can be no part of any "common good." Such actions "harm the character" of those voluntarily choosing them. In taking the actions, a person becomes a slave to his passions, allowing his reason to be overridden by his raw desire for sensuous pleasure.

On Finnis's account, when consensual sexual conduct is private, government may not outlaw it, but government "can rightly judge that it has a compelling interest in denying that 'gay lifestyles' are a valid and humanly acceptable choice and form of life". And for Finnis, Lee and George, equal treatment of same-sex and heterosexual relations is out of the question due to the morally defective character of same-sex relations. Macedo responds to Finnis by arguing that "all of the goods that can be shared by sterile heterosexual couples can also be shared by committed homosexual couples". Macedo points out that Finnis does not condemn sexual intercourse by sterile heterosexual couples.

But Finnis replies that there is a relevant difference between homosexual couples and sterile heterosexual ones: the latter but not the former are united "biologically" when they have intercourse. Lee and George make essentially the same point: only heterosexual couples can "truly become one body, one organism". But Macedo points out that, biologically, it is not the man and woman who unite but the sperm and the egg. It can be added that the "biological unity" argument seems to run contrary to Finnis's claim that his position "does not seek to infer normative ceases from non-normative premises". More importantly, Macedo and Koppelman make the key point that the human good possible through intimate relations is a function of "mutual commitment and stable engagement" and that same-sex couples can achieve "the precise kind of human good" that is available to heterosexual ones. Equal treatment under the law for same-sex couples, including the recognition of same-sex marriage, would remove unjustifiable obstacles faced by same-sex couples to the achievement of that human good.

DISABILITY

During the 1970's and 80's, persons with disabilities increasingly argued that they were second-class citizens. They organized into a civil rights movement that pressed for legislation that would help secure for them the status of equal citizens. Protection against discrimination based on disability was written into the Canadian Charter of Rights and Freedoms and The Charter of Fundamental Rights of the European Union. The disability rights movement in the U.S. culminated with the passage of the Americans With Disabilities Act of 1990. The ADA has served as a model for legislation in countries such as Australia, India and Israel

The Medical and Social Models

The traditional model for understanding disability is called the "medical model." It is reflected in many pre-ADA laws and in some philosophical discussions of disability which treat it as an issue of the just distribution of health care. The medical model, a disabled person is one who falls below some baseline level that defines normal human functioning. That level is a natural one, on this view, in that it is determined by biological facts about the human species. Thus, the medical model supposes that the question of who counts as disabled can be answered in a way that is value-free and that abstracts from existing social practices and the physical environment those practices have constructed. It also gives the medical profession a privileged position in determining who is disabled, as the study and treatment of normal and subnormal human functioning is the specialty of that profession.

The consensus among current disability theorists is that the medical model should be rejected. Any determination that a certain level of function is normal for the species will presuppose judgments that do not simply describe biological reality but impose on them some system of evaluation. Moreover, the level of functioning a person can achieve does not depend solely on her own individual abilities: it depends as well on the social practices and the physical environment those practices have shaped.

Disability theorists thus posit an important analogy between the categories of 'race' and 'disability'. As they understand it, neither category refers to any real distinctions in nature. Just as there is variation in skin colour, there is variation in acuity of vision, physical strength, ability to walk and run and so on. And just as there is no natural line dividing one "race" from another, there is no natural line dividing those who are functionally "abnormal" from those who are not so. The rejection of the medical model has led to a "social model," according to which certain physical or biological properties are turned into dysfunctions by social practices and the socially-constructed physical environment.

For example, lack of mobility for those who are unable to walk is not simply a function of their physical characteristics: it is also a function of building practices that employ stairs instead of ramps and by automotive design practices that require the use of one's legs to drive a car. There is nothing necessary about such practices. The social model conceives of disability as socially-imposed dysfunction. The social model brings attention to how engineering and design practices can work to the disadvantage of persons with certain physical characteristics. And the idea of dysfunction is certainly a value-laden one. But it seems no more accurate to think that dysfunction is entirely imposed by society than it is to think that it is entirely the product of an individual's physical or mental characteristics. Individual characteristics in the context of the socially-constructed environment determine the level of functioning that a person can achieve. And some individual characteristics would impair a person's functioning under all or almost all practicable alternatives to current social practices. Moreover, despite the fact that "normal human functioning" is a value-laden concept, it does not follow that it is entirely subjective or that reasonable efforts to specify the elements of some morally acceptable level of human functioning are misguided. Indeed, some defensible understanding of what counts as better or worse human functioning would seem to be necessary to determine when some social practice has turned a physical characteristic into a significant disadvantage for a person.

In addition, the social model's conception of what it is to be a disabled person seems overbroad. The social practice of requiring students to pass courses in order to receive a degree creates a barrier that some persons cannot surmount. It does not seem that such people are, *ipso facto,* disabled. Such examples of "exclusionary" social practices could be multiplied indefinitely. Some thinkers may not be troubled by the implication that everyone is disabled in every respect in which she is excluded or otherwise disadvantaged by some social practice. But it is difficult to see how the idea of disability would then be of much use.

Race, Disability, and Discrimination

The disability rights movement began with the idea that discrimination on the basis of disability was not different in any morally important way from discrimination based on race. The aim of the movement was to enshrine in law the same kind of antidiscrimination principle that protected persons based on their race. But some theorists have questioned how well the analogy holds. They point out that applying the antidiscrimination norm to disability requires taking account of physical or mental differences among people. This seems to be treatment based on a person's physical features, apparently the exact opposite of the ideal of "colourblindness" behind the traditional antidiscrimination principle.

Even race-based affirmative action does not really seem to be parallel to antidiscrimination policies that take account of disability. Advocates of affirmative action assert that the social ideal is for persons not to be treated on the basis of their race or colour at all. Race-conscious policies are seen as instruments that will move society towards that ideal.

In contrast, policies designed to counter discrimination based on disability are not sensibly understood as temporary measures or steps towards a goal in which people are not treated based on their disabilities. The policies permanently enshrine the idea that in designing buildings or buses or constructing some other aspect of our physical-social environment, we must be responsive to the disabilities people have in order for the disabled to have "fair equality of opportunity". The need for a permanent "accommodation" of persons with disabilities seems to mark an important difference in how the antidiscrimination norm should be understood in the context of disability, as opposed to the context of race.

However, it is important to recognize that, at the level of fundamental principle, the reasons why disability-based discrimination is morally objectionable and even unjust are essentially the same as the reasons why racial discrimination is so. At the individual level, disadvantageous treatment of the disabled is often rooted in ill-will, disregard, and moral arbitrariness. At the systemic level, such treatment creates a social pattern of disadvantage that reduces the disabled to second-class status. In those two respects, the grounds of civil rights law are no different when it comes to the disabled. Another way in which disability is thought to be fundamentally different from race concerns the special needs that the disabled often have that make life more costly for them. These extra costs would exist even if the socially-constructed physical environment were built to provide the disabled with fair equality of opportunity and their basic civil and political liberties were secured. In order to function effectively, disabled persons may need to buy medications or therapies or other forms of assistance that the able-bodied do not need for their functioning. And there does not seem to be any parallel in matters of race to the special needs of some of those who are disabled. The driving idea of the civil rights movement was that blacks did not have any special needs: all they needed was to have the burdens of racism lifted from them and, once that was accomplished, they would flourish or fail like everyone else in society. However, Silvers argues that the parallel between race and disability still holds: all the disabled may claim from society as a matter of justice is that they have fair equality of opportunity and the same basic civil rights as everyone else. Any special needs that the disabled may have do not provide the grounds of any legitimate claims of justice.

On the other hand, Kittay argues that the special needs of the disabled are a matter of basic justice. She focuses on the severely mentally disabled, for whom fair opportunity in the labour markets and political rights in the public sphere will have no significance, and on the families which have the responsibility of caring for the severely disabled. Pogge also questions Silvers' view, suggesting that it is implausible to deny that justice requires that society provide resources for meeting the needs of the severely disabled.

Still, it may be the case that some version of Silvers' approach may be justifiable when it comes to disabled persons who have the capacity "to participate fully in the political and civic institutions of the society and, more broadly, in its public life". In the case of such persons, the basic civil right to equal citizenship would require that they have the equal opportunity to participate in such institutions, regardless of their disability. Although there may be some aspects of the racial model that cannot be applied to persons with severe forms of mental disability, the principles behind the American civil rights struggles of the 1950's and 60's remain crucial normative resources for understanding and combating forms of unjust discrimination that have only more recently been addressed by philosophers and by society more broadly.

Contractarianism and the Disabled

The emergence of the issue of disability rights has posed an important challenge for versions of liberalism inspired by the social contract tradition. One of the putative advantages of such forms of liberalism is that they better reflect strong and widely held intuitions about justice and individual rights than does utilitarianism.

As Rawls famously wrote, "Each person possesses an inviolability founded on justice that even the welfare of society as a whole cannot override". However, several thinkers have argued that Rawls's own contractarian theory does not make adequate room for the severely disabled. These arguments are not about the rights of the severely disabled, but rather begin from the assumption that those who are so disabled do have robust moral rights and then proceed to the question whether contractarianism can account for those rights. The problem for Rawls derives from the conception of personhood that accompanies his idea that society should be conceived as a fair system of cooperation among free and equal persons, extending over generations. On that conception, "a person is someone who can be a citizen, that is, a normal and fully cooperating member of society over a complete life." Additionally, persons are represented as having two "moral powers," the capacities for a sense of justice and for a conception of the good. The parties to Rawls's original position choose principles of justice with such a conception of the person in mind.

Critics have argued that Rawls's principles of justice fail to take adequate account of the legitimate claims of the severely disabled and that the heart of the problem is Rawls's contractarianism. Nussbaum claims that Rawls goes astray in following traditional contractarianism and conceiving of society as a scheme of cooperation for mutual advantage. Yet, Becker defends mutual-advantage theories, arguing that they can incorporate a conception of reciprocity sufficiently rich to underwrite principles that truly do justice to the disabled. Stark and Brighouse argue that Rawls's theory, in particular, can be extended or modified to take account of disabled, without repudiating its contractarian core.

Kittay agrees with the liberal idea that justice must not be sacrificed for other values, but she doubts that any form of liberalism can make adequate room for the claims of justice made on behalf of the severely disabled. In contrast, Silvers and Francis defend a form of contract theory in which the parties seek to build mutual trust. They argue that the interests of disabled would not be discounted in such a contract.

LEGAL CASES AND STATUTES

- Americans With Disabilities Act. 42 U.S.C. §§12101-12213.
- Bowers v. Hardwick 478 U.S. 186.
- Boy Scouts v. Dale, No. 99-699.
- Civil Rights Act of 1866. 42 U.S.C §1981.
- Civil Rights Act of 1964. 42 U.S.C. §§2000e et seq.
- Defence of Marriage Act 28 U.S.C. §1738c.
- Ex Parte Crow Dog 109 U.S. 556.
- Indian Civil Rights Act of 1968. 28 U.S.C. §§1301-1303.
- Oklahoma Tax Commission v. Citizen Band, Potawatomi Indian Tribe 498 U.S. 505.
- Pregnancy Discrimination Act 42 U.S.C. §2000 (e)(k).
- Romer v. Evans 517 U.S. 620.
- Santa Clara Pueblo v. Martinez 436 U.S. 49.
- Thomasson v. Perry 80 F.3d 915

CIVIL LIBERTIES

Civil liberties are rights and freedoms that protect an individual from the state. Civil liberties set limits on the government so that its agents cannot abuse their power and interfere unduly with the lives of private citizens. Common civil liberties include the rights of people, freedom of religion, and freedom of speech, and additionally, the right to due process, to a trial, to own property, and to privacy. The formal concept of civil liberties dates back to the English legal charter the Magna Carta 1215, which in turn was based on pre-existing documents namely the English Charter of Liberties, a landmark document in English legal history.

Many contemporary states have a constitution, a bill of rights, or similar constitutional documents that enumerate and seek to guarantee civil liberties. Other states have enacted similar laws through a variety of legal means, including signing and ratifying or otherwise giving effect to key conventions such as the European Convention on Human Rights and the International Covenant on Civil and Political Rights. It might be said that the protection of civil liberties is a key responsibility of all citizens of free states, as distinct from authoritarian states.

The existence of some claimed civil liberties is a matter of dispute, as are the extent of most civil rights. Controversial examples include property rights, reproductive rights, civil marriage, and the right to keep and bear arms. Whether the existence of victimless crimes infringes upon civil liberties is a matter of dispute. Another matter of debate is the suspension or alteration of certain civil liberties in times of war or state of emergency, including whether and to what extent this should occur. An individual who "actively supports or works for the protection or expansion of civil liberties" is called a civil libertarian.

UNITED STATES

The United States Constitution, especially its Bill of Rights, protects civil liberties. Human rights within the United States are often called civil rights, which are those rights, privileges and immunities held by all Americans, in distinction to political rights, which are the rights that inhere to those who are entitled to participate in elections, as candidates or voters. Before universal suffrage, this distinction was important, since many people were ineligible to vote but still were considered to have the fundamental freedoms derived from the rights to life, liberty and the pursuit of happiness.

This distinction is less important now that Americans enjoy near universal suffrage, and civil liberties are now taken to include the political rights to vote and participate in elections.

CANADA

The Constitution of Canada includes the Canadian Charter of Rights and Freedoms which guarantees many of the same rights as the U.S. constitution, with the notable exceptions of protection against establishment of religion. However, the Charter does protect freedom of religion. The Charter also omits any mention of, or protection for, property.

EUROPEAN CONVENTION ON HUMAN RIGHTS

The European Convention on Human Rights, to which most European countries, including all of the European Union, belong, enumerates a number of civil liberties and is of varying constitutional force in different European states.

UNITED KINGDOM

While the United Kingdom has no codified constitution, relying on a number of legal conventions and pieces of legislation, it is a signatory to the European Convention on Human Rights which covers both human rights and civil liberties. The Human Rights Act 1998 incorporates the great majority of Convention rights directly into UK law.

Britain has what is called an unwritten constitution: centuries of legislation and legal precedent dating back to before the Magna Carta guarantee the rights of her subjects. Recently Shadow Home Secretary David Davies resigned his parliamentary seat over what he described as the "erosion of civil liberties" by the current government, and successfully won re-election on a civil liberties platform. This was in reference to the recent anti-terrorism laws and in particular the extension to pre-trial detention, that is perceived by many to be an infringement of Habeas Corpus established in the Magna Carta in 1215.

CHINA

The Constitution of People's Republic of China, especially its Fundamental Rights and Duties of Citizens, claims to protect many civil liberties, although in practice dissidents may find themselves without the protection of the rule of law.

INDIA

The Fundamental Rights — embodied in Part III of the constitution — guarantee civil liberties such that all Indians can lead their lives in peace as citizens of India. The six fundamental rights are right to equality, right to freedom, right against exploitation, right to freedom of religion, cultural and educational rights and right to constitutional remedies. These include individual rights common to most liberal democracies, incorporated in the fundamental law of the land and are enforceable in a court of law.

Violations of these rights result in punishments as prescribed in the Indian Penal Code, subject to discretion of the judiciary. These rights are neither absolute nor immune from constitutional amendments. They have been aimed at overturning the inequalities of pre-independence social practises. Specifically, they resulted in abolishment of untouchability and prohibit discrimination on the grounds of religion, race, caste, sex, or place of birth. They forbid human trafficking and unfree labour.

They protect cultural and educational rights of ethnic and religious minorities by allowing them to preserve their languages and administer their own educational institutions. All people, irrespective of race, religion, caste or sex, have the right to approach the High Courts or the Supreme Court for the enforcement of their fundamental rights. It is not necessary that the aggrieved party has to be the one to do so. In public interest, anyone can initiate litigation in the court on their behalf. This is known as "Public interest litigation". High Court and Supreme Court judges can also act on their own on the basis of media reports.

The Fundamental Rights emphasise equality by guaranteeing to all citizens the access and use of public institutions and protections, irrespective of their background. The rights to life and personal liberty apply for persons of any nationality, while others, such as the freedom of speech and expression are applicable only to the citizens of India. The right to equality in matters of public employment cannot be conferred to overseas citizens of India. Fundamental Rights primarily protect individuals from any arbitrary State actions, but some rights are enforceable against private individuals too. For instance, the constitution abolishes untouchability and prohibits begar.

These provisions act as a check both on State action and actions of private individuals. Fundamental Rights are not absolute and are subject to reasonable restrictions as necessary for the protection of national interest. In the Kesavananda Bharati vs. state of Kerala case, the Supreme Court ruled that all provisions of the constitution, including Fundamental Rights can be amended.

However, the Parliament cannot alter the basic structure of the constitution like secularism, democracy, federalism, separation of powers. Often called the "Basic structure doctrine", this decision is widely regarded as an important part of Indian history. In the 1978 Maneka Gandhi v. Union of India case, the Supreme Court extended the doctrine's importance as superior to any parliamentary legislation. The verdict, no act of parliament can be considered a law if it violated the basic structure of the constitution. This landmark guarantee of Fundamental Rights was regarded as a unique example of judicial independence in preserving the sanctity of Fundamental Rights. The Fundamental Rights can only be altered by a constitutional amendment, hence their inclusion is a check not only on the executive branch, but also on the Parliament and state legislatures. The imposition of a state of emergency may lead to a temporary suspension of the rights conferred by Article 19 to preserve national security and public order. The President can, by order, suspend the right to constitutional remedies as well.

RUSSIA

The Constitution of Russian Federation guarantees in theory many of the same rights and civil liberties as the U.S. except to bear arms, *i.e.*: freedom of speech, freedom of religion, freedom of association and assembly, freedom to choose language, to due process, to a fair trial, privacy, freedom to vote, right for education, etc.

However, human rights groups like Amnesty International have warned that Putin has seriously curtailed freedom of expression, freedom of assembly and freedom of association amidst growing authoritarianism.

BUSINESS AND HUMAN RIGHTS

Non-state actors, particularly multinational or trans-national corporations have become important players throughout the world. As the influence and reach of corporations has grown as a result of globalization and other global developments, there is an increasing debate about the roles and responsibilities of corporate actors with regard to human rights.

International human rights standards have traditionally been the responsibility of governments, aimed at regulating relations between the state and individuals/groups. In view of the increased role played by corporate actors at both the national and international level, the United Nations human rights machinery is considering the scope of business' human rights responsibilities and exploring ways for corporate actors to be accountable for the impact of their activities on human rights. However, the practical meaning of the link between business and human rights remains unclear for many and substantial debates over which human rights can and should apply to business, and in what way are ongoing.

OHCHR's work on the issue of business and human rights is focused on three areas:

1. Advocacy by the High Commissioner;
2. Support to the Special Representative of the Secretary-General on the issue of transnational corporations and other business enterprises;
3. Active involvement in the United Nations Global Compact;

The High Commissioners has expressed support for the development of human right standards applicable to the business sector, while at the same time advocating the implementation of voluntary initiatives towards corporate social responsibility.

OHCHR is providing ongoing support and advice to the work of the Special Representative of the Secretary-General on the issue of transnational corporations and other business enterprises with regard to human rights. The mandate was established by the United Nations Commission on Human Rights in 2005 by resolution 2005/69 and was extended by the Human Rights Council.

In resolution 2005/69, the Commission on Human Rights mandated the High Commissioner, in collaboration with the SRSG, to convene annually a consultation with executives from a particular business sector to discuss the human rights challenges faced by that sector. In November 2005, the High Commissioner convened a consultation with representatives from the extractive sector. In January 2007, the High Commissioner convened a consultation with representatives from the finance sector.

The UN Global Compact is certainly the most prominent voluntary initiative in the field of business and human rights. It is a personal initiative of the United Nations Secretary-General dating from 2000, aimed at getting business leaders to voluntarily promote and apply within their corporate domains 10 principles relating to human rights, labour standards, the environment, and anti-corruption. At present, thousands of companies, many of them large trans-national companies, from all continents have signed on to the Global Compact.

OHCHR is one of now 6 UN agencies which work in partnership with the Secretary-General's Global Compact office. Since the launch of the Global Compact, OHCHR has been requested by the United Nations Secretary-General to serve as "guardian" of the human rights principles and to contribute to efforts made to encourage companies to implement these principles in their core operations and business model.

OHCHR activities have been grouped around the themes of learning and dialogue. OHCHR is involved in Global Compact governance through its membership of the Global Compact Inter-Agency Team which is responsible for ensuring coherent support for the internalization of the principles within the United Nations and among all participants. The 18th of June 2008 the Human Rights Council was unanimous in "welcoming" the policy framework for business and human rights the SRSG proposed in his final report under the 2005 mandate.

The policy framework comprises three core principles: the State duty to protect against human rights abuses by third parties, including business; the corporate responsibility to respect human rights; and the need for greater access by victims to effective remedies.

The Human Rights Council has renewed the mandate for a period of 3 years with the new resolution A/HRC/8/L.8 that requests the Special Representative of the Secretary General to operationalize the framework elaborated and specifically:

- To provide views and recommendations on ways to strengthen the fulfillment of the duty of the State to protect all human rights from abuses by transnational corporations and other business enterprises, including through international cooperation;
- To elaborate further on the scope and content of the corporate responsibility to respect all human rights and to provide concrete guidance to business and other stakeholders;
- To explore options and make recommendations, at the national, regional and international levels, for enhancing access to effective

remedies available to those whose human rights are impacted by corporate activities;

- To integrate a gender perspective throughout his work and to give special attention to persons belonging to vulnerable groups, in particular children;
- To liaise closely with the efforts of the human rights working group of the Global Compact in order to identify, exchange and promote best practices and sessions learned on the issue of transnational corporations and other business enterprises;
- To work in close coordination with United Nations and other relevant international bodies, offices, departments and specialized agencies, and in particular with other special procedures of the Council;
- To continue to consult on the issues covered by the mandate on an ongoing basis with all stakeholders, including States, national human rights institutions, international and regional organizations, transnational corporations and other business enterprises, and civil society, including academics, employers' organizations, workers' organizations, indigenous and other affected communities and non-governmental organizations, including through joint meetings;
- To report annually to the Council and the General Assembly;

In Resolution 2005/69 The Commission on Human Rights requested the Secretary-General to appoint a special representative on the issue of human rights and transnational corporations and other business enterprises, for an initial period of two years, with the following mandate:

- To identify and clarify standards of corporate responsibility and accountability for transnational corporations and other business enterprises with regard to human rights; To elaborate on the role of States in effectively regulating and adjudicating the role of transnational corporations and other business enterprises with regard to human rights, including through international cooperation;
- To research and clarify the implications for transnational corporations and other business enterprises of concepts such as "complicity" and "sphere of influence";
- To develop materials and methodologies for undertaking human rights impact assessments of the activities of transnational corporations and other business enterprises;
- To compile a compendium of best practices of States and transnational corporations and other business enterprises.

HUMAN RIGHTS AND CLIMATE CHANGE

It is becoming apparent that climate change will have implications for the enjoyment of human rights. The United Nations Human Rights Council recognized this in its resolution 7/23 "Human rights and climate change", expressing concern that climate change "poses an immediate and far-reaching threat to people and communities around the word" and requesting the Office of the United Nations High Commissioner to prepare a study on the relationship between climate change and human rights.

The Fourth Assessment Report of the Intergovernmental Panel on Climate Change put it beyond doubt that the global climate system is warming and doing so mainly because of man-made greenhouse gas emissions. IPCC reports and other studies document how global warming will affect, and already is affecting, the basic elements of life for millions of people around the world. Effects include an increasing frequency of extreme weather events, rising sea levels, droughts, increasing water shortages, and the spread of tropical and vector born diseases.

Viewing the data through a human rights lens, it is clear that projected climate change-related effects threaten the effective enjoyment of a range of human rights, such as the right to safe and adequate water and food, the right to health and adequate housing. Equally, the human rights perspective brings into focus that climate change is set to hit the poorest countries and communities the hardest.

The international human rights standards serve as a guide for measures to tackle climate change, underscoring the fundamental moral and legal obligations to protect and promote full enjoyment of the rights enshrined in the Universal Declaration of Human Rights and in the core universal human rights treaties.

ACTION BY THE HUMAN RIGHTS COUNCIL

On 28 March 2008, the Human Rights Council adopted its first resolution on "human rights and climate change". In implementation of that resolution, OHCHR prepared and submitted a study on the relationship between climate change and human rights to the tenth session of the Council held in March 2009.

On 25 March 2009, the Council adopted resolution 10/4 "Human rights and climate change" in which it, inter alia, notes that "climate change-related impacts have a range of implications, both direct and indirect, for the effective enjoyment of human rights ..."; recognizes that the effects of climate change "will be felt most acutely by those segments of the population who are already in a vulnerable situation ...", recognizes that "effective international cooperation to enable the full, effective and sustained implementation of the United Nations Framework Convention on Climate Change ... is important in order to support national efforts for the realization of human rights implicated by climate change-related impacts", and affirms that "human rights obligations and commitments have the potential to inform and strengthen international and national policy-making in the area of climate change".

In resolution 10/4, the Council decided to hold a panel discussion on the relationship between climate change and human rights at its eleventh session in order to contribute to the realization of the goals set out in the Bali Action Plan. In implementation of resolutions 7/23 and 10/4, the OHCHR study and a summary of the Council's discussions will be made available to the Conference of Parties to the United Nations Framework Convention on Climate Change for its consideration.

CULTURAL RIGHTS

The cultural rights movement has provoked attention to protect the rights of groups of people, or their culture, in similar fashion to the manner in which the human rights movement has brought attention to the needs of individuals throughout the world. Cultural rights are different from human rights specifically because they are vested in groups of people, whereas human rights deal with individuals.

PROTECTING A CULTURE

Cultural rights focus on groups such as religious and ethnic minorities and indigenous societies that are in danger of disappearing. Cultural rights include a group's ability to preserve its way of life, such as child rearing, continuation of language, and security of its economic base in the nation, which it is located.

The related notion of indigenous intellectual property rights has arisen in attempt to conserve each society's culture base and essentially prevent ethnocide. The cultural rights movement has been popularized because much traditional cultural knowledge has commercial value, like ethno-medicine, cosmetics, cultivated plants, foods, folklore, arts, crafts, songs, dances, costumes, and rituals. Studying ancient cultures may reveal evidence about the history of the human race and shed more light on our origin and successive cultural development. However, the study, sharing and commercialization of such cultural aspects can be hard to achieve without infringing upon the cultural rights of those who are a part of that culture.

CULTURAL BIGOTRY

The notion of cultural rights is not too cultural. Cultural rights has many ways that it can be looked upon. "Cultural rights are vested not in individuals but in groups, such as religious and ethnic minorities and indigenous societies." All cultures are brought up differently, therefore cultural rights include a group's ability to preserve its culture, to raise its children in the ways its forebears, to continue its language, and to not be deprived of its economic base by the nation in which it is located."

Anthropologist sometimes choose not to study some cultures beliefs and rights, because they believe that it may cause misbehaviour, and they choose not to turn against different diversities of cultures. Although anthropologist sometimes do turn away from studying different cultures they still depend a lot on what they study at different archaeological sites.

DEMOCRACY

Human rights and democracy have historically been viewed as separate, albeit parallel, concepts. However, understandings of both human rights and democracy are dynamic and varied, and recent re-conceptualizations of both ideas have led to the emergence of a discourse that recognizes their interdependence.

Specifically, definitions of democracy have expanded from the traditional procedural democracy to encompass the ideals of a substantive, liberal democracy. Likewise, the human rights framework has begun to further develop conceptions of social, economic, and cultural rights, in addition to civil and political rights, thus expanding the notion of human rights to include human security, and extending human rights to the collective as well as the individual level. These renewed definitions present opportunities for recognizing the convergence of the theories and fields related to human rights and democracy.

The necessity of acknowledging the interdependence of democracy and human rights is becoming especially important in emerging democracies such as Palestine. In these cases, in which the development and reform of democratic institutions is starting to take place, it is imperative to ensure that such institutions are built on foundations of both human rights and democracy if they are to be sustainable. To be sure, previous attempts at democracy by the Palestinian Authority in the 1990s proved to be ephemeral, largely due to the absence of protection for human rights.

Likewise, human rights advocates have found it difficult to affect systemic change in the absence of a legitimate democracy. Thus, as Palestine looks ahead to new opportunities for democracy in the future, it is necessary to integrate the broadened human rights framework, including human security, with the ideals and institutions of a liberal, participatory democracy.

This text begins with a theoretical discussion of the principles of democracy, distinguishing between substantive and procedural democracy and identifying key elements and institutions inherent in a liberal democracy. The emerging re-conceptualization of the human rights framework, including the human security perspective, which has enhanced the complementarity between human rights and democracy.

The following part discusses the convergence of the democracy and human rights fields and theories, and concludes that the two concepts are not only complementary, but are indeed interdependent. The second half of the text focuses on the application of this theory in the case of Palestine by analysing past and present experiences with democracy and human rights in the Occupied Territories, including obstacles and points of progress, and discussing recommendations for future implementation.

THEORETICAL ANALYSIS

Defining Democracy: Principles and Institutions

The idea of democracy has been understood and applied in different ways, both temporally and culturally, with democracy taking various forms in different societies. From a historical perspective, the direct democracy of ancient Athens has been transformed into the representative democracy that is common today. Likewise, former restrictions on the political participation of women and other marginalized groups have been challenged in modern times to allow for more inclusive democracies.

Most recently, both theorists and practitioners of democracy are starting to further articulate differences between procedural democracies and substantive, liberal democracies. However, all of these forms of democracy are based to some extent on the original Greek notion of demokratia, that is, "government by the people," from the words demos and kratos.

This core concept still forms the crux of modern definitions of democracy, including the 1993 Vienna Declaration's statement that "democracy is based on the freely expressed will of the people to determine their own political, economic, social and cultural systems and their full participation in all aspects of their lives."

From this starting point, it is possible to identify several key principles and institutions that are inherent to a sustainable democracy. While historically there has been more emphasis on the political institutions and procedures that comprise democracy, namely elections, political parties, and governmental bodies, increased attention has recently been given to the ideals and principles that underscore those mechanisms. As stated by David Beetham, Director of the Centre for Democratization Studies at the University of Leeds, "to define democracy simply in institutional terms is to elevate means into ends, and to concentrate on the forms without the substance."

Jack Donnelly, International Studies at the University of Denver, agrees, noting that "pure procedural democracy can easily denigrate into non-democratic or even anti-democratic formalism," thus, "substantive conceptions rightly insist that we not lose sight of the core values of popular authority and control over government." However, Donnelly also notes that purely substantive approaches fail to recognize the "idea of the people ruling rather than just benefiting... The term 'democratic' easily slides into an essentially superfluous synonym for 'egalitarian.'"

That is, government for the people is not synonymous with government by the people, and therefore may or may not be democratic. To be sure, substantive conceptions risk being susceptible to normative associations that identify any positive sociopolitical elements as indicators of democracy. This text takes the position that neither "substantive" nor "procedural" conceptions of democracy should be considered more important than the other; indeed, it is questionable if the two notions can even be separated. Instead, substantive and procedural elements should be viewed as complementary and in fact essential to each other. The principles that underscore substantive democracy will only remain theoretical ideals unless mechanisms are present for translating those ideals into reality, while procedural institutions, however democratic in form, are meaningless if they do not yield ends that reflect democratic values.

For the remainder of this text, the term "substantive democracy" will refer to democracies that embody both the principles and the institutions that form the foundation of democracy, in contrast to "electoral democracies," which may be democratic in name and form but not in practice. The basic elements of a substantive democracy, Beetham, "are that the people have a right to a controlling influence over public decisions and decision makers, and that they should be treated with equal respect and as of equal worth in the context of such decisions."

Beetham refers to these concepts as popular control and popular equality, both of which contribute to the foundation of the principles and institutions that inform democracy. These primary elements, in conjunction with the rule of law, open government, and public participation, form the core of substantive democracies, as reflected in their mechanisms and institutions, and the presence of civil society and citizen rights.

Mechanisms

The primary indicator of democracy is the presence of popular elections. Beetham, "popular authorization is achieved through regular competitive elections according to universal secret ballot, which ensures voters a choice of candidates and policies and gives them the opportunity to dismiss politicians who no longer command their confidence." As Shadrack Gutto, Director of the Centre for Applied Legal Studies at the University of Witwatersrand in Johannesburg, states however, "for elections to be substantially 'free and fair,' it is imperative that enabling principles and rights be observed," including "the rights to or freedom of association, opinion, expression, and assembly."

Gutto also notes the importance of available and adequate material and human resources to educate voters, register voters, monitor the voting process, count election results, and reconcile disputes. Indeed, the democratic nature of an electoral process should be assessed by "the reach, inclusiveness, independence, integrity, and impartiality of elections, as well as how equally the electoral process treats citizens, how much effective choice it offers them, how far the government actually fulfills the electoral choices made, and how many people in practice exercise the right to vote." In addition, political parties function as a mechanism within electoral systems by organizing different policies into cohesive programmes, nominating appropriate candidates, and advocating for the implementation of decisions supported by the electorate.

Institutions

As Beetham articulates, "although elections form a key mechanism for the popular control of government, they are of limited effectiveness on their own without institutions that secure a government's continuous accountability to the public." Gutto agrees, noting how "elected representatives can play a democratic role only to the extent that enabling institutions of governance with clear systems and procedures that are secured by a normative framework and laws exist." Open and accountable political institutions depend primarily on the decentralization of governance and the separation of powers between the executive, legislative, and judiciary spheres. These branches should be monitored through a system of checks and balances by each other, through horizontal accountability, and also be answerable to the people as a whole through vertical accountability. These institutions' specific roles and functions can be best understood and implemented when articulated in a constitution or equivalent "rule of law." The constitution should also articulate the financial responsibilities of the legislature, as well as allow for a system of regional and local government.

Civil Society

As Gutto notes, "however effective public institutions and accountability processes may be in any society aspiring to democracy, their effectiveness and impact would nevertheless be diminished in the absence of a vibrant and activist civil society." Civil society, sometimes referred to as "democratic society," creates opportunities for active citizenship and direct involvement in the functioning of a democracy. The key elements of civil society include an independent media, sources of policy expertise independent of the state, and associations that may include organizations dedicated to social services, development, health, education, human rights, women's empowerment, or other issues. An active civil society has the additional benefit of fostering respect for the rights of other citizens by creating environments of diversity and dialogue.

Citizen Rights

Democracy also includes the presence of political and civil rights for citizens, especially freedom of expression, association, and assembly, which require the guarantee of due legal process and liberty and security of person to be effective. There has been recent debate on the necessity of economic, social, and cultural rights as conditions of democracy, however, it is becoming more widely accepted that "for civil and political rights and freedoms to have any value, citizens must possess the capacity to exercise them." The majority of political, civil, economic, social, and cultural rights at the national level relate directly or indirectly to the international human rights framework, as will be discussed further.

The Dynamism of Democracy

It should be noted that, despite these common elements, democracy can take a variety of forms; there is no "one size fits all" democracy. As Beetham explains, "different societies and diverse circumstances require different arrangements if democratic principles are to be effectively realised." Abdul Aziz Said, International Peace and Conflict Resolution at American University, agrees, noting that "the form of democracy is always cast in the mold of the culture of a people;" he thus urges a "more democratic theory of democracy" that recognizes its potential for variation and dynamism.

Relatedly, Said specifically emphasizes that "democracy is not a western product." The principles and institutions that inform substantive democracy are based on tenets that transcend national and political ideologies; thus, democracy is not exclusive to the West. This point has several implications. First, it implies that there is no fundamental incompatibility between democracy and the Arab world, nor between democracy and Islam.

As Said notes, "the lack of democracy in the Middle East is due more to a lack of preparation for it than to a lack of religious and cultural foundations." Secondly, the idea that democracy is not exclusive to the West can serve to caution superpowers to avoid imposing their models of democracy on other societies, and encourage them to instead assume a supportive role in developing democracy in local contexts. Likewise, superpowers should be cautious of pursuing national interests under the guise of democracy to prevent the association of democracy with western imperialism. At the same time, local democracy advocates are called upon to consider how their social mechanisms, values, and contexts can inform culturally sustainable democracies.

Defining Human Rights: the Human Security Perspective

As Donnelly summarizes, "human rights are, literally, the rights that one has simply as a human being. As such they are equal rights, because we are all equally human beings. They are also inalienable rights, because no matter how inhumanely we act or are treated we cannot become other than human beings."

Human rights are defined in several key documents, namely, the Universal Declaration of Human Rights, adopted by the United Nations General Assembly in 1948; the International Covenant on Civil and Political Rights, adopted in 1966; and the International Covenant on Economic, Social, and Cultural Rights, also adopted in 1966. The Vienna Declaration, adopted at the World Conference on Human Rights in 1993, further expanded the meaning of human rights. Originally, human rights were developed to outline a set of individual rights that states were required to respect or provide for their citizens.

The framework not only included the prohibition of certain acts, but also the "imposition of the duty to perform certain obligations in order to promote and protect the enjoyment of certain rights." In other words, abuse of human rights can take the form of both violations and denials. While the full realization of human rights is still an ideal, much has been achieved in the name of human rights.

Anthony Langlois, International Relations at Flinders University in Adelaide, Australia, achievements include "international recognition of human rights as the basic set of norms of human behaviour, the internationalization of human rights institutions of various types, and the development of International Human Rights Law." The notion of human rights has begun to be broadened in recent years.

First, the responsibility of ensuring human rights has been expanded beyond only state governments to include individuals, groups of people, and other non-state actors. Secondly, the common association of human rights law with peacetime has given way to the widespread recognition that human rights law applies in conflict situations, just as it does in periods of stability.

Finally the past ten years have seen increased acknowledgment of the interdependence and indivisibility of human rights. While this has always been true in theory, in the past the two separate Covenants suggested divisions between political and civil rights and economic, social, and cultural rights. While some divisions still exist, the gaps between the two fields of rights were largely bridged in 1993 at Vienna, where it was declared that "human rights are universal, indivisible and interdependent and interrelated" and that the international community "must treat human rights globally in a fair and equal manner."

In other words, the notion of human rights is expanding to include the concept of human security in a more conscious and deliberate manner. The United Nations Development Report of 1994, "human security can be said to have two main aspects. It means, first, safety from such chronic threats as hunger, disease and repression. And second, it means protection from sudden and hurtful disruptions in the patterns of daily life—whether in homes, in jobs or in communities." This renewed interest in human security and development has accordingly placed increased emphasis on economic and social rights, thus contributing to the re-conceptualization of the human rights framework.

As Beetham summarizes: The idea of economic and social rights as human rights expresses the moral intuition that, in a world rich in resources and the accumulation of human knowledge, everyone ought to be guaranteed the basic means for sustaining life, and that those denied these are victims of a fundamental injustice. Expressing this intuition in the form of human rights both gives the deprived the strongest possible claim to that of which they are deprived and emphasizes the duty of responsible parties to uphold or help them meet their entitlement.

Democracy and Human Rights

Democracy and human rights are clearly different notions; "they are distinct enough for them to be viewed as discreet and differentiated political concepts." Whereas democracy aims to empower "the people" collectively, human rights aims to empower individuals. Similarly, human rights is directly associated with the how of ruling, and not just the who, which may be the case in an electoral democracy, though not in a substantive democracy.

Thus, "democracies" exist that do not necessarily protect human rights, while some non-democratic states are able to ensure some, though not all, human rights. These distinctions have influenced the traditional separation of the theories and fields of human rights and democracy. From the human rights perspective, many have adhered to the separationist theory, which argues that "democracy is not immediately needed for the observation of human rights and that the maintenance of an essential link between human rights and democracy may well have the effect of delaying the implementation of human rights norms in various states." A recent corollary of the separationist theory is the "democracy as neo-imperialism" notion that charges that "democracy is a 'Western-centric' approach to government that is not found indigenously in all societies and is not desirable for all peoples."

These arguments are subject to several key counter arguments that emphasize the interdependence of human rights and democracy. First, in terms of the neo-imperialist argument, it is certainly true that Western superpowers should not impose their particular forms of democracy on other societies and expect them to be accepted and sustainable. However, it is equally culturally insensitive to claim that democracy is only an option in the West, or that it is incompatible with other cultures.

Secondly, in reference to the separationist theory, while it would be unwise to "wait" for democracy to start promoting human rights, it must also be recognized that some human rights are intrinsically linked with institutions and principles of democracy. Furthermore, separating human rights from democracy undermines opportunities for implementation, in that it reduces human rights to standards or norms; as Langlois states, "human rights amount to little more than charity if they are not functioning in a democratic framework."

Essentially, the inclination to separate human rights from democracy is rooted in the acceptance of their traditional definitions. An electoral democracy that lacks the other institutions and principles of a substantive democracy can function without necessarily guaranteeing human rights, just as some narrowly defined human rights can still be realised in the absence of democracy.

However, the re-conceptualization of democracy as substantive, and of human rights as being more far-reaching and inclusive, underscores the necessity of linking the two. This interdependence occurs on the levels of principle, enforcement, and specific rights. On the conceptual level, as Langlois notes, "both contemporary liberal democracy and human rights are derived from and express the assumptions of liberalism," which include individualism, egalitarianism, and universalism. Furthermore, both democracy and human rights pursue a common agenda, and it is "only within a democracy [that] human rights standards or norms transcended such that the values articulated by these norms or standards are genuine rights." In addition, it is only in a well-functioning democracy that individual citizens have access to mechanisms to ensure the implementation of their rights.

The relationship between human rights and democracy is perhaps most clear through an examination of civil and political rights, especially those articulated in Article 21 of the UDHR and Article 25 of the ICCPR, both of which ensure citizen participation in government through free and fair elections and through direct service and participation. These rights are related to the rights of expression, association, assembly, and movement, which are also interdependent with democracy, as well as the rights to liberty, security of person, and the guarantee of due process of the law.

Economic, social, and cultural rights are also being increasingly recognized as being mutually dependent, if not integral, with democracy. As Gutto writes, "the pursuit of the right to development and socio-economic rights is strongly associated with the social democracy vision of poverty eradication and the equitable distribution of ownership, control, and the benefits of wealth." Indeed, political and civil rights can best be realised by citizens who meet a basic level of physical security in terms of access to shelter, water, sanitation, and food, as well as education, healthcare, and employment or income.

Socially, democracy is interrelated with rights to equality and non-discrimination, especially for marginalized groups including women and minorities. Culturally, the respect for diversity and pluralism inherent to democracy is linked to the protection of rights related to language, religion, or ethnicity. It is thus clear that human rights and democracy are interdependent, especially when defined in the broader conceptualizations of democracy as substantive democracy, and human rights as civil, political, economic, social, and cultural rights. These different kinds of rights cannot be realised in a non-democratic system, and likewise, no democracy is sustainable without the presence of these rights. While this relationship is evident in theory, it is perhaps more useful to consider the interdependence of human rights and democracy through the case study of an emerging democracy.

HUMAN RIGHTS AND DEMOCRACY IN PALESTINE

The status of democracy in Palestine is somewhat open to interpretation. Many democracy advocates agree that Palestine is moving in the direction of becoming a substantive democracy, but that it still has ways to go.

Specifically, the will of the people reflects a keen desire for democracy, but that has yet to translate into viable democratic institutions and principles.As Nathan J. Brown of the Carnegie Endowment for International Peace states, "Palestine is... a model liberal democracy. Its most significant flaw is that it does not exist." That is, democracy in Palestine is evident in theory, but it has not been able to fully manifest itself in practice.

Obstacles to realizing both human rights and democracy are rooted in both external and internal factors. In terms of external factors, the Israeli occupation and the protracted Israeli-Palestinian conflict have posed obvious challenges to the development of democracy and human rights in Palestine. To start with democracy, political reform is difficult in the midst of any ongoing violent conflict.

In the case of Israel-Palestine, the challenge of political reform is further exacerbated by the nature of the occupation, which creates a complicated system of dual authority between Israel and the PA. Indeed, according to democracy advocates interviewed for this report, the occupation remains the most prominent obstacle to Palestinian democracy. Challenges resulting from the external influence of the occupation are interrelated with internal factors as well, most notably corruption in the executive branch of the PA under Arafat and the failure of the security services to be effective. Indeed, the Oslo Accords "were predicated on the ability of the PA to enhance Israeli security and thus focused on enabling the executive and placing few fetters on the security services in internal matters." In addition to, and perhaps, because of the fact that the PA lacked sovereignty, it also lacked legitimacy. This problem emerged not only from the external fact of the occupation however, but also from internal shortcomings such as centralization of power, lack of accountability and transparency, corruption, and human rights violations. To be sure, human rights, like democracy, have suffered from both internal and external factors.

On the one hand, numerous human rights violations by Israel against Palestinians have been cited, including targeted assassinations, restrictions on movement, collective punishment, and home demolitions. On the other hand, Palestinian security forces under the PA have also been guilty of numerous human rights violations, including detention without trial and/or specific charges, improper trials, torture, maltreatment, and use of the death penalty. Both human rights and democracy have also been hindered by poverty and the lack of human security in many communities in Palestine. As George Giacaman of Muwatin stated, "the democratic system is not sustainable with rampant poverty. Democracy requires a more equitable economic system based on a fair distribution of wealth." Khalid Nassif of the Civic Forum Institute agreed, noting that democracy regresses in the absence of economic and social rights that ensure human security.

Nassif, "when the economy improves, people have a greater sense of freedom and safety, and they can give more time and attention to joining parties and organizations and taking an interest in democracy." Clearly then, both human rights and democracy in Palestine have been hindered by both internal and external factors, primarily, the conflict with Israel and the limitations of the PA, and also by regional and international influences. Nevertheless, the will for both democracy and human rights in Palestine is strong on both individual and collective levels, and in fact, both exist to some extent in theory and on paper.

The current key issue before Palestinians at this time is to translate those conceptualizations into realised practices and institutions, which can only be possible through an integrative approach that recognizes the interdependence of human rights and democracy. At the same time, Israel and the international community must acknowledge that a democratic state in Palestine requires the existence of a state, as well as democracy.

Elections

The presidential elections of January 2005 were a major step towards procedural democracy. The elections followed the death of president Yasser Arafat, who had been elected in January 1996, and provided an opportunity for new leaders and parties to emerge. Though the election of Mahmoud Abbas was predicted, the elections saw widespread participation, with 71 per cent of registered voters casting ballots, and were declared free and fair by local and international monitors.

To refer to Beetham's standards for democratic electoral processes, the January elections were deemed successful in terms of their reach, inclusiveness, independence, integrity, and impartiality. The Central Elections Commission was credited with making laudable efforts in registering voters, coordinating the monitoring of the voting process, and counting and implementing results.

While the process was far from flawless, it was considered to be an overall success, and resulted in a smooth transfer of power and authority. The success of the election was largely made possible by pressure on both Israeli and Palestinian officials to protect rights to association, assembly, and expression, and the process itself underscored the procedural rights defined in Article 21 of the UDHR and Article 25 of the ICCPR. The municipal elections of May

2005 were likewise considered to be successful overall. In addition to being another step towards procedural democracy, these elections also affirmed support in the electoral system and thus contributed to the strengthening of substantive democracy.

As journalist Bakr Abu Bakr wrote in the Palestinian daily Al-Hayat Al-Jadidah: It is important...to point out what these elections represent to a Palestinian people still struggling to be free, still fighting Israeli occupation, and exercising democracy... They represent: first, an assertion of a course and a way of life chosen by the Palestinian people exemplified by freedom, dignity, dialogue, responsibility, and respect for the will of the people; second, the will and aspiration of many popular leaderships to serve the people...; third, a demonstration of Palestinian solidarity...; fourth, the continuity of Palestinian political struggle towards common goals; fifth, a renewal of societal leaderships.

Clearly, the elections represented more than simply a procedure; they were a tangible expression of democratic ideals and principles. These ideals were intertwined with human rights, including the rights to dignity, freedom, and political participation. Furthermore, the electoral process, while reflecting human rights, also served to facilitate human rights by functioning as an expression of Palestinian unity. The next phase of elections, for the Palestinian Legislative Council, were originally scheduled for July 2005 but were postponed to allow more time to formalize amendments to the proposed new electoral law.

While most democracy advocates support the adoption of the new law and recognize the need for giving ample time for its passage, most view the indefinite postponement as a setback to democratic processes and momentum. Furthermore, the postponement was interpreted by many as an attempt by Fatah to consolidate its support to secure a victory over Hamas in particular. This widely accepted theory, regardless of its veracity, has unfortunately undermined the apparent commitment to democratic procedures established in the presidential and municipal elections.

Political Parties

Political parties are a mechanism that can facilitate free and fair elections, and thus contribute significantly to a sustainable procedural democracy. Likewise they provide opportunities for citizen participation and expression, and thus contribute to the development of a substantive, liberal democracy as well. As Giacaman stated, "a multi-party system is essential for establishing a sustainable democracy."

In Palestine, there exists some foundation for a pluralist party structure. Although Fatah has remained the dominant party for some time, and has at times been difficult to distinguish from the PLO and the PA, other political parties have always remained in existence, and Islamist parties like Hamas in particular have gained considerable support in the past ten years.

Thus, it is clear that "there is a plurality of parties; the parties are based on ideological differences but still operate within a national consensus; and they generally accept one another's legitimacy. Missing, of course, are the democratic institutions that would induce existing parties to channel their energies towards electioneering and governance." That is, while various groups have long existed in Palestine, until recently they have lacked the electoral processes within which to operate.

To be sure, the majority of parties in Palestine have traditionally considered themselves "movements" or "fronts," and thus focus their attention on activities not necessarily related to electoral processes. In addition, the historical dominance of Fatah, and more recently, Hamas, have created challenges for the development of electoral parties in that "Fatah is too indistinguishable from the PA and Hamas too removed from it."

Indeed, while Fatah has traditionally identified itself as the primary force for Palestinian liberation, its loose cohesion has suffered from various fractions, due both to its position as the central party of the PA and to its handling of the second intifada. In contrast, Hamas has distanced itself from the PA, identifying itself as an "alternative to the status quo" and "the main opposition to Fatah and the PA." This contrast was not only established on the conceptual level but on the direct level as well, as Hamas provided numerous social services to communities that Fatah and the PA had been unable to supply. Also, Hamas has distinguished itself from Fatah by intentionally using religious rhetoric, in contrast to Fatah's secular nature.

In the past six months however, the nature of Hamas's political involvement has been shifting from that of an independent movement to a perhaps viable party in that members participated for the first time in municipal elections and plan to participate in PLC elections. Many democracy advocates are now calling for a "third movement" that would provide an alternative to the so-called "old guard" of Fatah and the PA, and to fundamentalist groups like Hamas. As Mustafa Barghouthi, Director of the Health, Development, Information, and Policy Institute on Palestine commented, "Palestinians do not have to choose between autocracy and fundamentalism.

There is a democratic alternative. Palestine could be a state that is independent and sovereign." Dr. Lily Feidy of MIFTAH agreed, advocating for a third movement that is secular and democratic. Nassif, who has observed numerous town meetings through the work of the Civic Forum Institute, it is evident that "people want change, and want more participation by political parties. They want real democracy, and they want political parties to function as a fundamental part of that democracy."

It should be noted that electoral party systems can take many forms, and in fact, a strictly organized party system could actually be detrimental in Palestine since many active reformists in the PLC have functioned essentially as independents, in practice at least if not in name. However, it is clear that the development of institutions to support electoral parties is becoming a necessity. Brown suggests three minimal steps to further democratic transition in the area of electoral parties. First, Fatah must be disentangled from the PA, for "when politicization of official positions runs deeply throughout the bureaucracy, and where there is a conflation of roles and ruling bodies... mechanisms of horizontal and vertical accountability begin to break down."

Secondly, parties need to develop clear structures of internal governance and take "significant organizational steps, such as determining their membership, internal procedures, selection of candidates, and decision-making structures." Third, organizations need to re-orient themselves to function in electoral competition, that is, groups need to consciously decide if they are primarily violent movements or if they are electoral parties.

In order for these steps to take place, certain human rights must be ensured. The rights to assembly and movement are inherent to political party organization, and the rights to opinion and expression are necessary for allowing diverse parties to develop and mature. These rights must be protected by both the PA and by Israel. As Barghouthi stated, "[Israeli] suppression of secular democratic forces in Palestine will lead to a polarization... between Hamas fundamentalists and the PA." Indeed, the protection of human rights are essential for the emergence of a third movement.

Separation of Powers

As Hussein Sirriyeh, Arabic and Middle Eastern Studies at the University of Leeds, writes, "the definition of democracy should not merely be restricted to the narrower sense of free elections and a multi-party system. It should also encompass a broader spectrum of ingredients, including government by consent and accountability..." To be sure, in order for political parties to function in effective institutions, especially the legislature, there needs to be a clear separation of power between the executive, legislative, and judiciary branches, with a viable system of checks and balances between them, articulated in a Constitution. This is necessary for ensuring transparency and accountability, and for enabling the different branches to fulfill their respective duties. In Palestine, power was largely concentrated in the executive branch under the leadership of Arafat, who developed a highly personalized system of authority. Under this system, Arafat managed to bypass the majority of institutions to extend his personal influence.

While this strategy was arguably motivated by Arafat's attempt to unite various factions of Palestinians with different opinions and interests, and to bolster his status as the unifying symbol of Palestine, the centralization of power proved detrimental and only further crippled the already limited legitimacy of the PA.

This centralization manifested itself in various ways. The most measurable indication was evident in the PA budget, in which over one quarter of the PA revenues were placed under the direct and unaccountable control of Arafat by 1997. The executive's domination was also felt strongly by the legislative and judiciary branches. While the PLC had the authority to draft and pass laws, it had no mechanism to ensure that the president would approve them. Thus, numerous bills and laws that were passed by the PLC, including the Basic Law, were subject to interminable waiting for Arafat's approval. Similarly, the executive responded to many court orders from the judiciary by simply ignoring them.

Sirriyeh proposes several theses to explain the authoritarian nature of the PA under Arafat. Some of these reasons include the desire of the PA to make an impression on the Israelis by suppressing anti-Oslo opposition, the issue of internalized PNA insecurity, the "outsider" status of the original PA leadership, the lack of political experience of the PA, and the desire to promote national unity by subordinating divisions within Palestine.

Whatever the reason, the failure to separate powers, compounded by widespread corruption within the PA, resulted in a system that lacked transparency, accountability, and ultimately, legitimacy. This crippled the development of democratic institutions in their early stages, and it is only recently that the new PA leadership under Abu Mazen has begun to confront the process of de-centralizing authority.

Judiciary

The branch of government that perhaps requires the most immediate attention is the judiciary. The judiciary was virtually nonexistent during the majority of the post-Oslo period, and it was only in 2002 with the passing of the judicial organizational law that the judiciary began to be managed by an independent judicial council.

However, to date the council has consisted of judges who, while inexperienced in administrative matters, are intent on preserving their autonomy, thus causing them to lose the support of the bar association. The judiciary has also been embroiled in rivalries with the PLC and the executive branch's Ministry of Justice, with disputes occurring most recently over a draft judicial law for reform introduced by a special committee under Abu Mazen and currently referred to the legislature.

Despite these challenges, the fact that an independent judiciary council does exist provides a foundation for starting judicial reform. Although building a strong judiciary is a long, complex process, it is imperative for several reasons. On the conceptual level, judicial reform is symbolically significant because it can address the general lawlessness that directly affected many Palestinian communities during the second intifada and can thus restore confidence in the PA. To be sure, an effective court system has the potential to restore order and thus serve as an indicator to Palestinians of the authenticity of reforms. Furthermore, "judicial reform is a logical priority because it can be a genuine tool—not simply a symbolic one—in addressing the corruption that is perhaps one of the most corrosive issues for Palestinian governance." Although laws exist regarding hiring for government positions, disclosing personal finances, and monitoring public funds, there have been no mechanisms for implementing them or prosecuting corrupt officials. This problem can be addressed by focusing initial reform efforts on the office of public prosecution. A strong judiciary can serve other important functions as well, including being a leading force in constitutional reform and the development and application of the Basic Law. It also can function as a key body for placing checks and balances on the executive and legislative branches.

Indeed, Hamdi Shaqqura of the Palestinian Centre for Human Rights, the empowerment of a strong and independent judiciary can alleviate current debates regarding concern over the popularity of Hamas as a political party. Shaqqura suggests that any hypothetical attempts by elected Hamas officials to "Islamicize" the system or re-introduce violence as an acceptable policy would be countered by the judiciary.

Finally, a strong, independent judiciary is necessary for preserving human rights. First, it would provide a legitimate institution for prosecuting cases of human rights abuses. Lamis Alami of the Palestinian Independent Commission for Citizens' Rights, ombudsmen and monitoring groups like PICCR can document human rights violations, but they currently lack effective institutions for addressing them. Furthermore, an effective judiciary branch is necessary for protecting rights to fair and public hearings and trials, as articulated in Articles 10 and 11 of the UDHR.

Security

Closely related to the topic of judicial reform is the issue of security. Indeed, in order to ensure due process and avoid violations such as arbitrary arrests or torture, it is necessary that an effective security apparatus, including a police force, operates with legitimacy. Viable security services are necessary for preserving the rule of law, which is essential in a sustainable democracy.

The issue of security is particularly important in Palestine, as security continues to play a vital role in many aspects of the Israeli-Palestinian conflict. To be sure, "for some external actors—especially Israel—security forms the basic logic of the reform process," and many of Israel's actions and policies are justified by concern for security. In the post-Oslo period however, many Palestinians perceived that the thrust of the so-called security reforms in the Occupied Territories was to protect Israeli security at the expense of Palestinian security. Inside Palestine, security concerns were not only associated with Israel but with internal elements as well, as the security services came to be associated with authoritarianism, corruption, and human rights violations against fellow Palestinians, including illegal detentions, improper trials, torture, and executions. The failure of the Palestinian security services after Oslo is largely attributable to other flaws within the PA. Primarily, "the absence of an effective control by an identifiable institution led to the excessive manipulation of responsibilities by members and leaders of these organizations." To be sure, "the security services effectively answered to the president regardless of the content of the Basic Law. When Arafat was president, he encouraged multiple security services but declined to draw clear divisions of responsibilities among them." This resulted in a lack of order and organization, lack of mandate, lack of professionalism, and consequently, lack of legitimacy.

Indeed, over a dozen security organizations were operating under Arafat, and none of them proved effective in providing either internal or external security. As Brown suggests, "the myriad layers of overlapping forces and command structures need to be replaced with a consolidated and transparent organization with clear lines of command to a democratically accountable official or set of officials." The president should still have some involvement, but other executive branch officials should include members of the Ministry of the Interior.

Furthermore, the PLC should be involved by finishing the draft of the legal framework for the security services' operation, as well as by examining the security budget. In addition to these top-down measures, reforms need to occur directly within the security services, first through consolidation and re-organization, and also through improved trainings. Specifically, security personnel trainings should be infused with human rights training, and ideally, should take place in conjunction with local human rights organizations.

This model is helpful for facilitating a professional ethos within the security services; that is, "their training should focus not only on developing technical expertise but also on fostering a sense of what security services should not do."

Steps should also be taken to establish a multi-level system of monitoring and accountability, including:

- A system for security personnel and officers to report human rights abuses and violations;
- A procedure for families to appeal for investigations;
- A joint investigative body at the local level consisting of senior and junior security officers, human rights activists, and jurists to review cases of abuse allegations;
- A stronger Committee on Human Rights within the PLC;
- A stronger PICCR or similar ombudsman institution. Some reforms have already taken place under Abu Mazen, but the process of security reform will inevitably be long and complex. Nevertheless, "Palestinian reform will clearly be moving forward if the Ministry

> of Interior exercises real oversight, if the PLC passes a set of laws governing security forces, and if the regular reporting of human rights groups and other NGOs suggests that the security forces are more respectful of the limits to their authority."

Civil Society

Democracy depends largely on the presence of a vibrant civil society. In Palestine, the presence of a strong civil society can be considered one of the most promising assets for the development of a sustainable democracy. Numerous civil organizations have existed since the early years of the occupation, essentially "keeping the country going before the PA, and still very active" after Oslo and during the present period. Dajani notes that, in Palestine, "in the absence of a state and central government, and without any formal, centrally organized political socialization via schools, the media, religion, friends or family, people began to organize themselves in civil groups—which subsequently became known as NGOs—and took over the role of a government." These organizations have assumed a variety of roles and duties, including the provision of social services, political activism, human rights monitoring, education and advocacy, media and outreach, and others.

Civil society groups have thus taken a number of forms, such as women's groups, media outlets, trade unions, human rights groups, religious groups, etc. While duplication, and at times, competition, are inevitable, many civil society organizations collaborate with each other and complement each others' work, and over 90 organizations belong to the Palestinian NGO Network, an umbrella group that seeks to support, strengthen, and consolidate Palestinian civil society. Organizations that focus on women's rights and empowerment are especially important for ensuring the viability of a sustainable democracy.

As Feidy explains, a strong Palestinian women's movement has existed since the 1920s, and women have been active in civil society throughout Palestinian history. However, women have been largely marginalized under the PA, with the old guard seeking to limit the participation of both women and youth. Alami, the women's agenda has lagged at times because many active women believe that political activism against the occupation deserves more attention than the women's movement, although one cannot really separate one agenda from the other.

Indeed, if women are to have an impact politically, they need to have the rights and access to participation. As Giacaman stated, "Equality is central to democracy." In addition to political marginalization, women also face challenges related to employment, education, violence, early marriage, and inheritance rights. Many Palestinian Muslim women also confront unique issues related to certain interpretations of Islam.

The range of challenges related to women has resulted in a variety of responses by different civil society groups. Some focus on advocating for legal reform, such as the establishment of a quota to ensure a certain percentage of local or PLC seats are reserved for women, while others focus more on assisting female candidates and encouraging women to run for office or to vote for candidates who are female or who support women's rights.

Other groups focus on making women aware of their civil and political rights through trainings, workshops, and conferences. As Mu'alim explains of his work with PCPD, "We are not speaking for people; rather, we empower people to speak on behalf of themselves. People have listened too long. They need to use their own voices now." This approach is especially important for women's empowerment.

An obvious institution for channeling these voices is the media, and indeed, newspapers and media outlets are important institutions within Palestinian civil society. A strong foundation exists in Palestine for a free press; according to Brown, "the basis for independent media that can facilitate reform [in Palestine] is solid." To be sure, the majority of media outlets in Palestine are privately owned, in contrast to the state-controlled media that dominates in some other parts of the Arab world and elsewhere.

Similarly, despite noted attempts by some PA officials to constrict discourse on certain topics such as Islamist parties, or certain stories, such as internal discord, the PA never fully stifled public expression. Nevertheless, there is still much room for improvement. Palestinian journalists should thus continue to build on their sound foundation of free media institutions to ensure that the media can function as a viable institution in a substantive democracy. Journalists and media outlets are not the only groups focusing on media concerns. Many organizations that advocate for democracy and reform are embracing media issues, as well as women's rights, as key areas of concentration for their work, under the larger goal of promoting democracy and working towards the development of sustainable institutions.

Some of the leading democracy organizations include MIFTAH, which focuses on democracy, human rights, gender equity, and participatory governance; Muwatin, which initiates intellectual debate on democratic issues and options; PCPD, which promotes human rights, tolerance, participation, accountability, empowerment, and rule of law; and Civic Forum Institute, which aims to increase citizens' awareness of democratic concepts and institutions and develop civil society institutions. This list is not intended to be exhaustive, but rather is meant to provide brief insight into the types of organizations that currently exist in the area of democracy advocacy.

Civil society is just one vital aspect of a participatory democracy, in which citizens are active participants in their government and communities, rather than just passive recipients. It should be noted that democratic participation can take many forms, including voting, holding public office, volunteering a service, writing letters to officials and/or newspapers, participating in marches, protests, and other forms of direct activism, and countless others. It is not the objective of this paper to evaluate the impact of various forms of participation; rather, it is to recognize the importance of citizen agency.

Perhaps the best indication of the potential for participatory democracy in Palestine was the early years of the first intifada, which saw widespread popular participation of different forms. Though the nonviolent "people power" strategies employed during that time have yet to be duplicated on the same scale, the spirit of that period is evident in the willingness of the people to express their opinions and voice their criticisms of both the PA and Israel.

Participatory democracy, and thus civil society, are both inputs and outputs of human rights. First of all, as an output, the emergence of civil society depends on the rights to freedom of thought, opinion, and expression, the right to assembly and association, and the right to participation and service in government or country.

As an input, many civil society groups adopt missions that help to ensure economic, social, and cultural rights such as access to social services like food, clothing, housing, and medical care, education, and human security and others focus on securing civil and political rights. In addition, human rights organizations in particular, as a part of civil society, play an important role in monitoring and documenting human rights violations and advocating for the protection of rights.

Assessment of Democracy and Human Rights in Palestine

Foundations clearly exist in Palestine for the emergence of a substantive democracy, but the process still has far to go. A helpful way of conceptualizing Palestine's current level of democracy is the transition theory, advocated by Dankwart Rustow.

This theory, democratic development occurs in four main stages: "a stage when a national unity is being established; a preparatory phase of prolonged and inconclusive political struggle; a decision phase when a historical movement of choosing a democratic path is taken; and a habituation phase witnessing a consolidation of democracy." In the case of Palestine, a national unity has long been established, and one might consider the post-Oslo period and second intifada to be periods of prolonged struggle.

It is possible that, at present, Palestine is transitioning into the third stage, embarking upon a path of decision to work deliberately towards democracy. Most democracy advocates interviewed agreed, suggesting that Palestine is in a middle stage, on the way to democracy. It is thus important at this stage to identify obstacles that prevent Palestine from fully realizing a substantive democracy. First, it should be noted that any transition to democracy is a long, slow process. In the case of Palestine, there have also been additional setbacks in the form of clashes in reform visions, both internally and between internal and external actors. Another obstacle is the persistence of the old guard, who continue to occupy many key positions. The past six months have seen hope for progress in both of these areas however, with the election of Abu Mazen. The new president has committed himself to reform, and in doing so has reconciled differences between international and domestic agendas, and has opened up the PA and Fatah to be more transparent and accountable.

As Brown notes however, "the primary obstacle to further Palestinian reform lies in the international context: Political reform is difficult in the midst of an ongoing conflict." Specifically, it is not possible to establish a substantive democracy under occupation. Unfortunately, international actors like the United States have to date have "approached diplomacy and reform as sequential rather than interdependent... [though] it is precisely the mutual dependence of reform and peace that make both so difficult achieve."

To be sure, the "peace now, democracy later" philosophy of Oslo proved to be ineffectual and perhaps even detrimental, and it is doubtful that the current logic of "democracy now, peace later" will be any different. As Brown notes, it is futile to build "public institutions that are expected to establish authority and accountability while placing them in a context of extremely limited autonomy."

Perhaps a better way to conceptualize the peace and democracy equation is to integrate the variable of human rights. Democracy is necessary for human rights, and human rights are necessary for democracy. Likewise, a real just peace cannot exist unless peace is integrated with the protection of human rights. Because human rights is thus a common variable to both peace and democracy, it makes sense to focus on the human rights framework when pursuing both diplomacy and institution-building. Only when human rights and democracy are pursued simultaneously will either be achieved, and it is only then that a just peace will be possible.

CEASE

Human rights and liberal democracy are not merely complementary, rather, they are interdependent. A democracy that is substantive as well as procedural cannot function without human rights, just as human rights, meaning civil, political, economic, social, and cultural rights, cannot be ensured in the absence of democracy.

In the case of Palestine, a foundation exists for both the realization of human rights and the development of a substantive democracy, but both internal and external factors have hindered the building of viable institutions to actualize those ideals. Greater attention thus needs to be given to the development of mechanisms such as elections, political parties, and separation of powers, and the restructuring of institutions including the judiciary branch and security sector. Despite the absence of these institutions to date, the will and perseverance of the Palestinian people, through both civil society and direct participation, has continued to push forward the democracy and human rights movements. Thus, attention must be given to these bottom-up efforts of popular participation, in addition to the top-down efforts of institution-building, if a liberal democracy is to be established. To be sure, no amount of institutional reform will be sustainable if it does not develop in tandem with popular will and public participation.

For this reason, it is necessary for civil society organizations and actors to continue to facilitate political participation and raise public awareness, and it is imperative that individuals and communities seize opportunities to demonstrate their will. Media institutions in particular can play a key role in this process by serving as a means of popular communication, education, and mobilization. The human rights framework can be helpful for developing direction and coordination for these efforts, and can integrate the distinct yet interdependent ideals of peace and justice, and human rights and democracy.

HUMAN RIGHTS AND DISABILITY

Until recently, the disabled have constituted a minority in obscurity. Unlike certain other groups that fall victim to discrimination, the disabled do not comprise a self-contained, close-knit social community. Instead, they populate every social sector, every class, every age group, every ethnic and religious community. And at every level, society has tended to ignore them, believing them incapable of participating in the community, or avoiding them as unpleasant reminders of the fragility of our existence.

Fortunately, this situation is beginning to change. Nations and localities are devoting steadily more attention to improving the plight of the disabled. Mr. Despouy's excellent interim report demonstrates the seriousness with which the international community too is finally addressing this important issue. The Bahá'í International Community welcomes the Special Rapporteur's study and would like to take a few minutes to comment on his report and on some of the issues it raises.

The plight of the disabled is a mirror reflecting the shortcomings of society. This fundamental observation holds true with respect to three major topics that the Special Rapporteur plans to treat at length in his final report: first, the causes of disability; second, prejudice and discrimination directed towards the disabled; and third, measures to ensure the equal enjoyment of human rights for the disabled.

First, with respect to the causes of disability, the list of injurious practices resulting in disability that the Special Rapporteur has compiled is thought provoking, ranging from amputations to civil war. Disability can be caused by the gamut of inhuman conduct perpetrated by human beings against one another. For that very reason, the international community must take aim at all human rights violations, for they can all result in the permanent mental or physical handicap of human beings. We fully agree with the Special

Rapporteur's observation, in paragraph 14 of his report, that any acts contrary to international law and violative of mental or physical integrity should be proscribed, not only those acts that rise to the level of torture or other cruel, inhuman or degrading treatment or punishment.

Secondly, the prejudice and discrimination that disabled people suffer is the product of the more general human tendency to label as "inferior" those who are somehow different. But the ostracism that disabled persons often experience can be even more intense, for it is founded on fear — fear on the part of the ostracizer that he, too, may someday become the victim of disability.

The only way to eradicate this fear is to educate every member of society to see disability for what it really is — a mental or physical condition that may make everyday life more challenging, but that cannot affect the disabled person's soul, spirit, creativity, imagination or determination — in short, some of the most valuable aspects of life.

At the same time, such an appreciation will enable individuals to see through the outward handicaps of disabled persons, to their inner reality. As we pointed out in our statements to the Sub-Commission last year, the reformation of social stereotypes and prejudices against the disabled requires education aimed at helping individuals to see the disabled as real people and to share in their triumphs. As Bahá'ís, we are working to implement this kind of education in our schools and in Bahá'í homes.

We are pleased to learn from the Special Rapporteur's report that a number of governments have reported that they are pursuing educational programmes with this goal directed towards young persons, teachers and the society as a whole. We hope that the Special Rapporteur will be in a position to elaborate Parts III and V of his final report, and to make specific recommendations on the form and content of educational programmes designed to combat prejudice against the disabled. We now turn to our third topic; ensuring equal rights for the disabled. Like many other groups, the disabled have been stigmatized and victimized by prejudice, preventing them from assuming their rightful places in society.

As pointed out by the Special Rapporteur, the elimination of traditional stereotypes and prejudices against the disabled is a sine qua non for their full enjoyment of fundamental human rights. We agree wholeheartedly with the Special Rapporteur that all sectors of society must work to integrate disabled persons into the life of society and give them equal opportunities in schools, the workplace and the community at large. Society will be the loser if it fails to benefit from the talents of disabled persons. Their resolute determination to overcome problems that most of us will never be forced to deal with should be a shining torch for us all.

We would only suggest that the Special Rapporteur emphasize the ideal of rehabilitation in the family as well as in the community. Family members should be trained, where possible, to help provide the support and encouragement that the disabled person requires to surmount his impairment. Moreover, we would add the right to freedom of religion to the list of those rights especially important for the disabled person. Disabled persons must be free to partake of the inspiration that religious beliefs can provide. We have described in more detail our views on these topics, and on the broad economic, social and cultural rights to which disabled persons are entitled, in our written statementto the current session of the Sub-Commission.

Finally, we welcome discussions on the possibility of drafting a convention on disabled persons' rights. Every effort to specify more clearly disabled persons' rights and entrench these rights in the legal order deserves to be commended. But the problem of finding the proper method for developing and entrenching these standards requires careful study. For this reason, we approve of the suggestion by the Secretary-General that the General Assembly consider forming a Working Group to examine the possibility of elaborating a convention and the steps involved in its preparation. Thanks in part to the devoted efforts of the Special Rapporteur, disabled persons will no longer have to cope with their handicaps in isolation, hidden behind a veil of intentional ignorance on the part of the society around them. We applaud efforts worldwide to help them surmount their disabilities and become fully-functioning members of their communities. Indeed, we all have much to learn from the disabled persons. Theirs is often an example worthy of emulation.

EDUCATION

The right to education is recognized as a human right by the United Nations and is understood to establish an entitlement to free, compulsory primary education for all children, an obligation to develop secondary education accessible to all children, as well as equitable access to higher education, and a responsibility to provide basic education for individuals who have not completed primary education.

In addition to these access to education provisions the right to education encompasses also the obligation to eliminate discrimination at all levels of the educational system, to set minimum standards and to improve quality. The right to education is enshrined in Article 26 of the Universal Declaration of Human Rights and Article 14 of the International Covenant on Economic, Social and Cultural Rights. The right to education has also been reaffirmed in the 1960 UNESCO Convention against Discrimination in Education, 1st Protocol of ECHR and the 1981 Convention on the Elimination of All Forms of Discrimination Against Women.

The right to education may also include the right to freedom of education. Education narrowly refers to formal institutional instructions. Generally, international instruments use the term in this sense and the right to education, as protected by international human rights instruments, refers primarily to education in a narrow sense. The 1960 UNESCO Convention against Discrimination in Education defines education in Article 1(2) as: "all types and levels of education, (including) access to education, the standard and quality of education, and the conditions under which it is given."

In a wider sense education may describe "all activities by which a human group transmits to its descendants a body of knowledge and skills and a moral code which enable the group to subsist". In this sense education refers to the transmission to a subsequent generation of those skills needed to perform tasks of daily living, and further passing on the social, cultural, spiritual and philosophical values of the particular community. The wider meaning of education has been recognised in Article 1(a) of UNESCO's 1974 Recommendation concerning Education for International Understanding, Co-operation and Peace and Education relating to Human Rights and Fundamental Freedoms.

The article states that education implies: "the entire process of social life by means of which individuals and social groups learn to develop consciously within, and for the benefit of, the national and international communities, the whole of their personal capabilities, attitudes, aptitudes and knowledge."

The European Court of Human Rights has defined education in a narrow sense as "teaching or instructions... in particular to the transmission of knowledge and to intellectual development" and in a wider sense as "the whole process whereby, in any society, adults endeavour to transmit their beliefs, culture and other values to the young."

FULFILLING THE RIGHT TO EDUCATION

The fulfilment of the right to education can be assessed using the 4 As framework, which asserts that for education to be a meaningful right it must be available, accessible, acceptable and adaptable. The 4 As framework was developed by the former UN Special Rapporteur on the Right to Education, Katarina Tomasevski, but is not necessarily the standard used in every international human rights instrument and hence not a generic guide to how the right to education is treated under national law. The 4 As framework proposes that governments, as the prime duty-bearer, has to respect, protect and fulfil the right to education by making education available, accessible, acceptable and adaptable.

The framework also places duties on other stakeholders in the education process: the child, which as the privileged subject of the right to education has the duty to comply with compulsory education requirements, the parents as the 'first educators', and professional educators, namely teachers.

The 4 As have been further elaborated as follows:

- *Availability*: Education is free and government-funded and there is adequate infrastructure and trained teachers able to support education delivery.
- *Accessibility*: The system is non-discriminatory and accessible to all, and positive steps are taken to include the most marginalised.

- *Acceptability*: The content of education is relevant, non-discriminatory and culturally appropriate, and of quality. The school itself is safe and teachers are professional.
- *Adaptability*: Education can evolve with the changing needs of society and contribute to challenging inequalities, such as gender discrimination, and can be adapted locally to suit specific contexts.

A number of international NGOs and charities work to realise the right to education using a rights-based approach to development.

DEVELOPMENT OF THE RIGHT TO EDUCATION

In Europe, before the Enlightenment of the eighteenth and nineteenth century, education was the responsibility of parents and the church. With the French and American Revolution education was established also as a public function. It was thought that the state, by assuming a more active role in the sphere of education, could help to make education available and accessible to all. Education had thus far been primarily available to the upper social classes and public education was perceived as a means of realising the egalitarian ideals underlining both revolutions.

However, neither the American Declaration of Independence (1776) nor the French Declaration of the Rights of Man (1789) protected the right to education as the liberal concepts of human rights in the nineteenth century envisaged that parents retained the primary duty for providing education to their children. It was the states obligation to ensure that parents complied with this duty, and many states enacted legislation making school attendance compulsory. Furthermore child labour laws were enacted to limit the number of hours per day children could be employed, to ensure children would attend school.

States also became involved in the legal regulation of curricula and established minimum educational standards. In On Liberty John Stuart Mill wrote that an "education established and controlled by the State should only exist, if it exists at all, as one among many competing experiments, carried on for the purpose of example and stimulus to keep the others up to a certain standard of excellence." Liberal thinkers of the nineteenth century pointed to the dangers to too much state involvement in the sphere of education, but relied on state intervention to reduce the dominance of the church, and to protect the right to education of children against their own parents.

In the latter half of the nineteenth century, educational rights were included in domestic bills of rights. The 1849 Paulskirchenverfassung, the constitution of the German Empire, strongly influenced subsequent European constitutions and devoted Article 152 to 158 of its bill of rights to education. The constitution recognised education as a function of the state, independent of the church. Remarkable at the time, the constitution proclaimed the right to free education for the poor, but the constitution did not explicitly require the state to set up educational institutions.

Instead the constitution protected the rights of citizens to found and operate schools and to provide home education. The constitution also provided for freedom of science and teaching, and it guaranteed the right of everybody to choose a vocation and train for it. The nineteenth century also saw the development of socialist theory, which held that the primary task of the state was to ensure the economic and social well-being of the community through government intervention and regulation. Socialist theory recognised that individuals had claims to basic welfare services against the state and education was viewed as one of these welfare entitlements. This was in contrast to liberal theory at the time, which regarded non-state actors as the prime providers of education.

Socialist ideals were enshrined in the 1936 Soviet Constitution, which was the first constitution to recognise the right to education with a corresponding obligation of the state to provide such education. The constitution guaranteed free and compulsory education at all levels, a system of state scholarships and vocational training in state enterprises. Subsequently the right to education featured strongly in the constitutions of socialist states. As a political goal, right to education was declared in F. D. Roosevelt's 1944 speech on the Second Bill of Rights.

IMPLEMENTATION

International law does not protect the right to pre-primary education and international documents generally omit references to education at this level. The Universal Declaration of Human Rights states that "everybody" has the right to education, hence the right accures to all individuals, although children are understood as the main beneficiaries.

The rights to education are separated into three levels:

1. Primary (Elemental or Fundamental) Education. This shall be compulsory and free for any child regardless of their nationality, gender, place of birth, or any other discrimination. Upon ratifying the International Covenant on Economic, Social and Cultural Rights States must provide free primary education within two years.
2. Secondary (or Elementary, Technical and Professional in the UDHR) Education must be generally available and accessible.
3. Higher Education (at the University Level) should be provided according to capacity. That is, anyone who meets the necessary education standards should be able to go to university.

Both secondary and higher education shall be made accessible "by every appropriate means, and in particular by the progressive introduction of free education". The only country that has declared reservations about introducing free secondary or higher education is Japan.

Role of the State

Today education is considered an important public function and the state is seen as the chief provider of education through the allocation of substantial budgetary resources and regulating the provision of education. The pre-eminent role of the state in fulfilling the right to education is enshrined in the 1966 International Covenant on Economic, Social and Cultural Rights.

Traditionally, education has been the duty of a child's parents, however with the rise of systems of education, the role of parents has diminished. With regards to realising the right to education the World Declaration on Education for All, adopted at the 1990 World Conference on Education for All states that "partnerships between government and non-governmental organisations, the private sector, local communities, religious groups, and families" are necessary.

Compulsory Education

The realisation of the right to education on a national level may be achieved through compulsory education, or more specifically free compulsory primary education, as stated in both the Universal Declaration of Human Rights and the International Covenant on Economic, Social and Cultural Rights.

FREEDOM OF SPEECH

Freedom of expression is a cornerstone of democratic rights and freedoms. In its very first session in 1946, before any human rights declarations or treaties had been adopted, the UN General Assembly adopted resolution 59(I) stating "Freedom of information is a fundamental human right and... the touchstone of all the freedoms to which the United Nations is consecrated."

Freedom of expression is essential in enabling democracy to work and public participation in decision-making. Citizens cannot exercise their right to vote effectively or take part in public decision-making if they do not have free access to information and ideas and are not able to express their views freely. Freedom of expression is thus not only important for individual dignity but also to participation, accountability and democracy.

Violations of freedom of expression often go hand in hand with other violations, in particular the right to freedom of association and assembly. Progress has been made in recent years in terms of securing respect for the right to freedom of expression. Efforts have been made to implement this right through specially constructed regional mechanisms. New opportunities are emerging for greater freedom of expression with the internet and worldwide satellite broadcasting.

New threats are emerging too, for example with global media monopolies and pressures on independent media outlets. Concepts of freedom of speech can be found in early human rights documents and the modern concept of freedom of speech emerged gradually during the European Enlightenment. England's Bill of Rights 1689 granted 'freedom of speech in Parliament' and the Declaration of the Rights of Man and of the Citizen, adopted during the French Revolution in 1789, specifically affirmed freedom of speech as an inalienable right. The Declaration provides for freedom of expression in Article 11, which states that: "The free communication of ideas and opinions is one of the most precious of the rights of man. Every citizen may, accordingly, speak, write, and print with freedom, but shall be responsible for such abuses of this freedom as shall be defined by law."

Article 19 of the Universal Declaration of Human Rights, adopted in 1948, states that: "Everyone has the right to freedom of opinion and expression; this right includes freedom to hold opinions without interference and to seek, receive and impart information and ideas through any media and regardless of frontiers." Today freedom of speech, or the freedom of expression, is recognized in international and regional human rights law.

The right is enshrined in Article 19 of the International Covenant on Civil and Political Rights, Article 10 of the European Convention on Human Rights, Article 13 of the American Convention on Human Rights and Article 9 of the African Charter on Human and Peoples' Rights. Based on John Stuart Mill's arguments, freedom of speech is understood as a multi-faceted right that includes not only the right to express, or disseminate, information and ideas, but three further distinct aspects:

1. The right to seek information and ideas;
2. The right to receive information and ideas;
3. The right to impart information and ideas.

International, regional and national standards also recognize that freedom of speech, as the freedom of expression, includes any medium, be it orally, in written, in print, through the Internet or through art forms. This means that the protection of freedom of speech as a right includes not only the content, but also the means of expression.

RELATIONSHIP TO OTHER RIGHTS

The right to freedom of speech and expression is closely related to other rights, and may be limited when conflicting with other rights. The right to freedom of expression is also related to the right to a fair trial and court proceeding which may limit access to the search for information or determine the opportunity and means in which freedom of expression is manifested within court proceedings.

As a general principle freedom of expression may not limit the right to privacy, as well as the honour and reputation of others. However greater latitude is given when criticism of public figures is involved. The right to freedom of expression is particularly important for media, which plays a special role as the bearer of the general right to freedom of expression for all.

However, freedom of the press is not necessarily enabling freedom of speech. Judith Lichtenberg has outlined conditions in which freedom of the press may constrain freedom of speech, for example where the media suppresses information or stifles the diversity of voices inherent in freedom of speech. Lichtenberg argues that freedom of the press is simply a form of property right summed up by the principle "no money, no voice".

ORIGINS AND ACADEMIC FREEDOM

Freedom of speech and expression has a long history that predates modern international human rights instruments. It is thought that ancient Athens' democratic ideology of free speech may have emerged in the late 6th or early 5th century BC. In Islamic ethics, freedom of speech was first declared in the Rashidun period by the caliph Umar in the 7th century AD. In the Abbasid Caliphate period, freedom of speech was also declared by al-Hashimi in a letter to one of the religious opponents he was attempting to convert through reason. George Makdisi and Hugh Goddard, "the idea of academic freedom" in universities was "modelled on Islamic custom" as practiced in the medieval Madrasah system from the 9th century.

Islamic influence was "certainly discernible in the foundation of the first deliberately-planned university" in Europe, the University of Naples Federico II founded by Frederick II, Holy Roman Emperor in 1224.

FREEDOM OF SPEECH, DISSENT AND TRUTH

Before the invention of the printing press a writing, once created, could only be physically multiplied by the highly labourious and error-prone process of manual copying out and an elaborate system of censorship and control over scribes existed. Printing allowed for multiple exact copies of a work, leading to a more rapid and widespread circulation of ideas and information.

The origins of copyright law in most European countries lie in efforts by the church and governments to regulate and control the output of printers. In 1501 Pope Alexander VI issued a bull against the unlicensed printing of books and in 1559 the Index Expurgatorius, or List of Prohibited Books, was issued for the first time.

While governments and church encouraged printing in many ways, which allowed the dissemination of Bibles and government information, works of dissent and criticism could also circulate rapidly. As a consequence, governments established controls over printers across Europe, requiring them to have official licences to trade and produce books.

The notion that the expression of dissent or subversive views should be tolerated, not censured or punished by law, developed alongside the rise of printing and the press. Areopagitica, published in 1644, was John Milton's response to the Parliament of England's re-introduction of government licensing of printers, hence publishers. Milton made an impassioned plea for freedom of expression and toleration of falsehood, stating:

- "Give me the liberty to know, to utter, and to argue freely according to conscience."

Milton's defence of freedom of expression was grounded in a Protestant worldview and he thought that the English people had the mission to work out the truth of the Reformation, which would lead to the enlightenment of all people. But Milton also articulated the main strands of future discussions about freedom of expression. By defining the scope of freedom of expression and of "harmful" speech Milton argued against the principle of pre-censorship and in favour of tolerance for a wide range of views. As the "menace" of printing spread governments established centralised control mechanism. The French crown repressed printing and the printer Etienne Dolet was burned at the stake in 1546.

In 1557 the British Crown thought to stem the flow of seditious and heretical books by chartering the Stationers' Company. The right to print was limited to the members of that guild, and thirty years later the Star Chamber was chartered to curtail the "greate enormities and abuses" of "dyvers contentyous and disorderlye persons professinge the arte or mystere of pryntinge or selling of books."

The right to print was restricted to two universities and to the 21 existing printers in the city of London, which had 53 printing presses. As the British crown took control of type founding in 1637 printers fled to the Netherlands. Confrontation with authority made printers radical and rebellious, with 800 authors, printers and book dealers being incarcerated in the Bastille in Paris before it was stormed in 1789. A succession of English thinkers developed the idea of a right to freedom of expression, starting with John Milton, then John Locke and culminating in John Stuart Mill.

Locke established the individual as the unit of value and the bearer of rights to life, liberty, property and the pursuit of happiness. It was the role of Government to protect these rights and this belief was first enshrined in the US Constitution, with the First Amendment adding the guarantee that "Congress shall make no law... abridging the freedom of speech, or of the press". John Stuart Mill argued that human freedom is good and without it there can be no progress in science, law or politics, which according to Mill required free discussion of opinion. Mill's On Liberty, published in 1859 became a classic defence of the right to freedom of expression. Mill argued that truth drives out falsity, therefore the free expression of ideas, true or false, should not be feared. Truth is not stable or fixed, but evolves with time. Mill argued that much of what we once considered true has turned out false. Therefore views should not be prohibited for their apparent falsity. Mill also argued that free discussion is necessary to prevent the "deep slumber of a decided opinion".

Discussion would drive the onwards march of truth and by considering false views the basis of true views could be re-affirmed. In Evelyn Beatrice Hall's biography of Voltaire, she coined the following phrase to emphasize Voltaire's beliefs: "I disapprove of what you say, but I will defend to the death your right to say it." Hall's quote is frequently cited to describe the principle of freedom of speech. In the 20th Century Noam Chomsky states that: "If you believe in freedom of speech, you believe in freedom of speech for views you don't like. Stalin and Hitler, for example, were dictators in favour of freedom of speech for views they liked only. If you're in favour of freedom of speech, that means you're in favour of freedom of speech precisely for views you despise."

Lee Bollinger argues that "the free speech principle involves a special act of carving out one area of social interaction for extraordinary self-restraint, the purpose of which is to develop and demonstrate a social capacity to control feelings evoked by a host of social encounters." Bollinger argues that tolerance is a desirable value, if not essential. However, critics argue that society should be concerned by those who directly deny or advocate, for example, genocide.

DEMOCRACY

The notion of freedom of expression is intimately linked to political debate and the concept of democracy. The norms on limiting freedom of expression mean that public debate may not be completely suppressed even in times of emergency. One of the most notable proponents of the link between freedom of speech and democracy is Alexander Meiklejohn. He argues that the concept of democracy is that of self-government by the people. For such a system to work an informed electorate is necessary. In order to be appropriately knowledgeable, there must be no constraints on the free flow of information and ideas. Meiklejohn, democracy will not be true to its essential ideal if those in power are able to manipulate the electorate by withholding information and stifling criticism.

Meiklejohn acknowledges that the desire to manipulate opinion can stem from the motive of seeking to benefit society. However, he argues, choosing manipulation negates, in its means, the democratic ideal. Eric Barendt has called this defence of free speech on the grounds of democracy "probably the most attractive and certainly the most fashionable free speech theory in modern Western democracies".

Thomas I. Emerson expanded on this defence when he argued that freedom of speech helps to provide a balance between stability and change. Freedom of speech acts as a "safety valve" to let off steam when people might otherwise be bent on revolution. He argues that "The principle of open discussion is a method of achieving a moral adaptable and at the same time more stable community, of maintaining the precarious balance between healthy cleavage and necessary consensus." Emerson furthermore maintains that "Opposition serves a vital social function in offsetting or ameliorating (the) normal process of bureaucratic decay."

Research undertaken by the Worldwide Governance Indicators project at the World Bank, indicates that freedom of speech, and the process of accountability that follows it, have a significant impact in the quality of governance of a country. "Voice and Accountability" within a country, defined as "the extent to which a country's citizens are able to participate in selecting their government, as well as freedom of expression, freedom of association, and free media" is one of the six dimensions of governance that the Worldwide Governance Indicators measure for more than 200 countries.

SOCIAL INTERACTION AND COMMUNITY

Richard Moon has developed the argument that the value of freedom of speech and freedom of expression lies with social interactions. Moon writes that "by communicating an individual forms relationships and associations with others – family, friends, co-workers, church congregation, and countrymen. By entering into discussion with others an individual participates in the development of knowledge and in the direction of the community."

LIMITATIONS ON FREEDOM OF SPEECH

The Freedom Forum Organization, legal systems, and society at large, recognize limits on the freedom of speech, particularly when freedom of speech conflicts with other values or rights. Limitations to freedom of speech may follow the "harm principle" or the "offense principle", for example in the case of pornography or "hate speech". Limitations to freedom of speech may occur through legal sanction or social disapprobation, or both.

In "On Liberty" John Stuart Mill argued that "...there ought to exist the fullest liberty of professing and discussing, as a matter of ethical conviction, any doctrine, however immoral it may be considered." Mill argues that the fullest liberty of expression is required to push arguments to their logical limits, rather than the limits of social embarrassment. However, Mill also introduced what is known as the harm principle, in placing the following limitation on free expression: "the only purpose for which power can be rightfully exercised over any member of a civilized community, against his will, is to prevent harm to others.

In 1985 Joel Feinberg introduced what is known as the "offence principle", arguing that Mill's harm principle does not provide sufficient protection against the wrongful behaviours of others. Feinberg wrote "It is always a good reason in support of a proposed criminal prohibition that it would probably be an effective way of preventing serious offense to persons other than the actor, and that it is probably a necessary means to that end." Hence Feinberg argues that the harm principle sets the bar too high and that some forms of expression can be legitimately prohibited by law because they are very offensive. But, as offending someone is less serious than harming someone, the penalties imposed should be higher for causing harm.

In contrast Mill does not support legal penalties unless they are based on the harm principle. Because the degree to which people may take offense varies, or may be the result of unjustified prejudice, Feinberg suggests that a number of factors need to be taken into account when applying the offense principle, including: the extent, duration and social value of the speech, the ease with which it can be avoided, the motives of the speaker, the number of people offended, the intensity of the offense, and the general interest of the community at large.

FREEDOM OF RELIGION OR BELIEF

INTRODUCTION

Defining Religion or Belief

The word "religion," meaning to bind fast, comes from the Western Latin word religare. It is commonly, but not always, associated with traditional majority, minority or new religious beliefs in a transcendent deity or deities. In human rights discourse, however, the use of the term usually also includes support for the right to non-religious beliefs.

In 1993 the Human Rights Committee, an independent body of 18 experts selected through a UN process, described religion or belief as "theistic, non-theistic and atheistic beliefs, as well as the right not to profess any religion or belief." Religions and other beliefs bring hope and consolation to billions of people, and hold great potential for peace and reconciliation.

They have also, however, been the source of tension and conflict. This complexity, and the difficulty of defining "religion" and "belief," are emphasized by the still developing history of the protection of freedom of religion or belief in the context of international human rights.

A Complex and Contentious Issue

The struggle for religious liberty has been ongoing for centuries, and has led to innumerable, tragic conflicts. The twentieth century has seen the codification of common values related to freedom of religion and belief, though the struggle has not abated. The United Nations recognized the importance of freedom of religion or belief in the 1948 Universal Declaration of Human Rights, in which Article 18 states that "Everyone shall have the right to freedom of thought, conscience and religion.

This right shall include freedom to have a religion or whatever belief of his choice." Since the Universal Declaration, the attempt to develop an enforceable human rights instrument related to freedom of religion and belief has been unsuccessful. In 1966 the UN passed the International Covenant on Civil and Political Rights, expanding its prior statement to address the manifestation of religion or belief.

Article 18 of this Covenant includes four paragraphs related to this issue:

- Everyone shall have the right to freedom of thought, conscience and religion. This right shall include freedom to have or to adopt a religion or belief of his choice, and freedom either individually or in community with others and in public or private, to manifest his religion or belief in worship, observance, practice and teaching.
- No one shall be subject to coercion which would impair his freedom to have or to adopt a religion or belief of his choice.
- Freedom to manifest one's religion or belief may be subject only to such limitations as are prescribed by law and are necessary to protect public safety, order, health, morals or the fundamental rights and freedoms of others.
- The States Parties to the present Covenant undertake to have respect for the liberty of parents and, when applicable, legal guardians, to ensure the religious and moral education of their children in conformity with their own convictions.

Some of the articles of the Covenant on Civil and Political Rights regarding fundamental freedoms have become international conventions, which are legally binding treaties. In contrast, however, because of the complexity of the topic and the political issues involved, Article 18 of the Covenant on Civil and Political Rights has not been elaborated and codified in the same way that more detailed treaties have codified prohibitions against torture, discrimination against women, and race discrimination.

After twenty years of debate, intense struggle and hard work, the General Assembly in 1981 adopted without a vote the Declaration on the Elimination of All Forms of Intolerance and of Discrimination Based on Religion or Belief. While the 1981 Declaration lacks any enforcement procedures, it remains the most important contemporary codification of the principle of freedom of religion and belief.

RIGHTS AT STAKE

The 1981 UN Declaration on the Elimination of All Forms of Intolerance and of Discrimination Based on Religion or Belief contains eight articles, three of which define specific rights. The remaining articles act in a supportive role by outlining measures to promote tolerance or prevent discrimination.

Taken together, the eight articles constitute a paradigm, an overall concept, to advocate for tolerance and to prevent discrimination based on religion or belief. While human rights are individual rights, the 1981 UN Declaration also identifies certain rights related to states, religious institutions, parents, legal guardians, children, and groups of persons.

Article 1: Legal Definition

This article repeats several rights from the Covenant on Civil and Political Rights's Article 18:

- Right to thought, conscience, and religion or belief;
- Right to have a religion or whatever belief of your choice;
- Right either individually or in community with others, in private or public, to manifest a religion or belief through worship, observance, practice and teaching;
- Right not to suffer coercion that impairs the freedom to choose a religion or belief;
- Right of the State to limit the manifestation of a religion or belief if based in law, and only as necessary to protect public safety, order, health, morals and the fundamental rights and freedoms of others.

Article 2: Classification of Discrimination

This article identifies categories of potential discrimi-nators, affirming the right not to be subject to discrimination on the grounds of religion or belief by:

- States;
- Institutions;
- Groups of persons;
- Persons.

Article 3: Link to Other Rights

This article links the 1981 UN Declaration to other international documents. Article 3 declares that discrimination based on religion or belief constitutes an affront to human dignity and a disavowal of the principles of the Charter of the United Nations, and shall be condemned as a violation of the human rights and fundamental freedoms proclaimed in the Universal Declaration of Human Rights, and enunciated in detail in:

- The International Covenant on Civil and Political Rights;
- The International Covenant on Economic, Social and Cultural Rights.

Article 4: Possible Solutions

Article 4 declares that all States [including all sectors of civil society] shall take effective measures to prevent and eliminate discrimination based on religion or belief through:

- Actions in all fields of civil, economic, political, social, cultural life;
- Enacting or rescinding legislation where necessary to prohibit such discrimination;
- Taking all appropriate measures to combat intolerance based on religion or belief.

Article 5: Parents, Guardians, Children

At stake in the implementation of this article are the following rights:

- Right of parents or legal guardians to bring the child up in their religion or belief;
- Right of the child to education in religion or belief, in accordance with the wishes of parents, and the right not to be compelled to receive education against their wishes;
- Right of the child to protection from discrimination and to education for tolerance;
- Right of the child's wishes when not under the care of parents or legal guardians;
- Right of the State to limit practices injurious to child's development or health.

Article 6: Manifesting Religion or Belief

At stake in the implementation of this article are the following rights:

- Right to worship and assemble, and to establish and maintain places of worship;
- Right to establish and maintain appropriate charitable or humanitarian institutions;
- Right to make, acquire and use materials related to rites and customs;
- Right to write, issue and disseminate relevant publications in these areas;
- Right to teach a religion or belief in places suitable for these purposes;
- Right to solicit and receive voluntary financial and other contributions;
- Right to train, appoint, elect or designate appropriate leaders;
- Right to observe days of rest and celebrate holidays and ceremonies;
- Right to establish and maintain communication with individuals and communities at national and international levels.

Article 7: National Legislation

This article declares that all of the rights at stake in the 1981 UN Declaration need to be accorded in national legislation in such a manner that everyone shall be able to avail themselves of such rights and freedoms in practice.

Article 8: Existing Protections

This article specifies that the 1981 UN Declaration is non-binding on States so as to ensure that the Declaration does not negate existing legal protections on freedom of religion or belief. Article 8 states that nothing in the Declaration shall be construed as restricting or negating any right defined in the Universal Declaration of Human Rights and International Covenants on Human Rights.

The 1981 UN Declaration is a compromise between states after twenty years of complex discussion and debate, and after final passage by the General Assembly.

Several sensitive issues are still in need of further clarification, including:

- Religious or national law versus international law,
- Proselytism,
- Conscientious objection to military service,
- Status of women in religion or belief,
- Claims of superiority or inferiority of religions and beliefs,
- Choosing and changing a religious commitment,
- Religious registration and association laws,
- Public media and religion or belief, and the relationship of religion or belief to the state.

INTERNATIONAL AND REGIONAL INSTRUMENTS OF PROTECTION

International legal instruments take the form of a *treaty* which may be binding on the contracting states. When negotiations are completed, the text of a treaty is established as authentic and definitive and is *signed* by the representatives of states. There are various means by which a state expresses its consent to be bound by a treaty, with the most common being ratification or accession. A new treaty is *ratified* by those states that have negotiated the instrument, while a state that has not participated in the negotiations may, at a later stage, *accede* to the treaty. The treaty enters into force when a pre-determined number of states have ratified or acceded to the treaty.

When a state ratifies or accedes to a treaty, that state may make reservations to one or more articles of the treaty, unless the treaty prohibits this actions. Reservations are exceptions that a state makes to a treaty—provisions that it does not agree to follow—and may normally be withdrawn at any time. In some countries, international treaties take precedence over national law.

In others, a specific law may be required to give an international treaty, although ratified or acceded to, the force of law. Almost all states that have ratified or acceded to an international treaty may issue decrees, amend existing laws or introduce new legislation in order for the treaty to be fully effective on the national territory. While the 1981 Declaration was adopted as a non-binding human rights instrument, several states had reservations. Romania, Poland, Bulgaria, Czechoslovakia and the then U.S.S.R. said that the 1981 UN Declaration did not take sufficient account of atheistic beliefs. Romania, Syria, Czechoslovakia, and the U.S.S.R. made a general reservation regarding provisions not in accordance with their national legislation.

Iraq entered a collective reservation on behalf of the Organization of the Islamic Conference as to the applicability of any provision or wording in the Declaration which might be contrary to Shari'a law or to legislation or acts based on Islamic law, and Syria and Iran endorsed this reservation.

Monitoring Freedom of Religion or Belief

Many international treaties have a mechanism to monitor their implementation. As part of the Covenant on Civil and Political Rights, Article 18 is legally-binding and is monitored by the Human Rights Committee. As of 2002, there were 149 States Parties to this Covenant. Under an Optional Protocol, 102 States Parties recognize the authority of the Human Rights Committee to consider confidential communications from individuals claiming to be victims of violations of any rights proclaimed under the treaty.

The 1981 UN Declaration on the Elimination of All Forms of Intolerance and of Discrimination Based on Religion or Belief is a non-binding declaration, and does not, therefore, have a treaty mechanism. Instead, in what is called an extra-conventional mechanism, the UN Commission on Human Rights appointed a Special Rapporteur for the 1981 UN Declaration. The Special Rapporteur is mandated to report annually to the Commission on the status of freedom of religion or belief worldwide.

4

Globalization and Social Policy

INTRODUCTION

During the 1990s globalization became a buzzword that appeared to dominate political, popular, and academic discourse. It is now difficult to read a newspaper or a book, watch the television, surf the Internet, or participate in a demonstration without coming across references to how 'globalization' is affecting our lives. Globalization, it seems, is variously blamed and credited for an incredibly wide range of phenomena.

Social problems ranging from famine to floods, from pollution to poverty, and from rural depopulation to urban overcrowding are commonly cited examples of the many invidious effects of globalization on social welfare. Conversely, globalization is trumpeted as being central to many developmental successes, such as poverty reduction, increasing economic prosperity, better services, and enhanced concern with human rights. Even those who are sceptical of the benefits globalization has brought so far may point to the ways in which it has the potential to transform political, economic, and social relations within and between countries to the benefit of human welfare worldwide.

Indeed, globalization is now invoked in so many contexts and applied in so many ways to such a wide range of phenomena that one would be forgiven for questioning its value as an analytical construct. Is it nothing more than a load of 'globaloney', generative of more political heat than analytical light? Is it in fact a central reality of our time or the product of an overactive imagination? Is it the case that a concept which is used to explain so much as a result explains nothing? This stage aims to untangle the multiple ways in which 'globalization' intersects with social policy as a field of study and research as well as a political practice.

We consider how useful globalization is in helping us to make sense of the dynamics and directions of social policy and the causes of – and therefore the solutions to – national and global trends in inequality, insecurity, and poverty. We consider how it relates to the way we study social policy. Can we simply add 'globalization' to the pot and stir? Or does engaging with globalization necessitate a fundamental rethinking of the basic analytical frameworks and concerns of social policy? After initially setting out some points of contention with regard to the concept and the array of meanings, discourses, and relationships that globalization embodies, we explore some of the different ways in which globalization is said to affect the way we study social policy.

We then move on to review debates regarding what impact globalization has had on welfare states. Following that, we survey the role of supranational agencies in the making of social policy and some of the questions and issues that alise therefrom. The stage lays a good deal of emphasis on historicizing and internationalizing contemporary debates about globalization and social policy.

The importance of historical context is emphasized throughout the stage because of the tendency within 'globalization studies' to focus on the contemporary world to the neglect of longer historical trends: this results in an over-emphasis on the 'newness' of current circumstances and policy issues. By historicizing contemporary concerns we can better discern what is unprecedented as opposed to what is essentially a continuation of previous trends. The stage also employs an internationalist approach that is sensitive to diverse welfare arrangements and circumstances around the world and the ways in which different countries' social policies have responded to 'globalization'. This is necessary to avoid the trap of generalizing about the effects of globalization based on experiences of some of the advanced industrialized countries, which, after all, contain only a minority of the world's population.

'GLOBALIZATION': DEFINITIONS AND ISSUES

At its most basic, globalization is the term that has been given to a range of economic, technological, cultural, social, and political forces and processes that are said to have collectively produced the characteristic conditions of contemporary life. Foremost among these characteristics is a dense, extensive network of interconnections and interdependencies that routinely transcend national borders.

The interconnectedness is said not only to be more extensive in scope than in previous periods, but the connections are also more intensive and the speed at which such interactions occur is increasing. These interconnections have occurred and are expressed in ways that appear to 'bring together' geographically distant localities around the world, and events happening in one part of the world are able to quickly produce effects in other parts of it.

It is this enmeshment which gives rise to consciousness of the world as a single, shared place – a 'global village'. It is worth pointing out that the globalization gconcept itself is of relatively recent vintage. Globalization was first used in production management studies to describe the global spread of production systems facilitated by technological advances in telecommunications and transport systems whereby corporate headquarters were able to control production sites on the other side of the world.

The term then spread throughout economics and then the rest of the social sciences to explain changes believed to be occurring as a result of increasing interconnection of economic, social, political, and cultural systems throughout the world. Scholars were highlighting the apparent emergence of a 'new international division of labour' resulting from this industrial restructuring. This entailed the relocation of production away from 'core' urban areas by companies in certain labour-intensive sectors with unionized, protected labour forces towards weakly organized and cheaper labour forces in 'peripheral' communities in developing countries.

The establishment of export processing zones, the most notorious of which are the Mexican maquiladoras, was central to this process. Globalization entered more widely into popular discourse after the end of the Cold War. The collapse of the Berlin Wall and the end of the Soviet bloc in 1989 heralded what the US President, George Bush Senior, announced as a 'new world order' and it is the characteristics of this order that the term globalization partly attempts to explain.

A main feature of this order was the triumph of capitalism over authoritarian socialism, but beyond that there were many questions asked about what this implied for international relations between states given the absence of a countervailing power to constrain US imperialist ambitions in particular and those of the West more generally. Further issues included changes in North–South relations and the realignment of countries formerly allied with the Soviet bloc.

GLOBALIZATION DOMAINS

Globalization captures a range of elements and processes across a number of key domains—economic, political, cultural, social, ecological, and technological. Politically, globalization is thought to result in the erosion of nation states and national sovereignty by new international actors.

The state's control over its national economy is being lost through the activities of private business enterprises such as transnational corporations whose decisions are seen to be increasingly made in a global context, while economic policy formation is increasingly being influenced by multilateral economic institutions such as the IMF and WB.

The state's political sovereignty is seen as being impinged upon by regional formations, such as the EU; its regulatory functions are increasingly being determined by supranational organizations such as the ITU and WTO and by international trade agreements. On issues such as human rights and environmental and labour standards states are under increasing pressure from INGOs to maintain and improve on them. On the cultural level, local and national cultures are seen to be increasingly submerged in an undifferentiated global mass culture, described by Ritzer as 'McDonaldization'. This involves the replacement of indigenous, traditional, national, and local cultures by an international culture of consumerism, seen in the global spread of pop music and Hollywood films, the increasing control of mass media by Western conglomerates and the endangering and disappearance of minority languages and cultural practices.

On the economic level, control of the global economy is seen as being concentrated in a small number of massive transnational corporations, whose turnover may be greater than the GDP of many nations, which can pick and choose where to locate their production, administrative, and research and development centres. Countries are said to be forced to cut tariffs and taxes if they wish to attract foreign direct investment from these TNCs.

The increasing number of free trade agreements, whether global, regional, or bilateral, are reducing the ability of states to form economic policies to promote their national interests. Finally, MEIs, such as the IMF, WB, ADB, and the EBRD, are increasingly influential in policy formation, especially in the case of developing and transitional countries which are encouraged to remove protectionist tariffs, privatize state industries, abolish price controls, and lift restrictions on private investment in order to obtain loans.

Governments have come under pressure to increase labour flexibility by making it easier to hire and fire workers, introduce temporary and precarious working conditions, and remove various trade union, health and safety, and minimal wage protections.

While much writing on globalization has emphasized the diminishing capacities of the state, a more nuanced view recognizes that states have not been idle, passive, powerless actors in these processes. Indeed, different states have enthusiastically followed pro-globalization policies. Indeed, the state has often been a key creator, shaper, and mediator of globalization.

NEO-LIBERAL GLOBALIZATION AND ANTI-GLOBALIZATION

What has been described as globalization is in fact only one possible variant of globalization – the neo-liberal one, described by Chomsky as 'a particular form of globalization, that has been instituted by state and corporate power, with primacy given to the rights of investors, financial institutions and so on, and with people being incidental'.

This has been associated with the emergence of the New Right, the election of Reagan in the US and Thatcher in Britain whose governments pursued neo-liberal economic policies and radical programmes of socio-institutional reform in domestic and foreign arenas alike throughout the 1980s and 1990s; the dominance of a neo-liberal 'free trade' agenda within the Bretton Woods institutions that emphasized public sector reform, privatization, deregulation, and residualized public welfare provision; and the establishment of new international governmental organizations concerned with global trade and finance. For these reasons globalization is perhaps most often used to denote profound transformations to capitalism over the past several decades, including the opening up of non-capitalist countries and markets to capitalist values, institutions, and social relations. This globalization has not gone uncontested. Beginning with the anti-austerity protests opposing IMF-imposed structural adjustment programmes and drawing on a wide range of national and international social movements, including environmental, development, labour, and consumer movements, the 'anti-globalization movement' has grown in strength so that meetings of MEIs, from Seattle to Prague to Genoa to Gleneagles, have been met by determined mass demonstrations.

These opposition forces have also come together at various world, regional, and national forums, not just in the alternative summits that accompany MEI meetings but also in free-standing meetings such as the WSF and the ESF, to express alternative visions and engage in social dialogues in opposition to neo-liberal globalization. The reaction can also be seen in the growth of campaigns to regulate the practices of TNCs in areas such as sweatshops, environmental impact, and the introduction of new technologies such as genetically modified foods.

Many of these campaigns are organized on a transnational basis using the same technological advances, such as the Internet, that are exploited by the corporations whose activities they oppose. Other reactions to globalization include the growth of right-wing anti-immigration politics in Europe and North America and the global growth of nationalistic, ethnic, and xenophobic movements, while globalization has also spurred the growth of religious fundamentalist movements. Finally, reaction to globalization can be seen in various national and local initiatives such as the 'slow food' movement in Italy, the development of farmers' markets in the UK, and LETS schemes in many countries.

PROBLEMS WITH THE DEFINITION AND USE OF GLOBALIZATION

Major problems exist with the definition and use of globalization as an analytical category. What, for example, is the substantive difference between globalization, internationalization, westernization, or transnationalization? Or between globalization, capitalism, industrialization, or imperialism? In other cases, what is described as global turns out to be less than global since often what is involved relates only to the Triad.

Furthermore, much of the literature privileges economic and technological factors, at its worst resembling crude Marxism in its economic determinism. As problematic is the failure to distinguish between association and causation: often social changes are attributed to globalization without sufficient evidential basis; and social changes, which may only suggest association with globalization, are presumed to be caused by globalization.

A recent review of literature on globalization and social welfare found that only 30 per cent of the 161 studies surveyed demonstrated their claims with 'more systematic causal proof' and concluded the literature was in danger of producing 'globaloney', 'producing self- and internally referential chains of arguments about globalization's supposedly ineluctable welfare effects that do not stand on a firm inferential basis'. When we are faced with rhetoric rather than analysis these problems affect writings that both denigrate and celebrate globalization.

Globalization has been analysed from a wide variety of positions. The main positions have been characterized as 'technological enthusiasts', 'marxisant pessimists', 'plural pragmatists', and 'sceptic internationalists'. These disagreements emanate not only from different theoretical standpoints but also from the different disciplinary backgrounds that give rise to various approaches, emphases, and concerns.

Thus, one distinction is between accounts that emphasize lived experience and identity, and those that stress changes to world political and economic structures. Another distinction is between macro perspectives that locate the driving forces of globalization at the level of intersecting economics, technology, and politics, and micro perspectives that emphasize changes taking place at the level of firms and their business environments. These are compounded by the different referents and indicators used to 'measure' globalization. A further complication is the fact that while globalization is used descriptively to refer to actually occurring trends and phenomena, it is also used prescriptively to advocate how the world should be developing. This usage of the term may slip from a means of characterizing structures and experiences associated with contemporary existence or historical changes to it, into a normative statement of what ought to happen, and what courses of action or policies are preferable. The use of the term in the normative sense is quite common, highlighting the ideological agendas and projects which it is often mobilized to serve. So, to state that 'globalization is unavoidable' is often little more than a barely disgeuised call for governments to loosen or remove 'restrictive' trade, labour, social, health, and environmental regulations. Such may be the degree of conflation between description and prescription that 'globalization can be used to serve rhetorical objectives' and may be 'advocated or rejected merely to justify a particular strategy'. Notwithstanding these reservations, used carefully a globalization perspective offers many fruitful avenues for social policy. In the remainder of the stage we examine what these avenues are and where they lead us.

HOW IS GLOBALIZATION RELEVANT TO SOCIAL POLICY?

Although social policy has arrived relatively late to 'globalization studies' its engagement with this field has been substantial and productive. Indeed, whatever one's position in relation to globalization the concept/debate is a significant one for this field, and even 'sceptic internationalists' who otherwise deny the fundamental precepts of the globalization thesis would agree there is a need to address the wider global contexts and dimensions of social policy. In fact, used carefully, 'globalization' presents many new opportunities to critically interrogate social policy – to think about how we construct fields of enquiry, the concepts and theories we use, the areas and issues we examine, and the types of questions we ask.

QUESTIONING THE 'NATIONAL' FRAME

One basic illustration of how a globalization perspective 'disrupts' the precepts of social policy is to consider how it challenges the basic unit of analysis – the national welfare state. Thus, academic social policy has essentially been concerned with variations in how welfare services are financed, organized, delivered, and consumed within these political territories as well as with the effects of these services on the social structure, social relations, and quality of life of their resident populations. Whether the variations are between social groups, over time, or between countries, the nation-state and the social policies enacted within it have framed the analysis. In many ways, this is sensible: after all, most welfare services are organized, funded, regulated, and delivered by governmental and non-governmental entities based and operating within the territorial boundaries of individual countries, while the services provided are usually accessed by people living in those same countries.

Yet in other ways this orientation unnecessarily restricts, even distorts, the field of enquiry by focusing our gaze on the national context to the detriment of the transnational and global ones. In particular, it presumes that the forces shaping the social structure are primarily local and national ones and that the entities involved in formulating and implementing social policy operate purely on a national basis.

It obscures the various transnational sites and spaces in which social policies are formulated, and the social impacts of 'our' domestic and foreign economic and development policies on other countries and populations. In essence, it problematically assumes that social policy exists within an impermeable national container space, and that it develops with little or no reference to the global circumstances of 'our' country or its relationship to other countries, or to developments and events elsewhere in the world.

TRANSNATIONAL ASPECTS OF SOCIAL POLICY: SOME HISTORICAL EXAMPLES

It is possible to argue that it has never, in fact, been appropriate to think of welfare states and social policies as first and foremost the outcomes of national forces or divorced from the dynamics of the wider global geo-political order. During the nineteenth and twentieth centuries the forces behind welfare state-building and the social regulation of capitalism occurred within a world order characterized by extensive international trade and migration, transnational corporations, and developed international monetary and exchange rate regimes.

While much recent commentary focuses on contemporary transnational political mobilization in the 'anti-globalization movement', there are examples dating back two centuries of political mobilization that were international and extended beyond Europe. Two examples here are the anti–slave trade movement and the movement against Congo colonization. Colonialism was central to the international political order that underpinned the development of social policies and welfare states in a range of countries throughout the world.

The development of the British welfare state, for example, is intricately tied up with Britain's status as a colonial power; its colonies – Ireland, Australia, Canada, India, Hong Kong, and many African countries – sustained Britain's its economic foundations, constituted a destination to which criminal classes and other socially deviant groups and individuals could be exported and formed a labour pool from which Britain drew to staff its welfare services.

In turn, these countries' colonial histories impacted upon the development of their social policies, as Britain 'exported' welfare ideologies and systems influenced their social and political structures, and, together with local elites, subsumed their economic development interests to British interests. A tangible example of the transnational dimensions of welfare systems is the British social security system.

The Commonwealth spawned a global administrative network of offices involved in the processing of war pensions payments not only to British war pensioners living abroad and to residents of former British colonies, but also to those with no connection to the British state, such as Polish soldiers who fought in the Second World War under British command. Not all of these transnational influences were colonial. Japan imported Western models of welfare as early as the 1870s, while Western thinking influenced the development of welfare in Taiwan and Korea.

Eugenic and population control ideologies have been given particular expressions in a range of different countries. The so-called golden era of welfare state-building in western Europe was underwritten by economic and development aid from the US to Europe in the form of the Marshall plan. Although much recent critical attention has focused on the influence of the World Bank's approach to social security and poverty reduction in developing countries, similar policy transfer processes between other more 'progressive' IGOs and countries can be discerned. Thus, Western European social democratic approaches to social protection were transmitted through the ILO which was, for most of the twentieth century, the dominant IGO in the social security field and exerted considerable influence on the development of national social security systems around the world, in 'developed' and 'developing' countries alike. Overall, then, a globalization perspective suggests that 'national' welfare states have been more shaped by and enmeshed in a global order than prevailing accounts of welfare state development allow for. Even if these international forces are mediated by specific circumstances, institutions, and forces in individual countries.

At the same time, the focus of 'globalization studies' on the relatively recent erosion of the policy autonomy of states in the advanced industrialized countries by external forces is problematic. Not only does this emphasis on recent developments obscure the long historical influences of the global North on social policy in the global South, but it side-steps an established literature emphasizing how ostensibly 'national' social policies are the outcome of a combination of political forces, social structures, cultural traditions, and economic processes entangled in a matrix of intersecting multi-level, multi-scalar sites and spaces.

GLOBALIZATION BRINGS NEW CONCERNS AND PERSPECTIVES TO SOCIAL POLICY

A globalization perspective also brings new perspectives and subject matter to social policy, extending its field of enquiry. To begin with, it opens up to enquiry the ways in which the content of social policy and the distribution of welfare are shaped by: governmental and nongovernmental organizations responding not only to domestic issues and sources of pressure but also to circumstances, events, and developments in other countries; the policies of foreign governments, international organizations, and financial institutions; and the decisions and activities of overseas headquarters or branches of TNCs. In essence, then, globalization draws attention to the ways in which societies, economies, and polities – including labour markets and welfare systems – of different countries are entangled in one another.

This appreciation of the extent and dimensions of 'enmeshment' leads us to focus on the 'external' and global sources of what are seen as principally 'domestic' or 'national' social problems and policy issues. For example, the global causes of increasing mobility of people internationally, some of which is manifested in the North as the 'problem' of migrants, refugees and asylum-seekers, can be seen as residing in uneven development and geo-economic inequalities.

Similarly, the levels and distribution of employment and unemployment within countries and localities are at least in part related to the overseas investment decisions of TNCs as well as economic events. The 1997 Asian financial crisis illustrates this latter point, demonstrating as it did the extent to which 'national' economies are interconnected through finance and the internationalized social consequences of financial crises.

Amongst the effects of that crisis, which were felt worldwide, were massive job losses, a severe drop in wages and incomes, a sharp rise in the numbers of people in poverty, and the mass repatriation of foreign workers in some Asian countries to their countries of origin. The international response to the crisis focused wider attention on the need to reform institutions of global governance to better regulate global financial transactions and develop more effective social protection systems.

Of course, any analysis of the relationship between globalization and social policy must also attend to the policies and practices of 'core' country governments. In recent years the antiglobalization movement and international development campaign groups have done much to raise public awareness of the content of anti-poverty and social development policies pursued by national governments abroad. They have also drawn attention to the social dimensions and implications of 'our' government's foreign policy and practices as regards finance, trade, agriculture, and environment, whether pursued bilaterally through aid programmes, or multilaterally through world-regional or global institutions.

These groups' campaigns have exposed the adverse social impacts of government policies supportive of, for example, the privatization of public utilities, the industrialization of agriculture and food production, and international financing and debt relief mechanisms. These campaigns have brought underspread attention to the wider public policy context of and influences on health, social welfare, and livelihoods and the responsibilities on the part of richer-country governments and populations towards poorer ones.

GLOBALIZATION PROMPTS THE RETHINKING OF KEY CONCEPTS

A globalization perspective not only 'stretches' the scope of our field of enquiry to recognize the variety of welfare arrangements that exist worldwide and the ways in which 'national' systems are deeply interconnected; it also challenges us to rethink theoretical and conceptual constructs. Academic work has only recently begun on 'globalizing' the bodies of sociological, political, philosophical, and economic theory that informed explanations of national social policy and welfare state development.

At the level of concepts, though, there has been some progress in developing the idea that globalization entails 'the deterritorialization of traditional concepts, their diasaggre-gation and resynthesis'. That this reconceptualization work does not necessarily entail jettisoning existing concepts. While in some cases we need to rethink basic concepts such as citizenship, justice, efficiency, and altruism which were developed in national c ontexts, in other cases it may be more of a case of how we might apply existing concepts to global contexts. One illustration of how a central social policy concept, the welfare mix might be applied in a global context and the kinds of adaptations it might involve.

IMPACTS OF GLOBALIZATION ON WELFARE STATES AND SOCIAL POLICY

There is a wide divergence of views as to how globalization impacts on the welfare state. This is not surprising given, as we saw earlier in this stage, the fundamental disagreements as to the existence of globalization, the differences in opinion as to how it should be characterized, and the forces driving it. These disagreements are reflected in the growing body of scholarship on globalization and the welfare state. Making sense of this literature is further complicated by a number of problems.

First, much of the work turns out to be selective in its coverage of countries, confined as it is mainly to industrialized countries to the neglect of developing ones. Second, many studies focus only on specific sectors or services from which often inappropriate generalizations about the impact of globalization on the welfare state as a whole are made. Third, much of the discussion is still often speculative rather than evidence-based and it tends to be prescriptive rather than descriptive.

These problems reflect the deeply ideological, often politicized nature of writing in the area, both from the political Left and the political Right. Nonetheless, it is possible to put down some markers to guide us through the literature. First, most of those writing about the impacts of globalization on welfare states do so from one of the three broad positions on globalization outlined earlier in this stage—marxisant pessimist, plural pragmatist, or sceptic internationalist. Technological enthusiasts have been noticeably absent from this literature.

Second, the literature revolves around a core set of concerns and issues, such as:

- The extent to which globalization triggers a 'race to the bottom', in which nation states continue to reduce welfare and regulatory costs in a competition with other states to attract foreign investors;
- The extent to which comprehensive public provision is eschewed in favour of reliance on private provision, be it commercial, voluntary or informal, in meeting social needs;
- The extent to which such provision and regulation is made on a transnational scale, and
- The effects of regional and global supranational agencies' involvement in social policy on national welfare systems.

Third, the literature focuses to a large extent on the 'new' global institutional architecture of welfare, to the neglect of the less institutionalized and informal aspects of social welfare. These include the ways in which individuals, households, and communities manoeuvre, strategize, and organize to maximize their opportunities and minimize their risks under conditions of globalization. Below we examine some of the main perspectives on how globalization has impacted on welfare states, noting the strengths and weaknesses of each approach, including the evidential basis of the claims being made. We also note how each of these perspectives relate to the general positions on globalization outlined earlier in the stage.

DECLINE OF WELFARE STATE GLOBALLY ATTRIBUTED TO NEO-LIBERAL POLICIES

In the first perspective, represented by Mishra and Beck among others, globalization heralds the decline, if not end, of social democratic politics upon which the welfare state was built. Globalization in this account is often conflated with neo-liberalism and is said to curtail the autonomy of national governments, restricting their pursuit of comprehensive programmes of redistribution, full employment, and economic growth.

Global competition exerts downward pressures on wages and working conditions as workers and welfare states are locked into international competition to attract FDI, while governments steer clear of programmes and interventions of which globalizing capital does not 'approve'. As the boundaries of public responsibility are restricted, universalist welfare states with extensive public provision and spending programmes are replaced by selectivist welfare systems in which the state plays a greatly reduced role in welfare provision and non-state sectors assume a greater one. State action becomes a measure of last resort, to stimulate the supply of human capital necessary for economic growth and tackle inequities that interrupt the smooth operation of the economy. In this view, globalization has ushered in neo-liberalism in economic policy with the convergence of social policy 'on a right-of-centre position with global capitalism driving policy rightwards'. Although this view exhibits many of the tenets of the 'marxisant pessimist' position, its key tenets are shared by those writing outside marxian frameworks, as evidenced by the ways in which globalization is seen to be directly implicated in changing welfare ideology, rootand- branch welfare state reform, and welfare convergence.

Beck and Taylor-Gooby, for example, offer similar analyses of how globalization entails the 'prising open' of welfare states and the social pacts underpinning them with social policies expected to follow the same course: The premises of the welfare state and pension system, of income support, local government and infrastructural policies, the power of organized labour, industry-wide free collective bargaining, state expenditure, the fiscal system and 'fair' taxation – all this melts under the withering sun of globalization and becomes susceptible to political moulding. [E]conomic globalization, labour market flexibility, more complex patterns of family life and the dissolution of traditional class structures require a new welfare settlement.

Since full employment, redistribution and expensive universal services are no longer seen as feasible, the new welfare can only justify social spending as investment in human capital and the enhancement of individual opportunities. Welfare states are all driven in the same direction by the imperatives of international competition. This presentation of globalization as pretty much single-handedly driving welfare state change in a particular direction is deeply problematic due to its exaggerated claims of the overwhelming power of capital, the impoverished capacities of states, and the irrelevance of countervailing political forces. Indeed, these arguments tend to be speculative, predicting future changes, while providing little evidence that welfare states are being restructured in the ways claimed or that 'globalization' is causing the suggested changes.

That said, Mishra examines Japan, Germany, Sweden, and a number of Anglo-Saxon countries, both refuting and refining key propositions associated with this thesis. Importantly, he points out that 'there are substantial and continuing differences in the approaches, policies and outcomes concerning the welfare state between Anglo-Saxon countries on the one hand and those of Continental Europe and Japan on the other'.

RESILIENCE OF, AND CONTINUED DIVERGENCE ACROSS, WELFARE STATES

As these broad-brush claims have been discredited, so analyses which emphasize the general resilience of welfare states against the onslaught of globalization and the varied impacts and responses generated by it have commanded more attention. This focus on welfare state resilience and variation is illustrative of the plural pragmatist position that accepts the existence of 'globalization' but recognizes the continued importance of domestic factors in mediating the pressures it generates, together with dual forces of fragmentation and unification involved.

This body of scholarship tends to focus on the factors that account for continued divergence and often makes extensive use of cross-national comparisons to highlight the continued importance of domestic contexts in mediating the effects of globalization pressures and shaping welfare state responses to them. This perspective typically emphasizes factors such as: the nature and strength of ideologies, and cultural and religious values and traditions; the impact of social, religious, political, and environmental movements; the strength and balance of political power between political parties, and between labour, civil associations, and capital, and the political compromises between them. These approaches also locate welfare state reforms in the context of broader state globalization strategies, be they 'niche states' which promote themselves as tax and regulation havens or developmental states, and how these strategies reflect states' particular histories, 'factor endowments', and capacities as well as their 'rank' in the international political system.

Development studies research has usefully shown how the implementation of multilateral agreements, policies, and programmes nationally varies between policy areas and depends on a range of country characteristics such as government ideology, political and social institutional regimes, interest group organization and mobilization, state capacity, and strategic location. When developments in economic, demographic, and social structures are also taken into account, even broadly similar pressures may generate quite different national responses. Thus, while some governments are adopting similar strategies such as fiscal austerity, marketization, privatization, and economic openness in trade, investment, and finance, others have not followed the neoliberal route.

Moreover, if anything, there has been continued heterogeneity amongst the welfare states of the Triad countries, where economic globalization is at its most intense, and amongst countries of other regions, such as Latin America, where MEIs have been active in reshaping national social policy. One of the challenges to research in this area is the need to widen its focus. International comparisons tend to be confined to particular OECD countries such as Germany, Britain, Japan, Sweden, and the US, to the neglect of the smaller OECD countries and non-OECD 'developing' countries. Of course, this is a general problem with comparative welfare state researchers who rarely extend their beyond countries similar to their own. A further issue with much of this research is its tendency to conceive of globalization as an essentially 'external' phenomenon. In addition, globalization is too often treated as a monolithic phenomenon, reducible to its economic dimensions. A further problem is that there is often little attention to the distinction between causation and association. Thus, the effects of 'globalization' – which are in any case difficult to identify – are often insufficiently disentangled from the effects of other political, demographic, and social trends.

GLOBALIZATION AS TANGENTIAL TO WELFARE STATE CHANGE

It is this problem of establishing causal relationships between globalization and welfare state change that is addressed by the third main perspective in the field. This body of literature locates welfare state changes observed to factors located within the domestic arena rather than to 'globalization'. To an extent this perspective has much in common with the sceptic internationalists' position but is also advanced by those who broadly accept the 'globalization' thesis.

A notable exemplar here is Pierson who argues that globalization has had little effect on the content and direction of welfare state change:

- Welfare states indeed face unprecedented budgetary stress, but this is primarily related to endogenous processes of social change, as the economic profiles of affluent societies have become increasingly 'post-industrial' and as their welfare states have matured and their populations have grown older. These important shifts are related only loosely, if at all, to the changing international economy. To focus on globalization is to mistake the essential nature of the problem.

While acknowledging that globalization is associated with welfare state change, and that it may intersect with and complicate such changes, Pierson refutes the argument that globalization is the overarching determinant factor that explains those changes. Instead, he argues that although globalization has indeed accompanied transitions, accentuating and modifying pressures on welfare states, the root source of the transition pressures lies at national level. In particular, he cites the slowdown in the growth of productivity associated with the shift from manufacturing to services employment, the expansion and maturation of governmental commitments, and a demographic shift to an older population. In common with the sceptic internationalists, he claims that the focus on globalization distracts as from identifying the real source of these trends and pressures which, he argues, lie in the domestic arena.

Furthermore, blaming 'globalization' – be it the global economy, international organizations, or transnational corporations – enables politicians and other interest groups to argue there are overwhelming, immutable external forces over which they have no control and to which must yield. In common with the 'plural pragmatists', the importance of the domestic context and forces is emphasized to explain the incremental and piecemeal nature of reform and why we have not witnessed the wholesale dismantling of the welfare state predicted by marxisant pessimists.

In short, the major sources of pressure on the welfare state are decidedly endogenous or national in origin, and 'external' pressures – or 'globalization' – are at best of secondary importance. In sum, it is often difficult to evaluate what impacts globalization has on welfare states due to the problems associated with the use of the term globalization namely the monolithic and reductionist use of globalization, the way in which it is conceptualized as something that is done by 'them' to 'us', and the variety of positions on whether globalization is happening at all.

Not with standing, it is possible to identify three main arguments about the current and future condition of the welfare state under globalization: the first of these claims that globalization erodes the welfare states and its foundations; the second claims that globalization effects are absorbed and mediated by the welfare state; the third claims that globalization is of secondary importance in welfare state change compared with domestic sources of pressure.

We can discern a shift in this debate in recent years away from the crude economic determinism of 'strong' globalization that predicted the widespread rolling back and convergence of welfare states towards acceptance of more tempered, realistic accounts of globalization as a pluralistic phenomenon having multiple and uneven effects on welfare states. Thus, over time the literature has become more sophisticated in discerning the different, often contradictory, processes involved, identifying the various sources and manifestations of interests and forces that account for the content and direction of welfare state reforms. To sum up, the literature has come to eschew the edicts of the 'strong' globalization thesis and its accompanying mantra – 'TINA' – in favour of more nuanced thesis that is encapsulated by 'TAMA'.

GLOBAL SOCIAL POLICY

As indicated earlier, there is increasing awareness that people's life chances and the shape of welfare states are shaped by policies of international forums, institutions, and agencies. The importance of these organizations and their social policies has received more widespread attention in recent years, and has generated a new field of enquiry – 'global social policy'.

One reason for this increased awareness can be attributed to the activities of NGOs and social movements. These have organized a range of mass demonstrations at major MEI meetings and specific campaigns and have highlighted the role of these organizations in often adversely shaping economic and social development worldwide. In addition, over the last decade a number of financial crises have highlighted the degree of 'enmeshment' of national economies and societies.

These crises have heightened general awareness of the role of the policies of the IMF and WB in both contributing to those crises in the first place and alleviating their social effects subsequently. The mainstream media's reporting of these various events has also been instrumental in creating wider awareness of these institutions in social policy matters.

INTERNATIONAL CO-OPERATION ON SOCIAL POLICY – HISTORICAL ASPECTS

To begin with we must emphasize that international co-operation and action on social policy issues long predate the recent concern with globalization. International NGOs resulting from private initiatives can be traced back to 1863 when the precursor to the Red Cross, the International Committee for the Relief of the Military Wounded, was founded at the initiative of Henry Dunant, shocked by his experiences at the Battle of Solferino in 1859.

This led to the signing in 1864 of the Geneva Convention for the Amelioration of the Wounded in Armies in the Field, which is recognized as the beginning of international humanitarian law. War also provided the spur for the foundation of the Oxford Committee for Famine Relief, founded in 1943 and registered as a charity in 1945: its first concern was with famine in Greece caused by the military activities of the German army there during the Second World War and it subsequently developed into a charity concerned with famine relief in developing countries. Another example of an international NGO is the International Planned Parenthood Foundation, which was founded in 1952 at the Third International Conference on Planned

Parenthood in Bombay and jointly sponsored the first world conference on family planning in 1981.

These NGOs have pursued their objectives by trying to influence government policies and through direct service provision. There is also a long history of intergovernmental co-operation on social policy issues. The early part of the twentieth century saw the foundation of the International Labour Organization as an affiliated agency of the ill-fated League of Nations. Building on the work of the ILO, the establishment of the International Social Security Association brought together governmental organizations involved in social security and gave further substance to international co-operation in that policy arena by providing a forum for policy dialogue among governmental organizations involved in social security administration throughout the world and promoting appropriate development of social protection adapted to the needs of the population.

While this began as an intergovernmental body, over time it included non-governmental bodies involved in social protection, such as Provident Funds and Trust Funds, which are not traditional social security schemes. During the twentieth century the international institutional and political architecture has evolved into a highly complex system involving numerous international agreements, treaties, regulations, and accords agreed and implemented through a wide range of organizations, agencies, and alliances.

The numbers of international formations have increased dramatically: as Kaul, Grunberg, and Stern note, 'more treaties were signed during the four decades after the Second World War than in the previous four centuries', while the number of international organizations grew from around seventy in 1940 to over one thousand by 1992. With this proliferation, transnational co-operation and co-ordination have also intensified to the extent that national social policy is now framed to an ever greater extent by a dense web of international legal and political obligations.

Currently, the most prominent areas of such co-operation are trade, investment, finance, and macro-economic policy, as well as environmental policies and social policies in employment, migration, social security, education, health and social services, food security, population control, and humanitarian relief. Collectively, these global institutions and networks play a significant role in directly and indirectly shaping the distribution of resources worldwide through, for example, setting the terms of international trade, overseeing the use of aid funds, monitoring social standards, and influencing the nature of social provision made in national contexts.

INTERNATIONAL GOVERNMENTAL AND NON-GOVERNMENTAL ORGANIZATIONS

Supranational organizations operate at both regional and global levels and vary in terms of their resources, their power to effect policy change at national level, and their degree of autonomy from governments. Some aim to achieve their policy goals through powers of persuasion, others do so through conditionalities attached to loans, while others still may impose fines or force governments to provide compensation should they fail to implement agreements/law. Many governments belong to both regional and global IGOs, while regional formations engage in trans-regional collaboration around social and economic policy issues.

Governments also pursue their policy objectives through a complex system of bilateral agreements to pursue their trade, social, and other objectives. In addition to international governmental organizations and forums, mention must be made of networks of international non-governmental organizations monitoring and lobbying on social policy issues. INGOs embrace groups from trade unions and professional associations to employers' groups, industry groups, consumer groups, and groups working on issues of poverty, environment, development, and trade.

These organizations are involved in both the formulation of social policy and its implementation through service delivery. For example, the main MEIs have formal processes for the consultation of NGOs in decision-making, and many of the World Bank's development projects are delivered through local, national, and international NGOs.

FROM REGULATING TO TRANSFORMING GLOBAL CAPITALISM

One of the key questions policy-makers, activists and scholars are currently engaged in is that of how to steer 'globalization' in the public interest generally and in the interests of social welfare more specifically. There is a broad consensus now that the current system of global governance requires significant overhaul, necessitating far-reaching institutional and policy reforms.

However, as we would expect, there are a wide variety of positions and approaches as to what the aims of the reforms should be and how they should be achieved. We cannot deal with the various details of policy discussions and disagreements in the confines of this stage. Nevertheless, it is possible to note some key questions that are currently being debated. Regulatory reform issues, for example, tend to boil down to the question of how to maintain or improve social protection, labour, educational, and health standards. Thus, what kinds of controls should be placed on the activities of globalizing corporations in their pursuit of profit – should they be voluntary or mandatory, and who should oversee their implementation? How far should global markets in welfare and other basic services be permitted to develop?

To what extent should social welfare provision be subject to international trade agreements, such as the GATS? Should there be global and regional mechanisms of social redistribution, and what form might these take? More generally, is it possible to reform the existing international institutional architecture in the interests of global social justice or are more radical courses of action required? What would be the founding principles of such an order and how would these be realised? The answers to these questions are rendered all the more complicated by the wide variety of countries, actors, and interests involved, as well as by the global, regional, and national levels on which they are debated.

One of the more pressing challenges is to democratize global social policy debates so as to incorporate a wider range of voices and interests rather than leave these discussions in the hands of a small group of policy elites and experts. Grassroots globalization forums, such as the World Social Forum and the World Water Forum, constitute a productive source of often radical policy alternatives.

One difficulty facing those aiming to strengthen the role of such global social forums in global policy-making is the major division between those who believe the current system can be reformed and those who believe revolutionary change is necessary for the creation of a globally just social order. While this makes it highly unlikely that an overarching consensus on global social policy will be reached in the future, it does at least ensure that there is plenty of room for vigorous contestation and debate for many years to come.

CONCLUSION

In this stage we have examined the interconnections between globalization and social policy. We have seen that globalization is a highly contested concept and that 'globalization studies' displays a range of theoretical, ideological, and political perspectives.

We identified the four main positions in the globalization debate as technological enthusiast, marxisant pessimist, plural pragmatist, and sceptic internationalist, and highlighted the fact that debates about globalization have tended to centre on issues of the rise of international nongovernmental actors, state sovereignty, and changing policy formations processes and the implications of these for social and economic development. We then looked at the connections between globalization and social policy as a field of academic study and research.

Here, the idea that a globalization perspective has potentially profound implications for the theories and concepts used to analyse social policy, provision, and development was introduced. We also discussed how, despite the recent concerns with the influences of globalization on national institutions and policy autonomy, welfare states and social policies have historically been the result of decidedly global and transnational circumstances, and influences, as well as national and local ones.

We proceeded to review competing arguments about the possible impacts of globalization on welfare states. We saw how this debate has evolved from an emphasis on the convergence of welfare states and social policies and on the inevitability of lower social standards and the dismantling of public social provision, to one which emphasizes the relative resilience and continued diversity of welfare state forms. We also touched on debates about the balance between 'internal' and 'external' forces bearing on 'national' social policy development.

Finally, we reviewed the importance of international organizations in the making of social policy and briefly reviewed some current issues and approaches within global social policy. Overall, there is no doubt that the debates on which we have touched will continue to be fiercely waged over the coming years and that students, scholars, policy-makers, and activists will need to take cognizance of the ways in which local, national, and global forces intersect in shaping the development of welfare states and social policy. As suggested, all need increasingly to engage with the range of complex social policy issues that 'globalization' raises and actively participate in devising imaginative responses focused on maximizing the health and social welfare of everyone worldwide.

5

International Human Rights Law

INTRODUCTION

In June 1993 a United Nations World Conference was held in Vienna to address the differences in national perceptions of international human rights. The goal was to reach a mutual understanding and universal approach to human rights norms, fundamental freedoms and enforcement mechanisms

As a preliminary to this global gathering of nations, an Asian regional meeting was held in Bangkok, gathering together the respective governments. One premise was to challenge the idea of 'universal human rights standards', which the Vienna Conference sought to establish. To Asia, their language of human rights differed fundamentally to that defined by the international community of the United Nations, given their unique culture, history and economy. Their discussions culminated in the Bangkok Declaration, proposing a culturally relative approach in favour of globally applicable standards.

In the aftermath of the Vienna Conference there appeared to be no resolution that appeased all parties. Ambassador Kausikan summed this view up when he declared that the World Conference on Human Rights in Vienna, on June 1993 did not promote "a genuine and fruitful dialogue" between the West and East.

- The West went to Vienna accusing Asia of trying to undermine the ideal of universality and determined to blame Asia if the conference failed. Inevitably Asia resisted. The result after weeks of wrangling was a predictable diplomatic compromise ambiguous enough so that all could live with it, but settled very few things. There was no real dialogue between Asia and the West, no genuine attempt to address the issues or forge a meeting of minds. If anything, the Vienna Conference may have only hardened attitudes on both sides and increased the deep scepticism which many Asian countries regard Western posturing on human rights

Over a decade later the debate continues, aligning itself upon an East/ West axis, with the Western world cultivating a vision of human rights with a core of civil and political rights shaped by a liberal western tradition, and the East challenging this view with cultural, political and economic dimensions. Ultimately "What appears from the Western perspective, to be a noble campaign for universal rights is interpreted from the Asian perspective, as cultural imperialism".

China lies amid this opposing Eastern faction and although it has experienced enormous economic and social progress, political reform has lagged behind, and the repression of citizens seeking to exercise their internationally recognised fundamental freedoms continues to be problematic.

This document seeks to understand China's aversion to the application of international human rights principles by analysing the main opposing arguments. Given the apparent reluctance of accedence to universal standards the focus will then turn to the International Community and their proposed mechanisms of improving the human rights dilemma. Within this the action taking by America, the European Union and the United Nations will be specifically noted. In addition the mechanisms that are currently in place to deal with the human rights problem by China itself will be looked to, to assess their capability of truly rectifying the problem.

CHINA'S OPPOSITION TO A UNIVERSAL STANDARD OF HUMAN RIGHTS

As a full member of the United Nations and a signatory to the Charter of the United Nations' China have pledged themselves to co-operate with the international community to achieve universal respect for, and observance of human rights and fundamental freedoms, and to accept the jurisdiction of the UN in cases of human rights abuse. Considering China's apparent commitment to the international community, its opposition to a universal agreement on human rights calls for clarification.

DIFFERENCE IN CULTURE AND THE CONCEPTION OF HUMAN RIGHTS

It is the perception of western society and the majority of the international community that being human is reason enough to be attributed certain inalienable rights. China asserts a contrasting dogma whereby man is born only with social and political duties, which should be carried out in service to the community. Rights are not derived from ones' status as a human being but rather they "flow from the state in the form of a gratuitous grant that can be subjected to conditions or abrogation by the unilateral decision of the state". These views stem from the Confucian tradition in China that humanity is not an innate quality but rather something which is achieved through socialization and contribution to the harmony of society. The granting of inalienable rights at birth would be a considered a subversion of established Chinese ideals.

Democracy is a further facet of Western traditions that fits uneasily with Chinese heritage. The Western world favours a system with the population as a ruling class, and an ultimate goal of individual rights and political liberty.

From a western perspective the Confucian ideal could only be deemed corrupt as it mandates great discretionary power for one ruler, with a society accepting their decisions as being in the best interest of the community. There exists no need for political human rights as it is unnecessary to keep check on the authority of the leader. In principle, the teachings of Confucius are manifest in China's past only, but history produces tradition and tradition shapes people's thinking and behaviour. The rationality, morality, and values of human beings are embedded in the particular cultural tradition in which they find themselves and from this the picture of human rights is shaped. China has sculpted its view of human rights from a culture at variance with that of the west, and so it contends that it cannot be governed by the same standards. The situation of China sharpens a long standing dilemma amongst various regions such as Indonesia and Africa, who articulate their inability to subsume a universalistic approach to human rights on account of there culture and traditions.

The fundamental question is whether there can be a truly universal doctrine of human rights applicable to all nations, and to what extent culture can justify a different application of human rights thinking and discourse? This is not a problem to which the consensus can agree upon and it may be necessary for the West to accept that states can legitimately agree to disagree without being guilty of gross misdeeds. An attempt to impose the Western definitions of 'liberty' and 'freedom' may only prove to be destructive in the face of Chinese opposition, best foregone in the interest of promoting genuine human rights. What can be said is that culture should not be used as a device to commit human rights violations and to reject entirely political and civil rights; "abuse is not part of any nation's cultural heritage".

It is a point worth noting that a persuasive case exists by which China can create a strong human rights foundation in line with global standards by drawing on its own political culture and beliefs. There are many aspects of Chinese culture which are indicative of values akin to those of the west such as value for life, and strong familial bonds. What is more is that the traditional culture advanced to justify cultural relativism far too often no longer exists. It is important to be astute to cynical, manipulation of a dying cultural past, "communitarian rhetoric too often cloaks the depredations of corrupt and often Westernized or deracinated elites."

IMPORTANCE OF ECONOMICOVER SOCIAL RIGHTS

The 1948 Universal Declaration of Human Rights proclaimed both political and economic rights, but the subsequent drafting of two separate protocols divided rights into civil and political on one hand, and economic, social and cultural on the other. Although the preambles of both the International Covenant on Civil and Political Rights, and the International Covenant on Economic, Social and Cultural Rights refer to the enjoyment of both classes of rights many countries have advocated only one division. In 1998 China became a signatory to the ICCPR yet it makes the ongoing representation that given its poor economy it is unable to support the political freedoms mandated therein and instead chooses to advocate the economic and social rights embodied in the IESCR

In 2004, Liu Zhenghua spoke on behalf of Chinese Delegation on Economic, Social and Cultural Rights at the 60 Session of the Commission on Human Rights.

In his speech he called upon the International Community to:

- Respond positively to the legitimate demand of the developing countries for greater prominence to be given to economic, social and cultural rights so as to promote fuller enjoyment of all human rights and fundamental freedoms by all peoples.

During the same session Du Zhonxing, adviser of the Chinese delegation on Civil and Political Rights made the following statement:

- As a developing country with a large population, great regional disparities, and a comparatively low level of economic development and education, China is facing various difficulties and challenges in its effort to realise civil and political rights. No matter what method or model a country adopts in realising human rights, the enjoyment of civil and political rights by individuals in that country cannot possibly exceed the level of its overall social development.

Such proclamations affirm that China grants primacy to economic development to the detriment of political freedoms. In the past the government has stated that "it is a simple truth that, for any country or nation, the right of subsistence is the most important of all human rights, without which the other rights are out of the question." Such statements suppose a false dilemma of having to choose between starvation and oppression, as economic development flourishes when it is without the hindrance of political freedoms. There is a lack of empirical support for a contention that suppression of freedoms yields significant benefits in terms of economic performance.

In fact the opposite is more likely to be true, as countries with authoritarian governments are the only nations to have suffered famine. Promoting political rights if anything only proves to improve the economy, it allows the people to have a voice to define their economic needs, enabling a better government response. Academics continue to dispute the dichotomy of economic and political rights stating that economic development and freedoms are inseparable and that no country can legitimately prioritize economic conditions over political freedoms.

SOVEREIGNTY

China mandates that respect for each country's sovereignty and non-interference with their internal affairs is a universal principle, and that this principle extends to all fields of international relations, including human rights. Section 7 of Article 2 of the Charter of the United Nations provides foundation for this assertion, stipulating that "Nothing contained in the present charter shall authorize the United Nations to intervene in matters which are essentially within the domestic jurisdiction of the state".

China is weary of other countries using human rights as a guise so that they may impose upon them their own political standards and modes of development. Consequently any criticism of its human rights by the international community is deemed to impinge their sovereignty.

The weakness of China's objection is twofold. Firstly the issue is not whether the international protection of human rights infringes domestic sovereignty, but whether it does so unlawfully. Secondly, the question arises as to whether the benefits to the world community outweigh the measure of national sovereignty that is relinquished. In addressing human rights the international community is not unlawfully interfering with China's internal jurisdiction. Human Rights issues cross national boundaries and so are valid international concerns; they deal with interactions between states and individuals, not relations between nations. One need only look at the many Christians, Tibetans and Falun Gong practitioners that fled China under the regime of Jiang Zemin to escape religious persecution. They now reside as refugees in countries external to China, an example of the domestic affairs spilling into the international arena.

As already noted, China is a voluntary member of the UN and signatory to the UN Charter, and consequently subject to international human rights enforcement decisions. In pursuing a policy of fiercely protecting its domestic integrity, China ultimately ignores the element of sovereignty abdicated in becoming a full member of the International Community. It is suggested therefore that in resolving who should have ultimate control on these matters, a balancing test of potential benefits to harms tips the argument in favour of international protection and enforcement. To avidly protect the integrity of China's domestic sovereignty over human rights will lead to individual harm, thus negating the very fabric of the treaties to which China is a signatory.

RECTIFYING THE PROBLEM

China's human rights position is one requiring a delicate approach. Its preference may be one of isolation and entirely independent governing, but its poor human rights record and repressive regimes nullify such a prospect. In pressing for progress, the international community must be careful not to upset the fragile balance between enduring human rights and respecting cultural difference.

USA

The United States Department, as part of its Human Rights and

Democracy Fund Project assigned more than $12,000,000 to China in 2004 and approximately $19,000,000 in 2005. Such expenditure is intended to encourage innovative programmes to uphold democratic principles, support democratic institutions and improve human rights. A substantial proportion of this fund is assigned to develop law and governance so as to create greater transparency in government and increase public participation.

This form of contribution carries weighted benefit. China continually mandates that economic instability is a major reason why political rights cannot be fully realised by their citizens. In providing a fund that has a sole focus of promoting a foundation for political rights, the United States is helping to remove one of China's greatest obstacles to fully ratifying the ICCPR.

In addition to funding, the United States recently published a report aimed at supporting democracy and human rights. Therein the US affirmed its commitment to continue to urge China to bring its human rights standards in line with that of the international community. As a means of securing this endeavour, US officials at all levels regularly engage with Chinese officials and researchers to discuss legal reform. The US mission in China has also brought internationally recognized speakers to China to address audiences on various topics, including democracy, human rights, religious freedom, corporate social responsibility and rule of law.

Such mechanisms facilitate the mutual exchange of ideas and create greater trust between China and the Western world. For China to commit to evolving its human rights it is important to encourage internal understanding as to what this will entail, otherwise it will be categorised as hostile imposition of foreign ideologies.

THE EUROPEAN UNION

The European Union has continually stood against China on account of its poor human rights regime. In 1997 the EU clarified its position by refusing to sponsor a human rights resolution on China at the United Nations Human Rights Commission. 2005 brought with it greater stress on the importance of dialogue and compromise between the EU and China with the holding of the 8th EU-China Summit in Beijing. During this meeting both sides endorsed the importance of exchanges in the field of human rights on the basis of equality and mutual respect. The EU welcomed China's commitment to ratifying the ICCPR and both sides confirmed their commitment to co-operate with UN human rights and international human rights standards provided for in relevant international human rights instruments.

Debatably one of the greatest achievements of the rhetoric between these two parties has been the emergence of the EU-China Legal and Judicial Co-operation Programme. This has become one of the most important assistance programmes of its kind in China, aiming to support and strengthen the rule of law thorough citizen participation. This type of grass roots up approach grants greater insurance that the endeavours of the international community are in keeping with the best interests of the Chinese people. Smaller grass roots projects have also been established, such as the EU-China Village Governance Programme, so as to empower citizens with civil rights.

This programme aims to devolve power to small regions, so that they can establish their own 'mini government' in which they participate in voting and the election of representatives. Such a system allows a natural understanding of what political rights entail, and allows citizens to experience their values. If the ICCPR is ratified, the approaches endorsed by the European Union will greater allow for the practical application of the rights contained therein.

THE UN

The Office of the Hugh Commissioner for Human Rights has developed a Regional Programme with a main objective of providing support for the ratification and implementation of international human rights treaties through comparative analysis of law and practices in the regions. OHCHR's approach involves working closely with regional actors, including government, national institutions, international organisations and civil society. This type of programme acknowledges China's reluctance to fully engage with the international community on the grounds of cultural difference. By becoming more aware of the diversity of the East, and the practices of law already in place the UN is better equipping itself to encourage a culturally sensitive approach to treaty ratification. The effects of this regime are already resonating in the more formal steps that China took towards ratification of the ICCPR at the close of 2005. At this time, during a visit by the High Commissioner for Human Rights, Louise Arbour, China assented to an agreement that they would ratify the ICCPR in the near future.

CHINA

The People's Republic of China has made some positive moves towards the realisation of human rights. The United Nation's, China ranks seventh in the world in terms of the size of its economy· If we take the progress that China has made in terms of taking its people out of poverty, and compare it with the rest of the globe, statistics will show that in the last 20 years, China has been decreasing the number of poverty stricken people by 10 million per year. In 1999 the World Bank and the UN development programme issued a report stating that "the number of poverty stricken people in the world is increasing in many places in the world, but China is an exception and China has achieved world renowned progress in solving the poverty problem" This makes China the leader in the world at reducing the number of poverty stricken people The development of a comprehensive social security system and health service system is further affirmation of China's progression in terms of Socioeconomic Rights' as is the improved education system where the enrolment rate for primary school-age children now stands at 87.3 per cent. These figures exceed the average figures for developing countries in the corresponding period. China's efforts in the realm of social and economic rights are admirable, but the dubious aspect of its rights portfolio lies in the area of civil and political rights. In the 2004 White Paper entitled "Building of Political Democracy in China", China declared the adoption of a constitutional amendment by the Second Session of the 10th National People's Congress. The new addition proclaims that 'the state respects and protects human rights'. This insertion has been deemed by many as a positive move forward and is backed by Amnesty International, but it does negate the remaining inadequacy of the Constitution as a whole nor does it remedy the inadequate legal and institutional system which provides no practical mechanism for the Constitution's application.

China has become a signatory to the ICCPR, and although it has yet to be ratified, the intention to do so in the near future has been declared. There have already been some signs of a changing attitude towards political rights under the auspices of the Chinese authorities. At local levels democratic policy making is developing through the establishing of village committees.

Direct elections of members of villagers' committees take place and they themselves are encouraged to decide upon major affairs of their community through democratic dialogue. Since the promulgation of the new Organic Law on Villagers' Committees in 1999, nearly half of the provinces, municipalities directly under the Central Government and autonomous regions have published their own laws and regulations on the election of villagers' committees. Many of these improvements have been outlined in the Chinese White Papers, publications which boast of the human rights endeavours that China has undertaken. One should be weary of taking these proclamations at face value. Sidney Jones, the Asian Director of Human Rights Watch has made prior statements of concern as to the motives of these documents and the substantiality of their claims. He has termed them a 'white wash' and suggested that they are a tactic used to placate the international community even though the reality of the situation in China is very different.

The Standing Committee of the 10th National People's Congress, China's top legislature has also stipulated an amendment to the criminal procedure in its five year legislature plan. It has been predicted that the amendment will include presumption of innocence, the right of the defendant to keep silent and seek legal council during questioning. Such amendments are a clear move towards improving the judicial system so as to support the upholding of human rights. As yet though there has been no clear move towards defining these amendments, nor any definite announcement on the part of any Chinese Official, so it remains to be seen whether they will be put in place in actuality.

6

International Human Rights Instruments

International human rights instruments are treaties and other international documents relevant to international human rights law and the protection of human rights in general. They can be classified into two categories: *declarations*, adopted by bodies such as the United Nations General Assembly, which are not legally binding although they may be politically so as soft law; and *conventions*, which are legally binding instruments concluded under international law. International treaties and even declarations can, over time, obtain the status of customary international law.

International human rights instruments can be divided further into *global instruments*, to which any state in the world can be a party, and *regional instruments*, which are restricted to states in a particular region of the world.

Most conventions establish mechanisms to oversee their implementation. In some cases these mechanisms have relatively little power, and are often ignored by member states; in other cases these mechanisms have great political and legal authority, and their decisions are almost always implemented. Examples of the first case include the UN treaty committees, while the best exemplar of the second case is the European Court of Human Rights.

Mechanisms also vary as to the degree of individual access to them. Under some conventions – e.g. the European Convention on Human Rights – individuals or states are permitted, subject to certain conditions, to take individual cases to the enforcement mechanisms; under most, however (e.g. the UN conventions), individual access is contingent on the acceptance of that right by the relevant state party, either by a declaration at the time of ratification or accession, or through ratification of or accession to an optional protocol to the convention. This is part of the evolution of international law over the last several decades. It has moved from a body of laws governing states to recognizing the importance of individuals and their rights within the international legal framework.

The Universal Declaration of Human Rights, the International Covenant on Civil and Political Rights, and the International Covenant on Economic, Social and Cultural Rights are sometimes referred to as the *international bill of rights*.

DECLARATION OF THE RIGHTS OF THE CHILD

The Declaration of the Rights of the Child is the name given to a series of related children's rights proclamations drafted by Save the Children founder Eglantyne Jebb in 1923.

Jebb believed that the rights of a child should be especially protected and enforced, thus drafting the first stipulations for child's rights.

Jebb's initial 1923 document consisted of the following criteria:

- The child must be given the means requisite for its normal development, both materially and spiritually.
- The child that is hungry must be fed, the child that is sick must be nursed, the child that is backward must be helped, the delinquent child must be reclaimed, and the orphan and the waif must be sheltered and succored.
- The child must be the first to receive relief in times of distress.
- The child must be put in a position to earn a livelihood, and must be protected against every form of exploitation.
- The child must be brought up in the consciousness that its talents must be devoted to the service of its fellow men.

These ideas were adopted by the International Save the Children Union, in Geneva, on 23 February 1923 and endorsed by the League of Nations General Assembly on 26 November 1924 as the World Child Welfare Charter. However, these proclamations were not enforceable by international law, but rather only guidelines for countries to follow

The original document, in the archives of the city of Geneva, carries the signatures of various international delegates, including Jebb, Janusz Korczak, and Gustave Ador, a former President of the Swiss Confederation.

The SCIU merged into the International Union of Child Welfare by 1946, and this group pressed the newly formed United Nations to continue to work for war-scarred children and for adoption of the World Child Welfare Charter.

On 20 November 1959 the United Nations General Assembly adopted a much expanded version as its own Declaration of the Rights of the Child, adding ten principles in place of the original five. This date has been adopted as the Universal Children's Day. In 1989, the Convention on the Rights of the Child was adopted by UN General Assembly. On September 2, 1990 it became international law with one notable exception: the US signed the Charter but has not ratified it. The Convention consists of 54 articles that address the basic human rights to children everywhere are entitled:

- The right to survival;
- The right to develop to the fullest;
- Protection from harmful influences, abuse and exploitation;
- The right to participate fully in family, cultural and social life.

The four core principles of the Convention are non-discrimination; devotion to the best interests of the child; the right to life, survival and development; and respect for the views of the child. Under the Convention, a child is defined as "... every human being below the age of eighteen years unless, under the law applicable to the child, majority is attained earlier."

UNIVERSAL DECLARATION OF HUMAN RIGHTS

The Universal Declaration of Human Rights (UDHR) is a declaration adopted by the United Nations General Assembly on 10 December 1948 at Palais de Chaillot, Paris. The Declaration arose directly from the experience of the Second World War and represents the first global expression of rights to which all human beings are inherently entitled. The full text is published by the United Nations on its website.

It consists of 30 articles which have been elaborated in subsequent international treaties, regional human rights instruments, national constitutions and laws. The International Bill of Human Rights consists of the Universal Declaration of Human Rights, the International Covenant on Economic, Social and Cultural Rights, and the International Covenant on Civil and Political Rights and its two Optional Protocols. In 1966 the General Assembly adopted the two detailed Covenants, which complete the International Bill of Human Rights; and in 1976, after the Covenants had been ratified by a sufficient number of individual nations, the Bill took on the force of international law.

HISTORY

Precursors

During World War II, the allies adopted the Four Freedoms—freedom of speech, freedom of religion, freedom from fear, and freedom from want—as their basic war aims. The United Nations Charter "reaffirmed faith in fundamental human rights, and dignity and worth of the human person" and committed all member states to promote "universal respect for, and observance of, human rights and fundamental freedoms for all without distinction as to race, sex, language, or religion". A universal declaration that specified the rights of individuals was necessary to give effect to the Charter's provisions on human rights. At the time, Canadian legal scholar John Peters Humphrey was newly appointed as Director of the Division of Human Rights within the United Nations Secretariat. The Commission on Human Rights, a standing body of the United Nations, was constituted to undertake the work of preparing what was initially conceived as an International Bill of Rights. The membership of the Commission was designed to be broadly representative of the global community with representatives of the following countries serving: Australia, Belgium, Byelorussian Soviet Socialist Republic, Chile, China, Egypt, France, India,-family phrases were the result of the Christian Democratic movement's influence on Cassin and Malik.

Adoption

The Universal Declaration was adopted by the General Assembly on 10 December 1948 by a vote of 48 in favor, 0 against, with eight abstentions: the Soviet Union, Ukrainian SSR, Byelorussian SSR, People's Federal Republic of Yugoslavia, People's Republic of Poland, Union of South Africa, Czechoslovakia and the Kingdom of Saudi Arabia. Honduras and Yemen, both members of UN at the time, failed to appear for vote. The South African position can be seen as a kind of protection of the system of apartheid in South Africa, which clearly violated any number of articles in the declaration. The Saudi Arabian delegation abstained mostly for two reasons: because of Article 18 which states that everyone has the right "to change his religion or belief" and because of Article 16 on equal marriage rights. Eleanor Roosevelt attributed the abstention of the Soviet bloc nations to Article 13, which provided the right of citizens to leave their countries.

The following countries voted in favor of the Declaration:

- Afghanistan
- Argentina
- Australia
- Belgium
- Bolivia
- Brazil
- Burma
- Canada
- Chile
- Republic of China
- Colombia
- Costa Rica
- Cuba
- Denmark
- Dominican Republic
- Ecuador
- Egypt
- El Salvador
- Ethiopia
- France
- Greece
- Guatemala
- Haiti
- Iceland
- India
- Iran
- Iraq
- Lebanon

- Liberia
- Luxembourg
- Mexico
- Netherlands
- New Zealand
- Nicaragua
- Norway
- Pakistan
- Panama
- Paraguay
- Peru
- Philippines
- Siam
- Sweden
- Syria
- Turkey
- United Kingdom
- United States
- Uruguay
- Venezuela

Despite the central role played by Canadian John Humphrey, the Canadian Government at first abstained from voting on the Declaration's draft, but later voted in favor of the final draft in the General Assembly.

STRUCTURE

The underlying structure of the Universal Declaration was introduced in its second draft which was prepared by René Cassin. Cassin worked from a first draft prepared by John Peters Humphrey. The structure was influenced by the *Code Napoléon*, including a preamble and introductory general principles. Cassin compared the Declaration to the portico of a Greek temple, with a foundation, steps, four columns and a pediment. Articles 1 and 2 are the foundation blocks, with their principles of dignity, liberty, equality and brotherhood.

The seven paragraphs of the preamble, setting out the reasons for the Declaration, represent the steps. The main body of the Declaration forms the four columns. The first column (articles 3–11) constitutes rights of the individual, such as the right to life and the prohibition of slavery. Articles 6 through 11 refer to the fundamental legality of human rights with specific remedies cited for their defense when violated. The second column (articles 12–17) constitutes the rights of the individual in civil and political society. The third column (articles 18–21) is concerned with spiritual, public and political freedoms such as freedom of thought, conscience and religion, as well as freedom of association. The fourth column (articles 22–27) sets out social, economic and cultural rights. In Cassin's model, the last three articles of the Declaration provide the pediment which binds the structure together. These articles are concerned with the duty of the individual to society and the prohibition of use of rights in contravention of the purposes of the United Nations Organisation.

COMMEMORATION: INTERNATIONAL HUMAN RIGHTS DAY

The adoption of the Universal Declaration is a significant international commemoration marked each year on 10 December and is known as Human Rights Day or International Human Rights Day. The commemoration is observed by individuals, community and religious groups, human rights organisations, parliaments, governments and the United Nations. Decadal commemorations are often accompanied by campaigns to promote awareness of the Declaration and human rights. 2008 marked the 60th anniversary of the Declaration and was accompanied by year-long activities around the theme "Dignity and justice for all of us".

SIGNIFICANCE AND LEGAL EFFECT

Significance

The *Guinness Book of Records* describes the UDHR as the "Most Translated Document" in the world. In the preamble, governments commit themselves and their people to progressive measures which secure the universal and effective recognition and observance of the human rights set out in the Declaration. Eleanor Roosevelt supported the adoption of the UDHR as a declaration rather than as a treaty, because she believed that it would have the same kind of influence on global society as the United States Declaration of Independence had within the United States. In this, she proved to be correct. Even though it is not legally binding, the Declaration has been adopted in or has influenced most national constitutions since 1948. It has also served as the foundation for a growing number of national laws, international laws, and treaties, as well as regional, national, and sub-national institutions protecting and promoting human rights.

Legal Effect

While not a treaty itself, the Declaration was explicitly adopted for the purpose of defining the meaning of the words "fundamental freedoms" and "human rights" appearing in the United Nations Charter, which is binding on all member states. For this reason the Universal Declaration is a fundamental constitutive document of the United Nations. Many international lawyers, in addition, believe that the Declaration forms part of customary international law and is a powerful tool in applying diplomatic and moral pressure to governments that violate any of its articles. The 1968 United

Nations International Conference on Human Rights advised that it "constitutes an obligation for the members of the international community" to all persons. The declaration has served as the foundation for two binding UN human rights covenants, the International Covenant on Civil and Political Rights, and the International Covenant on Economic, Social and Cultural Rights and the principles of the Declaration are elaborated in international treaties such as the International Convention on the Elimination of All Forms of Racial Discrimination, the International Convention on the Elimination of Discrimination Against Women, the United Nations Convention on the Rights of the Child, the United Nations Convention Against Torture and many more. The Declaration continues to be widely cited by governments, academics, advocates and constitutional courts and individual human beings who appeal to its principles for the protection of their recognised human rights.

REACTION

Praise

The Universal Declaration has received praise from a number of notable people. Charles Malik, Lebanese philosopher and diplomat, called it "an international document of the first order of importance," while Eleanor Roosevelt, first chairwoman of the Commission on Human Rights (CHR) that drafted the Declaration, stated that it "may well become the international Magna Carta of all men everywhere." 10 December 1948. In a speech on 5 October 1995, Pope John Paul II called the UDHR "one of the highest expressions of the human conscience of our time". And in a statement on 10 December 2003 on behalf of the European Union, Marcello Spatafora said that "it placed human rights at the centre of the framework of principles and obligations shaping relations within the international community."

Criticism

Islamic countries

Most Islamic countries have signed the Universal Declaration of Human Rights and other human rights agreements. In 1948, Saudi Arabia abstained from the ratification vote on the declaration, claiming that it violated Islamic Sharia law.

However, Pakistan (which had signed the declaration) disagreed with and critiqued the Saudi position. In 1982, the Iranian representative to the United Nations, Said Rajaie-Khorassani, said that the UDHR was "a secular understanding of the Judeo-Christian tradition", which could not be implemented by Muslims without trespassing the Islamic law. On 30 June 2000, Muslim nations that are members of the Organisation of the Islamic Conference (now the Organisation of Islamic Cooperation) officially resolved to support the Cairo Declaration on Human Rights in Islam, an alternative document that says people have "freedom and right to a dignified life in accordance with the Islamic Shari'ah", without any discrimination on grounds of "race, colour, language, sex, religious belief, political affiliation, social status or other considerations".

As a secular state, Turkey has signed the declaration of Human Rights in 1948 and other European Human Rights agreements.

A number of scholars in different fields have expressed concerns with the Declaration's alleged western bias. These include Irene Oh (Religion and Ethics), Abdulaziz Sachedina (Religion), Riffat Hassan (Theology) and Faisal Kutty (Law). Riffat Hassan argues as follows:

"What needs to be pointed out to those who uphold the Universal Declaration of Human Rights to be the highest, or sole, model, of a charter of equality and liberty for all human beings, is that given the Western origin and orientation of this Declaration, the "universality" of the assumptions on which it is based is - at the very least - problematic and subject to questioning. Furthermore, the alleged incompatibility between the concept of human rights and religion in general, or particular religions such as Islam, needs to be examined in an unbiased way."

Irene Oh argues that one of the ways to reconcile the two is to approach it from the perspective of comparative ethics.

Kutty writes: "A strong argument can be made that the current formulation of international human rights constitutes a cultural structure in which western society finds itself easily at home... It is important to acknowledge and appreciate that other societies may have equally valid alternative conceptions of human rights."

The Right to Refuse to Kill

Groups such as Amnesty International and War Resisters International have advocated for "The Right to Refuse to Kill" to be added to the UDHR. War Resisters International has stated that the right to conscientious objection to military service is primarily derived from, but not yet explicit in, Article 18 of the UDHR: the right to freedom of thought, conscience and religion. Steps have been taken within the United Nations to make this right more explicit; but those steps have been limited to secondary, more "marginal" United Nations documents. That is why Amnesty International would like to have this right brought "out of the margins" and explicitly into the primary document, namely the UDHR itself.

- To the rights enshrined in the Universal Declaration of Human Rights one more might, with relevance, be added. It is "The Right to Refuse to Kill."— Assistant Secretary General of the United Nations, and Nobel Peace Laureate, Sean MacBride, *1974 Nobel Lecture*

Women

American feminist Catharine MacKinnon has asked the question "are women considered human?", focusing in part on the use of male-centric terms such as *brotherhood* in Article 1 and *himself and his family* in article 23.

Bangkok Declaration

In the Bangkok Declaration adopted by Ministers of Asian states meeting in 1993 in the lead up to the World Conference on Human Rights held in the same year, Asian governments reaffirmed their commitment to the principles of the United Nations Charter and the Universal Declaration of Human Rights. They stated their view of the interdependence and indivisibility of human rights and stressed the need for universality, objectivity and non-selectivity of human rights.

At the same time, however, they emphasized the principles of sovereignty and noninterference, calling for greater emphasis on economic, social, and cultural rights, particularly the right to economic development, over civil and political rights. The Bangkok Declaration is considered to be a landmark expression of the Asian Values perspective, which offers an extended critique of human rights universalism.

ORGANIZATIONS PROMOTING UDHR

International Federation for Human Rights

The International Federation for Human Rights (FIDH) is nonpartisan, nonsectarian, and independent of any government. Its core mandate is to promote respect for all the rights set out in the Universal Declaration of Human Rights, the International Covenant on Civil and Political Rights, and the International Covenant on Economic, Social and Cultural Rights.

Amnesty International

Director Stephen Johnson and 41 international animators, musicians and producers created a 20-minute video for Amnesty International to celebrate the 40th Anniversary of the Declaration of Human Rights in 1988, bringing to life the 30 articles of the Universal Declaration of Human Rights. Amnesty International celebrated Human Rights Day and the 60th anniversary of the Universal Declaration of Human Rights all over the world by organizing the Fire Up event.

American Library Association

The Council of the American Library Association endorsed Article 19 from the Universal Declaration of Human Rights in 1997. Along with Article 19, Article 18 and 20 are also fundamentally tied to the ALA Universal Right to Free Expression and the Library Bill of Rights. Censorship, the invasion of privacy, and interference of opinions are human rights violations according to the American Library Association.

AMERICAN DECLARATION OF THE RIGHTS AND DUTIES OF MAN

- All men are born free and equal, in dignity and in rights, and, being endowed by nature with reason and conscience, they should conduct themselves as brothers one to another.— *Preamble, American Declaration of the Rights and Duties of Man*

The American Declaration of the Rights and Duties of Man was the world's first international human rights instrument of a general nature, predating the Universal Declaration of Human Rights by less than a year.

The Declaration was adopted by the nations of the Americas at the Ninth International Conference of American States in Bogotá, Colombia, in April 1948, the same meeting that adopted the Charter of the Organization of American States and thereby created the OAS.

Chapter One of the Declaration sets forth a catalogue of civil and political rights to be enjoyed by the citizens of the signatory nations, together with additional economic, social, and cultural rights due to them. As a corollary, its second chapter contains a list of corresponding duties. As explained in the preamble:

- "The fulfillment of duty by each individual is a prerequisite to the rights of all. Rights and duties are interrelated in every social and political activity of man. While rights exalt individual liberty, duties express the dignity of that liberty."

Although strictly speaking a declaration is not a legally binding treaty, the jurisprudence of both the Inter-American Court of Human Rights and the Inter-American Commission on Human Rights holds it to be a source of binding international obligations for the OAS's member states. While largely superseded in the current practice of the inter-American human rights system by the more elaborate provisions of the American Convention on Human Rights (in force since 18 July 1978), the terms of the Declaration are still enforced with respect to those states that have not ratified the Convention, such as Cuba and the United States.

DECLARATION ON THE RIGHTS OF DISABLED PERSONS

The Declaration on the Rights of Disabled Persons was a declaration of the General Assembly of the United Nations, made on 9 December 1975. It is the 3447th resolution made by the Assembly. As a resolution of the Assembly, it is not binding on member nations, but it forms a framework that may be drawn on for the purposes of international and domestic law. It consists of a lengthy preamble, and thirteen clauses that broadly promote the rights of those with disabilities. In 2007 the Convention on the Rights of Persons with Disabilities was adopted.

CAIRO DECLARATION ON HUMAN RIGHTS IN ISLAM

The Cairo Declaration on Human Rights in Islam (CDHRI) is a declaration of the member states of the Organisation of the Islamic Conference adopted in Cairo in 1990, which provides an overview on the Islamic perspective on human rights, and affirms Islamic Shari'ah as its sole source. CDHRI declares its purpose to be "general guidance for Member States [of the OIC] in the Field of human rights". This declaration is usually seen as an Islamic response to the post-World War II United Nations' Universal Declaration of Human Rights (UDHR) of 1948.

HISTORY

Predominantly Muslim countries, such as Sudan, Iran, and Saudi Arabia, frequently criticized the Universal Declaration of Human Rights for its perceived failure to take into account the cultural and religious context of non-Western countries. In 1981, the post-revolutionary Iranian representative to the United Nations Said Rajaie-Khorassani articulated the position of his country regarding the Universal Declaration of Human Rights, by saying that the UDHR was "a secular understanding of the Judeo-Christian tradition", which could not be implemented by Muslims without trespassing the Islamic law. The CDHRI was adopted in 1990 by members of the Organisation of the Islamic Conference and in 1992 the CDHRI was presented to the United Nations Commission on Human Rights, where it was strongly condemned by the International Commission of Jurists.

INSIDE

The Declaration starts by forbidding (in terms of basic human dignity and basic obligations and responsibilities) " discrimination on the basis of race, colour, language, belief, sex, religion, political affiliation, social status or other considerations". It continues on to proclaim the sanctity of life, and declares the "preservation of human life" as "a duty prescribed by the Shariah". In addition the CDHRI guarantees "non-belligerents such as old men, women and children", "wounded and the sick" and "prisoners of war", the right to be fed, sheltered and access to safety and medical treatment in times of war.

The CDHRI gives men and women the "right to marriage" regardless of their race, colour or nationality, but not religion. In addition, women are given "equal human dignity", "own rights to enjoy", "duties to perform", "own civil entity", "financial independence", and the "right to retain her name and lineage", though not equal rights in general. The Declaration makes the husband responsible for the social and financial protection of the family. The Declaration gives both parents the rights over their children, and makes it incumbent upon both of them to protect the child, before and after birth. The Declaration also entitles every family the "right to privacy". It also forbids the demolition, confiscation and eviction of any family from their residence. Furthermore, should the family get separated in times of war, it is the responsibility of the State to "arrange visits or reunions of families".

Article 10 of the Declaration states: "Islam is the religion of unspoiled nature. It is prohibited to exercise any form of compulsion on man or to exploit his poverty or ignorance in order to convert him to another religion or to atheism."

The Declaration protects each individual from arbitrary arrest, torture, maltreatment and/or indignity. Furthermore, no individual is to be used for medical or scientific experiments. It also prohibits the taking of hostages of any individual "for any purpose" whatsoever. Moreover, the CDHRI guarantees the presumption of innocence; guilt is only to be proven through a trial in "which he [the defendant] shall be given all the guarantees of defence". The Declaration also forbids the promulgation of "emergency laws that would provide executive authority for such actions". Art. 19 stipulates that there are no other crimes or punishments than those mentioned in the Sharia, which include corporal punishment (whippings, amputations) and capital punishment. The right to hold public office can only be exercised in accordance with the Sharia, which forbids Muslims to submit to the rule of non-Muslims.

The Declaration also emphasizes the "full right to freedom and self-determination", and its opposition to enslavement, oppression, exploitation and colonialism. The CDHRI declares the rule of law, establishing equality and justice for all. The CDHRI also guarantees all individuals the "right to participate, directly or indirectly in the administration of his country's public affairs". The CDHRI also forbids any abuse of authority 'subject to the Islamic Shari'ah.'

Article 22(a) of the Declaration states that "Everyone shall have the right to express his opinion freely in such manner as would not be contrary to the principles of the Shari'ah." 22(b) states that "Everyone shall have the right to advocate what is right, and propagate what is good, and warn against what is wrong and evil according to the norms of Islamic Shari'ah." 22(c) states: "Information is a vital necessity to society. It may not be exploited or misused in such a way as may violate sanctities and the dignity of Prophets, undermine moral and ethical values or disintegrate, corrupt or harm society or weaken its faith." 22(d) states "It is not permitted to arouse nationalistic or doctrinal hatred or to do anything that may be an incitement to any form of racial discrimination."

Religious features

Though using a universalist language akin to the Universal Declaration of Human Rights, "quite a number of [its] features express an Islamic particularity." The preamble is mostly religious rhetoric, and the particulars of the CDHRI contain numerous references to the Quran, sharia and aspects of the Islamic faith that appear on no other similar international list. The CDHRI concludes in article 24 and 25 that all rights and freedoms mentioned are subject to the Islamic Shariah, which is the declaration's sole source. The CDHRI declares "true religion" to be the "guarantee for enhancing such dignity along the path to human integrity". It also places the responsibility for defending those rights upon the entire Ummah.

CRITICISM

The CDHRI has been criticized for being implemented by a set of states with widely disparate religious policies and practices who had "a shared interest in disarming international criticism of their domestic human rights record."

Article 24 of the declaration states: "All the rights and freedoms stipulated in this Declaration are subject to the Islamic Sharia." Article 19 also says: "There shall be no crime or punishment except as provided for in the Sharia."

The CDHRI has been criticised for failing to guarantee freedom of religion, in particular the right of each and every individual to change their religion, as a "fundamental and nonderogable right".

In a joint written statement submitted by the International Humanist and Ethical Union (IHEU), a non-governmental organization in special consultative status, the Association for World Education (AWE) and the Association of World Citizens (AWC), a number of concerns were raised that the CDHRI limits human rights, religious freedom, and freedom of expression. The statement concludes, "The Cairo Declaration of Human Rights in Islam is clearly an attempt to limit the rights enshrined in the UDHR and the International Covenants. It can in no sense be seen as complementary to the Universal Declaration."

The Centre for Inquiry in September 2008 in an article to the United Nations writes that the CDHRI "undermines equality of persons and freedom of expression and religion by imposing restrictions on nearly every human right based on Islamic Sharia law." Rhona Smith writes that because the CDHRI's reference to Shariah implies an inherent degree of superiority of men.

Adama Dieng, a member of the International Commission of Jurists, criticised the CDHRI. He argued that the declaration gravely threatens the inter-cultural consensus on which the international human rights instruments are based; that it introduces intolerable discrimination against non-Muslims and women. He further argued that the CDHRI reveals a deliberately restrictive character in regard to certain fundamental rights and freedoms, to the point that certain essential provisions are below the legal standards in effect in a number of Muslim countries; it uses the cover of the "Islamic Shari'a (Law)" to justify the legitimacy of practices, such as corporal punishment, which attack the integrity and dignity of the human being.

VIENNA DECLARATION AND PROGRAMME OF ACTION

The Vienna Declaration and Programme of Action, also known as VDPA, is a human rights declaration adopted by consensus at the World Conference on Human Rights on 25 June 1993 in Vienna, Austria. The United Nations High Commissioner for Human Rights was created by this Declaration endorsed by General Assembly Resolution 48/121.

The VDPA reaffirmed the Universal Declaration of Human Rights and the United Nations Charter. Its Preamble states "The World Conference on Human Rights, Considering that the promotion and protection of human rights is a matter of priority for the international community, and that the Conference affords a unique opportunity to carry out a comprehensive analysis of the international human rights system and of the machinery for the protection of human rights, in order to enhance and thus promote a fuller observance of those rights, in a just and balanced manner."

The Preamble also states: "Invoking the spirit of our age and the realities of our time which call upon the peoples of the world and all States Members of the United Nations to rededicate themselves to the global task of promoting and protecting all human rights and fundamental freedoms so as to secure full and universal enjoyment of these rights,"

LOOKING BACK

The VDPA reflects the fact that the World Conference on Human Rights marks a turning point for human rights, as the Cold War has ended. The VDPA looks back, with the Preamble stating:

- Recalling also the determination expressed in the Preamble of the Charter of the United Nations to save succeeding generations from the scourge of war, to establish conditions under which justice and respect for obligations arising from treaties and other sources of international law can be maintained, to promote social progress and better standards of life in larger freedom, to practice tolerance and good neighborliness, and to employ international machinery for the promotion of the economic and social advancement of all peoples.

HUMAN RIGHTS AS RELEVANT UNIVERSAL STANDARD

And the VDPA seeks to reaffirm human rights as universal and relevant standard. The Preamble states: "Emphasizing that the Universal Declaration of Human Rights, which constitutes a common standard of achievement for all peoples and all nations, is the source of inspiration and has been the basis for the United Nations in making advances in standard setting as contained in the existing international human rights instruments, in particular the International Covenant on Civil and Political Rights and the International Covenant on Economic, Social and Cultural Rights."

HUMAN RIGHTS AS INDIVISIBLE, INTERDEPENDENT AND INTERRELATED

The VDPA emphasizes that all human rights are of equal importance, seeking to end the qualitative division between civil and political rights and economic, social and cultural rights, which was pronounced during the Cold War era. Part I, para 5 states that "All human rights are universal, indivisible and interdependent and interrelated. The international community must treat human rights globally in a fair and equal manner, on the same footing, and with the same emphasis. While the significance of national and regional particularities and various historical, cultural and religious backgrounds must be borne in mind, it is the duty of States, regardless of their political, economic and cultural systems, to promote and protect all human rights and fundamental freedoms." This phrase is also cited by Declaration of Montreal as well as The Yogyakarta Principles and the Convention on the Rights of Persons with Disabilities. To this end, Part II, para 75 also encourages the Commission on Human Rights, in accordance with the Committee on Economic, Social and Cultural Rights, to continue the examination of Optional Protocol to the International Covenant on Economic, Social and Cultural Rights on equal basis of the Optional Protocols to the International Covenant on Civil and Political Rights.

DEMOCRACY, DEVELOPMENT AND HUMAN RIGHTS AGAINST TERRORISM

The VDPA also draws a direct connection between respect for human rights, democracy and international development, stating in Part I, para 8 that "8. Democracy, development and respect for human rights and fundamental freedoms are interdependent and mutually reinforcing. Democracy is based on the freely expressed will of the people to determine their own political, economic, social and cultural systems and their full participation in all aspects of their lives. In the context of the above, the promotion and protection of human rights and fundamental freedoms at the national and international levels should be universal and conducted without conditions attached. The international community should support the strengthening and promoting of democracy, development and respect for human rights and fundamental freedoms in the entire world." And in Part I, para 17 that "The act, methods and practices of terrorism in all its form" as well as the drug trafficking "are activities aimed at the destruction of human rights, fundamental freedom and democracy." and that "the international community should take necessary steps to enhance cooperation to prevent and combat terrorism."

POVERTY AND SOCIAL EXCLUSION

The VDPA makes a direct link between poverty and the realisation of human rights. Part I, para 14 states: "The existence of widespread extreme poverty inhibits the full and effective enjoyment of human rights; its immediate alleviation and eventual elimination must remain a high priority for the international community." The VDPA stops short of declaring poverty a human rights violation in itself, but states in Part I, para 25 that: "25. The World Conference on Human Rights affirms that extreme poverty and social exclusion constitute a violation of human dignity and that urgent steps are necessary to achieve better knowledge of extreme poverty and its causes, including those related to the problem of development, in order to promote the human rights of the poorest, and to put an end to extreme poverty and social exclusion and to promote the enjoyment of the fruits of social progress. It is essential for States to foster participation by the poorest people in the decision making process by the community in which they live, the promotion of human rights and efforts to combat extreme poverty."

THE RIGHT TO DEVELOPMENT

The VDPA reaffirms the right to development, which is regarded as controversial by some human rights scholars and UN member states. Part I, para 9 reaffirms that least developed countries committed to the process of democratization and economic reforms, many of which are in Africa, should be supported by the international community in order to succeed in their transition to democracy and economic development. And Part I, para 10 states: "The World Conference on Human Rights reaffirms the right to development, as established in the Declaration on the Right to Development, as a universal and inalienable right and an integral part of fundamental human rights. As stated in the Declaration on the Right to Development, the human person is the central subject of development.

While development facilitates the enjoyment of all human rights, the lack of development may not be invoked to justify the abridgement of internationally recognized human rights. States should cooperate with each other in ensuring development and eliminating obstacles to development. The international community should promote an effective international cooperation for the realization of the right to development and the elimination of obstacles to development. Lasting progress towards the implementation of the right to development requires effective development policies at the national level, as well as equitable economic relations and a favourable economic environment at the international level."

Part I, para 11 goes on to state: "The right to development should be fulfilled so as to meet equitably the developmental and environmental needs of present and future generations. The World Conference on Human Rights recognizes that illicit dumping of toxic and dangerous substances and waste potentially constitutes a serious threat to the human rights to life and health of everyone. Consequently, the World Conference on Human Rights calls on all States to adopt and vigorously implement existing conventions relating to the dumping of toxic and dangerous products and waste and to cooperate in the prevention of illicit dumping. Everyone has the right to enjoy the benefits of scientific progress and its applications. The World Conference on Human Rights notes that certain advances, notably in the biomedical and life sciences as well as in information technology, may have potentially adverse consequences for the integrity, dignity and human rights of the individual, and calls for international cooperation to ensure that human rights and dignity are fully respected in this area of universal concern."

RIGHT TO SEEK ASYLUM AND HUMANITARIAN AID

In Part I, para 23, the VDPA reaffirms that everyone, without distinction of any kind, is entitled to the right to seek and enjoy in other countries asylum from persecution, as well as the right to return to one's own country. In this respect it stresses the importance of the Universal Declaration of Human Rights, the 1951 Convention relating to the Status of Refugees, its 1967 Protocol and regional instruments. It expresses its appreciation to States that continue to admit and host large numbers of refugees in their territories, and to the Office of the United Nations High Commissioner for Refugees for its dedication to its task. It also expresses its appreciation to the United Nations Relief and Works Agency for Palestine Refugees in the Near East. And VDPA recognises that, in view of the complexities of the global refugee crisis and in accordance with the Charter of the United Nations, relevant international instruments and international solidarity and in the spirit of burden-sharing, a comprehensive approach by the international community is needed in coordination and cooperation with the countries concerned and relevant organisations, bearing in mind the mandate of the United Nations High Commissioner for Refugees.

This should include the development of strategies to address the root causes and effects of movements of refugees and other displaced persons, the strengthening of emergency preparedness and response mechanisms, the provision of effective protection and assistance, bearing in mind the special needs of women and children, as well as the achievement of durable solutions, primarily through the preferred solution of dignified and safe voluntary repatriations, including solutions such as those adopted by the international refugee conferences. And underlines the responsibilities of States, particularly as they relate to the countries of origin. And regarding disasters, that in accordance with the Charter of the United Nations and the principles of humanitarian law, VDPA emphasizes the importance of and the need for humanitarian aid to victims of all natural disaster and man-made disaster.

AGAINST RACISM, XENOPHOBIA AND INTOLERANCE

In Part II, para 20, the VDPA urges all governments to take immediate measure and to develop strong policies to prevent and combat all forms and manifestations of racism, xenophobia or related intolerance, where necessary by enactment of appropriate legislation, including penal measure. and also appeals to all States parties to the International Convention on the Elimination of All Forms of Racial Discrimination to consider making the declaration under article 14 of the Convention.

PERSONS BELONGING TO MINORITY GROUPS

In Part II, para 25, the VDPA calls on the Commission on Human Rights to examine ways and means to promote and protect effectively the rights of persons belonging to minorities as set out in the Declaration on the Rights of Persons belonging to National or Ethnic, Religious and Linguistic Minorities. In this context, VDPA calls upon the Centre for Human Rights to provide, at the request of Governments concerned and as part of its programme of advisory services and technical assistance, qualified expertise on minority issues and human rights, as well as on the prevention and resolution of disputes, to assist in existing or potential situations involving minorities. And at para 26, VDPA urges States and the international community to promote and protect the rights of persons belonging to national or ethnic, religious and linguistic minorities in accordance with the Declaration on the Rights of Persons belonging to National or Ethnic, Religious and Linguistic Minorities. And further at para 95, VDPA underlines the importance of preserving and strengthening the system of special procedures, rapporteurs, representatives, experts and working groups of the Commission on Human Rights and the Sub-Commission on the Prevention of Discrimination and Protection of Minorities, in order to enable them to carry out their mandates in all countries throughout the world, providing them with the necessary human and financial resources. The procedures and mechanisms should be enabled to harmonize and rationalize their work through periodic meeting. All States are asked to cooperate fully with these procedures and mechanisms.

INDIGENOUS PEOPLE

In Part II, para 29, the VDPA recommends that the Commission on Human Rights consider the renewal and updating of the mandate of the Working Group on Indigenous Populations upon complement of the drafting of the Declaration on the Rights of Indigenous Peoples. And further at para 32, recommend that the General Assembly proclaim an international decade of the World's indigenous people, to begin from January 1994, including action oriented programmes, to be decided upon in partnership with indigenous people. An appropriate voluntary trust fund should be set up for this purpose. In the framework of such a decade, the establishment of a permanent forum for indigenous peoples in the United Nations system should be considered.

RIGHTS OF MIGRANT WORKERS

In Part II, para 34, the VDPA invites States to consider the possibility of signing and ratifying on the earliest possible time, the United Nations Convention on the Protection of the Rights of All Migrant Workers and Members of Their Families.

WOMEN'S RIGHTS AND DOMESTIC VIOLENCE

The VDPA draws attention to the importance of women's rights and the rights of the "girl-child", Part I, para 18 stating: "The human rights of women and of the girl-child are an inalienable, integral and indivisible part of universal human rights. The full and equal participation of women in political, civil, economic, social and cultural life, at the national, regional and international levels, and the eradication of all forms of discrimination on grounds of sex are priority objectives of the international community."

The VDPA also explicitly recognising gender-based violence, sexual harassment and exploitation, with Part I, para 18 going on to state: "Gender-based violence and all forms of sexual harassment and exploitation, including those resulting from cultural prejudice and international trafficking, are incompatible with the dignity and worth of the human person, and must be eliminated. This can be achieved by legal measures and through national action and international cooperation in such fields as economic and social development, education, safe maternity and health care, and social support."

The VDPA concludes by proclaiming women's rights and gender-based exploitation as legitimate issues for the international community. Part I, para 19 concluding that: "The human rights of women should form an integral part of the United Nations human rights activities, including the promotion of all human rights instruments relating to women. The World Conference on Human Rights urges Governments, institutions, intergovernmental and non-governmental organizations to intensify their efforts for the protection and promotion of human rights of women and the girl-child."

The VDPA, at Part II, para 38, also calls upon the General Assembly to adopt the draft Declaration on the Elimination of Violence Against Women and urges States to combat violence against women in accordance with its provisions. And that "violations of the human rights of women in situations of armed conflict are violations of the fundamental principles of international human rights and humanitarian law. All violations of this kind, including in particular murder, systematic rape, sexual slavery, and forced pregnancy, require a particular effective response."

THE RIGHTS OF THE CHILD

In Part II, para 45, the VDPA reiterates the principle of "First Call for Children" and, in this respect, underlines the importance of major national and international efforts, especially those of the United Nations Children's Fund, for promoting respect for the rights of the child to survival, protection, development and participation. At para 46, VDPA affirms that measures should be taken to achieve universal ratification of the Convention on the Rights of the Child by 1995 and the universal signing of the "World Declaration on the Survival, Protection and Development of Children and Plan of Action" adopted by the World Summit for Children. And at para 47, VDPA urges all nations to undertake measures to the maximum extent of their available resources, with the support of international cooperation, to achieve the goals in the World Summit Plan of Action. And calls on States to integrate the Convention on the Rights of the Child into their national action plans.

By means of those national action plans and through international efforts, particular priority should be places on reducing infant mortality and maternal mortality rates, reducing malnutrition and illiteracy rates and providing access to safe drinking water and to basic education. Whenever so called for, national plans of action should be devised to combat devastating emergencies resulting from natural disasters and armed conflicts and the equally grave problem of children in extreme poverty. And at para 48, VDPA urges all States, to address the acute program of children under difficult circumstance. Exploitation and abuse of children should be actively combated, including by addressing their root causes.

Effective measure are required against female infanticide, harmful child labour, sale of children and organ, child prostitution, child pornography, as well as other forms of sexual abuse. And para 50, the VDPA strongly supports the proposal that the Secretary General initiate a study into means of improving the protection of children in armed conflicts. And that humanitarian norms should be implemented and measures taken in order to protect and facilitate assistance to children in war zone. Measure should include protection for children against indiscriminate use of all weapon of war, especially, anti-personnel mines. The need for aftercare and rehabilitation of children traumatized by war must be addressed urgently.

FREEDOM FROM TORTURE

In Part II, para 54, the VDAP welcomes the ratification by many Member States of the United Nations Convention Against Torture and at para 61, also reaffirm that effort to eradicate torture should, first and foremost, be concentrated on prevention and, therefore, calls for early adoption of an Optional Protocol to the Convention against Torture, which is intended to establish a preventive system of regular visits to places of detention.

ENFORCED DISAPPEARANCES

In Part II, para 62, the VDAP welcoming the adoption by the General Assembly of the Declaration on the Protection of All Persons from Enforced Disappearance, calls upon all States to take effective legislative, administrative, judicial on other measure to prevent, terminate and punish acts of enforced disappearance. This is the origin of the International Convention for the Protection of All Persons from Enforced Disappearance.

THE RIGHTS OF THE DISABLED PERSON

In Part II, para 63, the VDAP reaffirms that all human rights and fundamental freedoms are universal and thus unreservedly include persons with disabilities. Every person is born equal and has the same rights to life and welfare, education and work, living independently and active participation in all aspects of society. Any direct discrimination or other negative discriminatory treatment of a disabled person is therefore a violation of his or her rights. And at para 64, the VDAP affirms that the place of disabled person is everywhere. Persons with disabilities should be guaranteed equal opportunity through the elimination of all socially determined barriers, be they physical, financial, social or psychological, which exclude or restrict full participation in society.

HUMAN RIGHTS, THE RESPONSIBILITY OF THE STATE

Part I, para 1 of the VDPA starts with "The World Conference on Human Rights reaffirms the solemn commitment of all States to fulfill their obligations to promote universal respect for, and observance and protection of, all human rights and fundamental freedoms for all in accordance with the Charter of the United Nations, other instruments relating to human rights, and international law. The universal nature of these rights and freedoms is beyond question." The VDPA acknowledges that international cooperation to realise human rights is vital, Part I, para 1 going on to state: "In this framework, enhancement of international cooperation in the field of human rights is essential for the full achievement of the purposes of the United Nations." However, the VDPA firmly places the ultimate responsibility for realizing human rights with the State, or the respective governments, Part I, para 1 concluding that: "Human rights and fundamental freedoms are the birthright of all human beings; their protection and promotion is the first responsibility of Governments."

Recognising the rising importance of NGOs, the VDPA states in Part I, para 13: "There is a need for States and international organizations, in cooperation with non-governmental organizations, to create favourable conditions at the national, regional and international levels to ensure the full and effective enjoyment of human rights. States should eliminate all violations of human rights and their causes, as well as obstacles to the enjoyment of these rights." And on ratification of international treaties on human rights, the VDPA states in Part I, para 26 that it "welcomes te progress made in the codification of human rights instruments, which is a dynamic and evolving process, and urges the universal ratification of human rights treaties.

All States are encouraged to accede to these international instruments; all States are encouraged to avoid, as far as possible, the resort to reservations." And on remedy and redress of human rights violation, VDPA states in Part I, para 27 that "Evry States should provide an efective framework of remedies and redress human rights grievances or violations. The administration of justice, including law enforcement and prosecutorial agencies and, especially, an independent judiciary and legal profession in full conformity with applicable standards contained in international human rights instruments, are essential to the full and non-discriminatory realization of human rights and indispensable to the processes of democracy and sustainable development".

HUMAN RIGHTS EDUCATION

In Part II, para 78, the VDPA considers human rights education, training and public information essential for the promotion and achievement of stable and harmonious relations among communities and for fostering mutual understanding, tolerance and peace. And at para 79 that States should strive to eradicate illiteracy and should direct education towards the full development of the human personality and to the strengthening of respect for human rights and fundamental freedoms. The VDPA calls on all States and institutions to include international human rights law, international humanitarian law, democracy and rule of law as subjects in the curricula of all learning institutions in formal and non-formal settings. And, at para 80 that human rights education should include peace, democracy, development ans social justice, as set forth in international and regional human rights instruments, in order to achieve common understanding ans awareness with a view to strengthening universal commitment to human rights.

And further at para 81, the VDPA states that taking into account the World Plan of Action on Education for Human Rights and Democracy, adopted in March 1993 by the International Congress on Education for Human Rights and Democracy of the United Nations Educational, Scientific and Cultural Organization, and other human rights instruments, the VDPA recommends that States develop specific programmes and strategies for ensuring the widest human rights education and the dissemination of public information, taking particular account of the human rights needs of women.

IMPLEMENTATION AND MONITORING METHODS

In Part II, para 83, the VDPA urges Governments to incorporate standard as contained in international human rights instruments in domestic legislation and to strengthen national structures, institutions and organs of society which play a role in protecting and safeguarding human rights. And para 84 recommends the strengthening of United Nations activities and programmes to meet requests for assistance by States which want to establish or strengthen their own national human rights institutions for promotion and protection of human rights.

And Part II, para 92, the VDPA recommends that the Commission on Human Rights examine the possibility for better implementation of existing human rights instruments at the international and regional levels and encourages the International Law Commission to continue its work on an

International Criminal Court. And para 93 appeals to states which have not yet done so that accede to the Geneva Conventions of 12 August 1949 and the Protocols thereto, and to take all appropriate national measures, including legislative ones, for their full implementation. And para 96 recommends that the United Nations assume a more active role in the promotion and protection of human rights in ensuring full respect for international humanitarian law in all situations of armed conflict, in accordance with the purposes and principles of Charter of the United Nations. And para 97, the VDPA, recognizing the important role of human rights components in specific arrangements concerning some Peacekeeping Operations by United Nations, recommends that the Secretary-General take into account the reporting, experience and capabilities of the Centre for Human Rights and human rights mechanisms, in conformity with the Charter of the United Nations.

FOLLOWUP

United Nations High Commissioner for Human Rights

The VDPA considered the adaptation and strengthening of the United Nations machinery for human rights, including the question of the establishment of a United Nations High Commissioner for Human Rights. Part II, para 17 states that "The World Conference on Human Rights recognizes the necessity for a continuing adaptation of the United Nations human rights machinery to the current and future needs in the promotion and protection of human rights, as reflected in the present Declaration... In particular, the United Nations human rights organs should improve their coordination, efficiency and effectiveness."

Following this the VDPA states, Part II, para 18, that "The World Conference on Human Rights recommends to the General Assembly that when examining the report of the Conference at its forty-eighth session, it begin, as a matter of priority, consideration of the question of the establishment of a High Commissioner for Human Rights for the promotion and protection of all human rights." The United Nations General Assembly subsequently created the post of United Nations High Commissioner for Human Rights on 20 December 1993 (resolution 48/141).

Country Action Plans

The World Conference on Human Rights recommended that each State consider the desirability of drawing up a national action plan identifying steps whereby that State would improve the promotion and protection of human rights. VDPA, Part II, paragraph 71. To such ends, the Office of the High Commissioner on Human Rights has included field offices and technical expertise to its mission. Further, the United Nations Development Programme has identified promotion of national institutions as one of its primary concerns.

United Nations Human Rights Council

The United Nations Human Rights Council holds regular debates (under its agenda item 8) on follow-up to the VDPA. While the scope of issues that can be addressed under this heading was initially disputed, recent sessions of the Human Rights Council have shown increasing debate on systematic follow-up to the VDPA, with States and non-governmental organizations raising a broad range of issues, reflecting the universal scope of the VDPA. This included themes like gender equality, sexual orientation and gender identity and institutional issues such as the independence of the Office of the UN High Commissioner for Human Rights (OHCHR). In September 2012, the Human Rights Council decided to hold a panel debate, in March 2013, to commemorate the 20th anniversary of the VDPA.

DECLARATION OF HUMAN DUTIES AND RESPONSIBILITIES

The Declaration of Human Duties and Responsibilities (or DHDR) was written for reinforcing the implementation of human rights under the auspices of the UNESCO and the interest of the UN High Commissioner of Human Rights and was proclaimed in 1998 "to commemorate the 50th anniversary of the Universal Declaration of Human Rights"(UDHR) in the city of Valencia. Therefore it is also known as the Valencia Declaration.

Considering that the major challenge for this new century is the effective and efficient realisation of human rights for all people, and that at the same time is needed that all members of the human family strive for its fulfilment, the DHDR formulates related duties and responsibilities for our current interdependence. Its preamble states categorically: The effective enjoyment and implementation of human rights and fundamental freedoms is inextricably linked to the assumption of the duties and responsibilities implicit in those rights.....

After fifty years of the adoption of the UDHR and following human rights instruments, the point of departure of the DHDR Preamble is the shared concern regarding the lack of political will for enforcing globally human rights. Moreover, the DHDR takes into account the new challenges of the global scenario for translating semantically rights into duties and responsibilities. "Recognising the changes that new technologies, scientific development and the process of Mondialisation have brought about, and aware of the need to address their impact upon and potential consequences for human rights and fundamental freedoms", states in its Preamble.

Its 12 Chapters and 41 articles can be compared with the human rights such as formulated in the UDHR and recent initiatives that reflect a similar preoccupation for the formulation of duties and responsibilities, such as the United Nations Millennium Declaration, the Statute of Rome, the Global Compact, The Earth Charter, the Kyoto Protocol, and UNESCO declarations and conventions.

HISTORY

The drafting of the declaration has been the result of the committed and disinterested work of a group of experts integrated by Nobel laureates - Joseph Rotblat, Wole Soyinka and Darío Fo-, scientists, artists and philosophers representing all the regions of the world –among them, Federico Mayor Zaragoza, Richard Falk, Ruud Lubbers, Lord Frank Judd, Sergei Kapitsa, Jakob von Uexküll, Fernando Savater-, and the judicious chairmanship of Richard Goldstone from South Africa and among its members. This process was inspired by the need –in words of Justice Goldstone- of the transition from a "formal equality" to a "substantial equality, with a shared concern of the situation of millions of ignored and marginalised people in our globalised world: "the recognition of human rights is insufficient, … if such so rights are to be realized it is necessary that they are enforceable... There must be a duty on all relevant authorities and individuals to enforce those rights." With a convergent perspective, Norberto Bobbio has entirely supported the initiative and the text of the DHDR, in particular taking into account the main concern for humanity of reinforcing the international systems. In that context he has established an interesting comparison between the transition from "moral rights" to "legal rights" and the need to transform "moral duties" into "legal duties".

This Declaration proposes comprehensively the implicit system of duties and responsibilities contained in our human rights systems, in particular that enshrined in the Universal Declaration of Human Rights (UDHR) and in subsequent international human rights instruments and establishes consequently their bearers.

THE DHDR CHAPTER I: THE GENERAL PROVISIONS

In the DHDR Article 1 "duty" and "responsibility" are defined for the purpose of the declaration: "duty" means an ethical or moral obligation; and "responsibility", an obligation that is legally binding under existing international law. The DHDR explains in details the complexity of the exercise of responsibilities. The bearers are the members of the global community that have collective, as well as individual duties and responsibilities, to promote universal observance of human rights and fundamental freedoms. "Global community" means both States and non-States actors: international, regional and sub-regional intergovernmental organisations, non-governmental organisations, public and private sector (trans)national corporations, other entities of civil society, peoples, communities and individuals taken as a collective.

The DHDR reflects the gamma of both states and non-states actors that have to be mutual supportive bearers of duties and responsibilities. On the contrary, the UN Millennium Declaration (MD), recent international document of the governments, is focused primarily on the States responsibilities that is shared and collective: "We/heads of State and Government/ recognize that, in addition to our separate responsibilities to our individual societies, we have a collective responsibility to uphold the principles of human dignity, equality and equity at the global level. As leaders we have a duty therefore to all the world's people..."

The DHDR Article 2 is dedicated to postulate exhaustively the bearers of duties and responsibilities: "Members of the global community have collective, as well as individual duties and responsibilities, to promote universal respect for and observance of human rights and fundamental freedoms...." This declaration considers the existence of collective responsibilities inside the limits traced by the universally recognized rights, with the implicit consequences of accountability that would be fairly distributed. The DHDR addresses simultaneously the responsibilities of individuals and groups. It states: "As the holders of human rights and fundamental freedoms, all individuals, peoples and communities in the exercise of their rights and freedoms, have the duty and responsibility to respect those of others, and a duty to strive for the promotion and observance thereof". This statement continues appropriately the way initiated by the UDHR in Article 29 and reiterates the interaction of duties, responsibilities and rights of the International Covenants on Human Rights of 1966.

DHDR CHAPTER 2: THE RIGHT TO LIFE AND HUMAN SECURITY

Most of the titles of the DHDR chapters enunciate a right or fundamental freedom that will be the thematic focus of the related duties and responsibilities. Chapter 2 begins the list of duties and responsibilities with the right to life and human security, rights to be secure for the present and also future generations in the awareness that for the first time in human history the humankind survival is in peril due to human action. Following the UDHR Article 3 "Everyone has the right to life, liberty and security of person"; this chapter draws our attention to the intergenerational responsibility.

The DHDR Article 3 is dedicated to the duty and responsibility to protect the life of every member of the human family and ensure the survival of both present and future generations. That means "to take reasonable steps to help others whose lives are threatened, or who are in extreme distress or need". A key element of the formulation of the DHDR has been the present duty and responsibility for the potential consequences of our actions for the future generations. "The rights of these future generations are the duties of present generations" summarises correctly Federico Mayor, the then Director General UNESCO. Therefore, the right to peace and the right to live in a balanced ecological environment have to be recognized and guaranteed. In a broader sense, the Earth Charter, a declaration of principles for a sustainable world, emphasises the urgency of sharing responsibility for caring for the community of life, including the well-being of human family.

The DHDR Article 4 enunciates the duty and responsibility to promote collective security and a culture of peace of all members of the global community. War and conflict prevention, fostering international peace, global security and cooperation are needed for this purpose. The responsibility of States, according to UN Chapter 7, is underlined and also their duty strengthening mediation, conflict prevention and post-conflict peace-building mechanisms and peace-keeping capacities.

The DHDR Article 5 is dedicated to the duty and responsibility to promote rapid and effective disarmament in the interests of peace. Primarily the States are in charge of reducing military expenditure in favour of human development, and together with no-States actors to carry our nuclear disarmament, to cease any production or use of all chemical and biological weapons, and use of landmines.

The Duty to intervene to prevent gross human rights violations is stated in the DHDR Article 6 that means the commission of genocide, crimes against humanity, war crimes and other gross or systematic human rights abuses in all circumstances. States are mainly in charge of preventing and also punishing such violations, and there is also a collective duty of the States to intervene in the case where individual State fails to prevent such abuses. UN Chapter 7 remains general framework for this responsibility. For defining gross human rights violations and the need of prevention and punishment this chapter has been inspired by the Rome Statute that was adopted some months before this Declaration was finalised.

The DHDR Article 7 enunciates the duty and responsibility unconditionally and in all circumstances to respect international humanitarian law during times of armed conflict. This law, commonly infringed, means for the government forces and insurgents, military or paramilitary forces the obligation to refrain from committing acts of genocide; crimes against humanity, and war crimes, as mass killing, torture or rape.

The focus of DHDR Article 8 is the duty and responsibility of humanitarian assistance and intervention to those in need. In a globalised world with millions of displaced people, it is claimed for the adequate provision of food, shelter, health care and other essential requirements for survival to ensure the right to life for everyone on the world.

The DHDR Article 9 finishes this chapter with the duty and responsibility to protect and promote a safe, stable and healthy environment, promoting respect, protection and preservation of the uniqueness and diversity of all forms of life. An adequate use of resources avoiding excessive exploitation and consumption, and a collaborative scientific research and exchange of information are required. This article promotes similarly to the Kyoto Protocol, an international and legally binding agreement to reduce greenhouse gases emissions world wide, an urgent change of attitude towards the environment. This duty for the present and future generations has already been confirmed by a broad scientific consensus on the existence of climate change and the human responsibility.

DHDR CHAPTER 3: HUMAN SECURITY AND AN EQUITABLE INTERNATIONAL ORDER

The DHDR Article 10 emphasises the duty and responsibility to promote an equitable international order for the universal enjoyment of sustainable human, economic, social, cultural, political, scientific and technological development and equitably participation in the decision-making processes for an interdependent and technologically well equipped world, providing an extensive vision of the general formulation of the UDHR Article 28: "Everyone is entitled to a social and international order in which the rights and freedoms set forth in this Declaration can be fully realized". The DHDR statements are categorical: "Economic policies and development should not be pursued at the expense of human rights or social development" (6), "Economic and social development shall not be pursued at the expense of the environment and natural resources" (7), and "As sovereign and equal members of the international community, all States have the right to participate fully, equitably and effectively in international and global institutions and decision-making processes...(8)" Coincidently to the DHDR proposals the "millennium development goals" of the MD set an influential agenda for a global partnership to fight poverty, establishing shared goals for a better world by 2015. Their fulfilment is measurable indicated by a progress at quantitative level.

Following the previous article, the DHDR Article 11 enunciates the duty to alleviate usurious debt that would endanger human lives and impede economic and social development.

This Chapter continues with the DHDR Article 12 dedicated to the duty and responsibility to promote safe, responsible and equitable scientific and technological development for the benefit of all humankind. The UNESCO spirit of encouraging universally intellectual and moral solidarity is emphasised, in particular taking into account the condition of the lesser scientifically advanced States. In particular this article has received a good reception by several scientists and related people. Neutrality of science appears today as an illusion, in particular considering formerly scientific advances such as in genetics or cybernetics. This DHDR approach reinforces fully the importance of the recent UNESCO ethical documents for biosciences, and also other efforts for codifying ethical principles for the use of science.

The DHDR Article 13 enunciates duties and responsibilities of public and private sector corporations, indicating as common criteria the respect for sovereignty of host countries and simultaneously fully respect and promotion of universal human rights and international labour standards. For having an ethical code of the corporations and for promoting a more sustainable and inclusive global economy, the then UN General Secretary, Kofi Annan, has proposed the Global Compact, an international initiative bringing companies together with UN agencies, labour and civil society to support universal environmental and social principles, that was finally launched in 2000.

The DHDR Article 14 enunciates the duty and responsibility to prevent and punish international and organised crime as a shared task of the members of the global community. This article also has the innovative approach of global cooperation of the Statute of Rome, for combating of international crimes, transnational crimes and organised crime and assisting international criminal tribunals.

The focus of the DHDR Article 15 is the duty and responsibility to eradicate corruption and build an ethical society in both the public and private sectors, implementing codes of conduct and training programmes, and promoting accountability, transparency public awareness of the harm caused by corruption. This emphasis in code of ethics was also encouraged by the Global Compact, in particular for the private sector.

DHDR CHAPTER 4: MEANINGFUL PARTICIPATION IN PUBLIC AFFAIRS

The DHDR Article 16 expresses the duty and responsibility to ensure meaningful participation in public affairs, for ensuring that the authority of government is based upon the will of the people and the rule of law. This promoted participation reiterates the universal right to take part in the government of his country, directly or through freely chosen representatives of the UDHR Article 21 at different levels, in local, national and global governance.

DHDR CHAPTER 5: FREEDOM OF OPINION, EXPRESSION, ASSEMBLY, ASSOCIATION AND RELIGION

Following the content of the UDHR Article 19 on the right to freedom of opinion and expression, the DHDR Article 17 reformulates the duty and responsibility to respect and ensure freedom of opinion, expression, and the media, providing concrete measures for the world today, affirming the pursuit of truth as unhindered, and condemning any degrading treatment of individuals and the presentation of violence as entertainment. And Article 17 also insists that "the media and journalists have a duty to report honestly and accurately to avoid incitement of racial, ethnic or religious violence or hatred.

The DHDR Article 18 establishes duties and responsibilities concerning information and communications technologies with the aim of ensuring universal access to basic communication and information infrastructure and services. Similarly, UNESCO has already made a recommendation on information promoting universal access to cyberspace.

Complementing the UDHR Article 20 on the right to freedom of peaceful assembly and association the DHDR Article 19 enunciates the duty and responsibility to take all necessary steps to ensure the substantive realisation of the rights to free assembly and freedom of association.

Finally, the DHDR Article 20, following the UDHR Article 18 on the right to freedom of thought, conscience and religion, formulates the related duty and responsibility to respect and ensure freedom of religion, belief and conscience, and of having or not having a religion or belief.

DHDR CHAPTER 6: THE RIGHT TO PERSONAL AND PHYSICAL INTEGRITY

The DHDR Article 21 focused on formulating the duty and responsibility to respect and ensure the physical, psychological and personal integrity of all members of the human family in all circumstances, including in situations of armed conflict, reformulate the UDHR articles 10-12 dedicated to the rights to personal integrity and respect for privacy.

The DHDR Article 22 enunciates the duty and responsibility to take all necessary measures to respect and ensure the right to personal liberty and physical security, in first place by the States, preventing arbitrary arrest and detention and ensuring that all arrests and detentions are carried out in accordance with universally recognised standards of fairness and due process.

The DHDR Article 23 emphasises today the duty and responsibility to prohibit and prevent slavery and institutions and practices similar to slavery and slave-like practices including child prostitution, child exploitation, enforced prostitution, debt bondage, serfdom, and other forms of enforced labour inconsistent with international law, punishing such practices; instituting effective controls to prevent the illegal trafficking of persons; creating greater public awareness through education of the human rights abuses associated with such practices. The UDHR Article 4 states that "no one shall be held in slavery or servitude; slavery and the slave trade shall be prohibited in all their forms". Today slavery is still not eradicated from the world, although universally condemned.

The DHDR Article 24 enunciates the duty and responsibility to condemn torture and to take all necessary measures to prevent torture, cruel, inhuman and degrading treatment or punishment, declaring criminal and punishing all acts of torture, cruel and inhuman and degrading treatment or punishment, enforcing strict controls over places and conditions of custody of persons deprived of their liberty. This enunciation specifies the duty for achieving the content of UDHR Article 5: "No one shall be subjected to torture or to cruel, inhuman or degrading treatment or punishment".

DHDR Article 25: The duty and responsibility to condemn and to prevent and eradicate enforced disappearances declaring criminal and punishing all acts of forced disappearances, ensuring that persons deprived of their liberty are only held in officially recognised places of detention, and that they have adequate access to judicial officers, legal representation, medical personnel and family members during the course of their detention.

DHDR CHAPTER 7: EQUALITY

After trying to meet the major global challenges of our interdependent world, that are affecting today humankind as a whole. The DHDR Chapter 7 rethinks the principle of equality, such as states in the first UDHR articles. With a similar approach the UNESCO has already approved two meaningful documents promoting cultural diversity, the UNESCO Universal Declaration on Cultural Diversity (2001) and the Convention on the Protection and Promotion of the Diversity of Cultural Expressions (2005). The DHDR Article 26 enunciates in general the duty to respect, ensure and promote the right to equal treatment and to eradicate discrimination in all its forms.

The DHDR Article 27 states the duty and responsibility for the States, in primary place, to respect and ensure the substantive equality of every member of human family, not only ensuring equality before the law, but also taking positive action to prevent direct or indirect discrimination.

In the DHDR Article 28 is enunciated the duty and responsibility to ensure substantive racial and religious equality, that means to ensure the effective enjoyment of all human rights and fundamental freedoms without discrimination on the basis of race, religion or ethnicity, and to condemn all forms of racial and religious discrimination and respect racial, ethnic and religious diversity; promoting equal opportunities for all.

The DHDR Article 29 formulates the duty and responsibility to ensure sex and gender equality and the recognition of women's rights as human rights. In particular the States have to ensure the effective enjoyment of all human rights and fundamental freedoms without discrimination on the basis of sex or gender, promoting the equality in the representation and participation of women in the public and political life, the eradication of cultural, religious and social practices which discriminate against women; the economic empowerment of women and the recognition of the full legal capacity of women. The DHDR Article 30 is dedicated to the duty and responsibility to ensure the substantive equality of persons with a disability, and to ensure the enjoyment and exercise of all human rights and fundamental freedoms without discrimination on the basis of disability. Some progress towards the accomplishment of this duty can be observed at international level. In March 2006, the UN Programme on Disability has been consolidated into the Secretariat for the Convention on the Rights of Persons with Disabilities.

DHDR CHAPTER 8: PROTECTION OF MINORITIES AND INDIGENOUS PEOPLES

Reinforcing the fulfilment of equality, the aim of the Chapter 8 is to emphasise the need for protection of minorities and indigenous peoples. Both the global community and the States are considered by this Declaration as the major responsible, collectively and individually for ensuring the rights of these vulnerable groups.

The DHDR Article 31 formulates the duty and responsibility to respect and protect the existence, identity and rights of national, ethnic, religious and linguistic minorities, having the States a primary duty and responsibility to take adequate measures. The above referred efforts of the UNESCO for protecting the value of cultural diversity and cultural expressions are a reflection of this obligation. The DHDR Article 32 enunciates the duty and responsibility to respect, protect and promote the rights of indigenous peoples, in particular their right to preserve, maintain and develop their identities and to protect their means of livelihood, in a general context of respect of universal human rights. Indigenous rights are diversely protected at national level, but it is much needed that the international community assumes collectively their responsibility. It is also expected that the proposed declaration on the rights of indigenous peoples will be again considered for approval in September 2007 by the UN General Assembly in order to protect these rights universally.

DHDR CHAPTER 9: RIGHTS OF THE CHILD AND THE ELDERLY

The chapter 9 deals also with the implementation of the principle of equality taking into account the primary responsibilities of the States for the children and elderly rights. The DHDR Article 33 emphasises the duty and responsibility to respect, protect and promote the rights of the child, following the content of the almost universally ratified UN Convention on the Right of the Child (1989) and aware, that although this excellent document is shared broadly by the international community, today million of children are still innocent victims of armed conflict, extreme poverty and hunger.

The DHDR Article 34 is dedicated to the formulation of the duty and responsibility to promote and enforce the rights and wellbeing of the elderly, trying to ensure the full and effective enjoyment by elderly people of all human rights and fundamental freedoms without discrimination on the basis of age, and to respect the well-being, dignity and physical and personal integrity of the elderly. Although major efforts are being made by the United Nations, such as the International Year of Older Persons (1999) and the formulation UN Principles addressing the independence, participation, care, self-fulfillment and dignity of older persons, and regional and national efforts, it does not exist by now a recognised framework for securing their rights. Therefore, the DHDR constitutes a very interesting contribution for enforcing the rights of the elderly.

DHDR CHAPTER 10: WORK, QUALITY OF LIFE AND STANDARD OF LIVING

The DHDR Chapter 10 complements the system of duties and

responsibilities related to the right to work, quality of life and standard of living. For doing that, the DHDR take into account at the same time, the responsibility of the States and the shared responsibility of the world community in the context of the global interdependence.

The DHDR Article 35 formulates the duty and responsibility to promote the right to justly remunerated work, following considerately the UDHR Article 23. Measures such adopting policies designed to promote productive work; ensuring employment security, in particular protection against arbitrary or unfair dismissal; and ensuring equality of opportunity and conditions of work, are proposed by the DHDR.

The DHDR Article 36 emphasises the postponed duty and responsibility to promote quality of life and an adequate standard of living for all. Although in the UDHR Article 22 it states the States obligation of fulfilling "the economic, social and cultural rights indispensable for his dignity and the free development of his personality", today our interdependent world is not free from hunger and there is not universal access to adequate food and clean water for everyone. The DHDR reiterates the shared responsibility for eradicating extreme poverty from the world, in particular if we consider the sufficiency of material resources for meeting this challenge. Similarly, but with a more pragmatic approach, the Millennium Development Goals (2000) establishes an intergovernmental agreement for realising globally human rights. These transitional goals indicate indubitably the correct course for implementing human rights in a continuous process with measurable criteria. However, it would be positive to promote a dialogue on the achievement and evolution of the achievement of those goals with the help of this systematised view on universal duties and responsibilities.

DHDR CHAPTER 11: EDUCATION, ARTS AND CULTURE

The DHDR Chapter 11 is dedicated to formulate duties and responsibilities on the promotion of education, arts and culture, major topics of the UNESCO, such as the programmes "education for all" and its various instruments for securing adequate conditions for education and artistic and cultural activities.

The DHDR Article 37 enunciates the duty and responsibility to promote and enforce the right to education, taking into account that illiteracy still affects millions of people in the developing countries and that is coincident with the already referred Millennium Development Goals.

The DHDR Article 38 emphasises the duty and responsibility to foster arts and culture by the States and the global community in general, similarly to the UNESCO statements.

– — ° ″ ′ ≈ ≠ ≤ ≥ ± − × ÷ ← → · § ==Declaration of Human Duties and Responsibilities Chapter 12: Right to a remedy== The DHDR finishes with the Chapter 12 dedicated to the right to a remedy where a human right or fundamental freedom is threatened or has been violated. The DHDR Article 39 enunciates the duty and responsibility, primarily of the States, to provide for and enforce effective national judicial, administrative, legislative and other remedies for these cases, in similarity with the UDHR Article 8.

This Chapter proposes, finally, in article 40 the duty to monitor and implement the Declaration of Human Duties and Responsibilities, by establishing tripartite councils composed of State, civil society and private sector representatives in cooperation with States, relevant civil society organisations, national, regional and international inter-governmental organisations.

The DHDR Article 41 with a non-derogation clause where it states: "Nothing in this Declaration shall be interpreted as impairing or restricting the rights contained in the Universal Declaration of Human Rights and other international and regional human rights instruments."

UNESCO UNIVERSAL DECLARATION ON CULTURAL DIVERSITY

The Universal Declaration on Cultural Diversity is a declaration adopted by the General Conference of the United Nations Educational, Scientific and Cultural Organization (UNESCO) at its thirty-first session on 2 November 2001 This Declaration is constituted by 12 Articles; Article 1 titled "Cultural diversity, the common heritage of humanity" states that "As a sorce of exchange, innovation and creativity, cultural diversity is as necessary for humankind as biodiversity is for the nature. In this sense, it is the common heritage of humanity and should be recognized and affiemed for the benefit of present and future generations." Article 6 affirms the freedom of expression, media pluralism and multilingualism. And Article 12 defines on the role of the UNESCO.

DECLARATION ON THE RIGHTS OF INDIGENOUS PEOPLES

The United Nations Declaration on the Rights of Indigenous Peoples was adopted by the United Nations General Assembly during its 61st session at UN Headquarters in New York City on 13 September 2007.

While as a General Assembly Declaration it is not a legally binding instrument under international law, according to a UN press release, it does "represent the dynamic development of international legal norms and it reflects the commitment of the UN's member states to move in certain directions"; the UN describes it as setting "an important standard for the treatment of indigenous peoples that will undoubtedly be a significant tool towards eliminating human rights violations against the planet's 370 million indigenous people and assisting them in combating discrimination and marginalisation." UNDRIP which codifies "Indigenous historical grievances, contemporary challenges and socio-economic, political and cultural aspirations" is a "culmination of generations-long efforts by Indigenous organizations to get international attention, to secure recognition for their aspirations, and to generate support for their political agendas. " Canada Research Chair and faculty member at theUniversity of Saskatchewan, Ken Coates, argues that UNDRIP resonates powerfully with Indigenous peoples, while national governments have not yet fully understood its impact.

PURPOSE

The Declaration sets out the individual and collective rights of indigenous peoples, as well as their rights to culture, identity, language, employment, health, education and other issues. It also "emphasizes the rights of indigenous peoples to maintain and strengthen their own institutions, cultures and traditions, and to pursue their development in keeping with their own needs and aspirations". It "prohibits discrimination against indigenous peoples", and it "promotes their full and effective participation in all matters that concern them and their right to remain distinct and to pursue their own visions of economic and social development". The goal of the Declaration is to encourage countries to work alongside indigenous peoples to solve global issues, like development, multicultural democracy and decentralization. According to Article 31, there is a major emphasis that the indigenous peoples will be able to protect their cultural heritage and other aspects of their culture and tradition, which is extremely important in preserving their heritage. The elaboration of this Declaration had already been recommended by the Vienna Declaration and Programme of Action

The Declaration is structured as a United Nations resolution, with 23 preambular clauses and 46 articles. Articles 1–40 concern particular individual and collective rights of indigenous peoples; many of them include state obligations to protect or fulfil those rights. Article 31 concerns the right to protect cultural heritage as well as manifestations of their cultures including human and genetic resources.CITEREFUN200811 Articles 41 and 42 concern the role of the United Nations. Articles 43–45 indicate that the rights in the declaration apply without distinction to indigenous men and women, and that the rights in the Declaration are "the minimum standards for the survival, dignity and well-being of the indigenous peoples of the world," and do not in any way limit greater rights. Article 46 discusses the Declaration's consistency with other internationally agreed goals, and the framework for interpreting the rights declared within it.

NEGOTIATION AND ADOPTION

The Declaration was over 25 years in the making. The idea originated in 1982 when the UN Economic and Social Council (ECOSOC) set up its Working Group on Indigenous Populations (WGIP), established as a result of a study by Special Rapporteur José Ricardo Martínez Cobo on the problem of discrimination faced by indigenous peoples. Tasked with developing human rights standards that would protect indigenous peoples, in 1985 the Working Group began working on drafting the Declaration on the Rights of Indigenous Peoples. The draft was finished in 1993 and was submitted to the Sub-Commission on the Prevention of Discrimination and Protection of Minorities, which gave its approval the following year. During this the International Labour Organisation adopted the Indigenous and Tribal Peoples Convention, 1989.

The Draft Declaration was then referred to the Commission on Human Rights, which established another Working Group to examine its terms. Over the following years this Working Group met on 11 occasions to examine and fine-tune the Draft Declaration and its provisions. Progress was slow because of certain states' concerns regarding some key provisions of the Declaration, such as indigenous peoples' right to self-determination and the control over natural resources existing on indigenous peoples' traditional lands. The final version of the Declaration was adopted on 29 June 2006 by the 47-member Human Rights Council (the successor body to the Commission on Human Rights), with 30 member states in favour, 2 against, 12 abstentions, and 3 absentees.

The Declaration (document A/61/L.67) was then referred to the General Assembly, which voted on the adoption of the proposal on 13 September 2007 during its 61st regular session. The vote was, *in favour* 144 countries: Afghanistan, Albania, Algeria, Andorra, Angola, Antigua and Barbuda, Argentina, Armenia, Austria, Bahamas, Bahrain, Barbados, Belarus, Belgium, Belize, Benin, Bolivia, Bosnia and Herzegovina, Botswana, Brazil, Brunei Darussalam, Bulgaria, Burkina Faso, Cambodia, Cameroon, Cape Verde, Central African Republic, Chile, China, Comoros, Congo, Costa Rica, Croatia, Cuba, Cyprus, Czech Republic, Democratic People's Republic of Korea, Democratic Republic of the Congo, Denmark, Djibouti, Dominica, Dominican Republic, Ecuador, Egypt, El Salvador, Estonia, Finland, France, Gabon, Germany, Ghana, Greece, Guatemala, Guinea, Guyana, Haiti, Honduras, Hungary, Iceland, India, Indonesia, Iran, Iraq, Ireland, Italy, Jamaica, Japan, Jordan, Kazakhstan, Kuwait, Lao People's Democratic Republic, Latvia, Lebanon, Lesotho, Liberia, Libya, Liechtenstein, Lithuania, Luxembourg, Madagascar, Malawi, Malaysia, Maldives, Mali, Malta, Mauritius, Mexico, Micronesia (Federated States of), Moldova, Monaco, Mongolia, Mozambique, Myanmar, Namibia, Nepal, Netherlands, Nicaragua, Niger, Norway, Oman, Pakistan, Panama, Paraguay, Peru, Philippines, Poland, Portugal, Qatar, Republic of Korea, Saint Lucia, Saint Vincent and the Grenadines, San Marino, Saudi Arabia, Senegal, Serbia, Sierra Leone, Singapore, Slovakia, Slovenia, South Africa, Spain, Sri Lanka, Sudan, Suriname, Swaziland, Sweden, Switzerland, Syria, Thailand, the Republic of Macedonia, Timor-Leste, Trinidad and Tobago, Tunisia, Turkey, United Arab Emirates, United

Kingdom, United Republic of Tanzania, Uruguay, Venezuela, Viet Nam, Yemen, Zambia, Zimbabwe.

- *Against*: Australia, Canada, New Zealand, United States. All four member states that voted against have their origins as colonies of the United Kingdom, and have large non-indigenous immigrant majorities and small remnant indigenous populations. Since then, all four countries have moved to endorse the declaration.
- *Abstaining*, 11 countries: Azerbaijan, Bangladesh, Bhutan, Burundi, Colombia, Georgia, Kenya, Nigeria, Russian Federation, Samoa and Ukraine. Colombia and Samoa have since endorsed the document.
- *Absent*: Chad, Côte d'Ivoire, Equatorial Guinea, Eritrea, Ethiopia, Fiji, Gambia, Grenada, Guinea-Bissau, Israel, Kiribati, Kyrgyzstan, Marshall Islands, Mauritania, Montenegro, Morocco, Nauru, Palau, Papua New Guinea, Romania, Rwanda, Saint Kitts and Nevis, São Tomé and Príncipe, Seychelles, Solomon Islands, Somalia, Tajikistan, Togo, Tonga, Turkmenistan, Tuvalu, Uganda, Uzbekistan, Vanuatu.

REACTION

Support

In contrast to the Declaration's initial rejection by Australia, Canada, New Zealand and the United States over legal concerns (all 4 countries later switched their positions to supporting the declaration), United Nations officials and other world leaders expressed pleasure at its adoption. Secretary-General Ban Ki-moon described it as a "historic moment when UN Member States and indigenous peoples have reconciled with their painful histories and are resolved to move forward together on the path of human rights, justice and development for all." Louise Arbour, a former justice of the Supreme Court of Canada then serving as the UN's High Commissioner for Human Rights, expressed satisfaction at the hard work and perseverance that had finally "borne fruit in the most comprehensive statement to date of indigenous peoples' rights." Similarly, news of the Declaration's adoption was greeted with jubilation in Africa and, present at the General Assembly session in New York, Bolivian foreign minister David Choquehuanca said that he hoped the member states that had voted against or abstained would reconsider their refusal to support a document he described as being as important as the Universal Declaration of Human Rights. Bolivia has become the first country to approve the U.N. declaration of indigenous rights. Evo Morales, President of Bolivia, stated, "We are the first country to turn this declaration into a law and that is important, brothers and sisters. We recognize and salute the work of our representatives. But if we were to remember the indigenous fight clearly, many of us who are sensitive would end up crying in remembering the discrimination, the scorn."

Stephen Corry, Director of the international indigenous rights organization Survival International, said, "The declaration has been debated for nearly a quarter century. Years which have seen many tribal peoples, such as the Akuntsu and Kanoê in Brazil, decimated and others, such as the Innu in Canada, brought to the edge. Governments that oppose it are shamefully fighting against the human rights of their most vulnerable peoples. Claims they make to support human rights in other areas will be seen as hypocritical."

Criticism

Prior to the adoption of the Declaration, and throughout the 62nd session of the General Assembly, a number of countries expressed concern about some key issues, such as self-determination, access to lands, territories and resources and the lack of a clear definition of the term *indigenous*. In addition to those intending to vote against the adoption of the declaration, a group of African countries represented by Namibia who proposed to defer action, to hold further consultations, and to conclude consideration of the declaration by September 2007. Ultimately, after agreeing on some adjustments to the Draft Declaration, a vast majority of states recognized that these issues could be addressed by each country at the national level.

The four states that voted against continued to express serious reservations about the final text of the Declaration as placed before the General Assembly. As mentioned above, all four opposing countries have since then changed their vote in favour of the Declaration.

Australia

Australia's government opposed the Declaration in the General Assembly vote of 2007, but has since endorsed the declaration. Australia's Mal Brough, Minister for Families, Community Services and Indigenous Affairs, referring to the provision regarding the upholding of indigenous peoples' customary legal systems, said that, "There should only be one law for all Australians and we should not enshrine in law practices that are not acceptable in the modern world."

Marise Payne, Liberal Party Senator for New South Wales, further elaborated on the Australian government's objections to the Declaration in a speech to the Senate as:

- Concerns about references to self-determination and their potential to be misconstrued.
- Ignorance of contemporary realities concerning land and resources. "They seem, to many readers, to require the recognition of Indigenous rights to lands which are now lawfully owned by other citizens, both Indigenous and non-Indigenous, and therefore to have some quite significant potential to impact on the rights of third parties."

- Concerns over the extension of Indigenous intellectual property rights under the declaration as unnecessary under current international and Australian law.
- The potential abuse of the right under the Declaration for indigenous peoples to unqualified consent on matters affecting them, "which implies to some readers that they may then be able to exercise a right of veto over all matters of state, which would include national laws and other administrative measures."
- The exclusivity of indigenous rights over intellectual, real and cultural property, that "does not acknowledge the rights of third parties – in particular, their rights to access Indigenous land and heritage and cultural objects where appropriate under national law." Furthermore, that the Declaration "fails to consider the different types of ownership and use that can be accorded to Indigenous people and the rights of third parties to property in that regard."
- Concerns that the Declaration places indigenous customary law in a superior position to national law, and that this may "permit the exercise of practices which would not be acceptable across the board", such as customary corporal and capital punishments.

In October 2007 former Australian Prime Minister John Howard pledged to hold a referendum on changing the constitution to recognise indigenous Australians if re-elected. He said that the distinctiveness of people's identity and their rights to preserve their heritage should be acknowledged. On 3 April 2009, the Rudd government formally endorsed the Declaration.

Canada

Anishinabek spiritual leader, Chief William Commanda (1908-3 August 2011) was honoured at the 21st annual week-long First Peoples Festival held in Montreal from 2–9 August 2011, celebrating Canada's 2010 adoption of the U. N. declaration. AFN Innu representative, Ghislain Picard's tribute praised Grandfather Commanda for his work that was "key not only in the adoption of the U.N. declaration, but in all the work leading up to it throughout the last 25 years."

The Canadian government said that while it supported the spirit of the declaration, it contained elements that were "fundamentally incompatible with Canada's constitutional framework", which includes both the Charter of Rights and Freedoms and Section 35, which enshrines aboriginal and treaty rights. In particular, the Canadian government had problems with Article 19 (which appears to require governments to secure the consent of indigenous peoples regarding matters of general public policy), and Articles 26 and 28 (which could allow for the re-opening or repudiation of historically settled land claims). Minister of Indian Affairs and Northern Development Chuck Strahl described the document as "unworkable in a Western democracy under a constitutional government." Strahl elaborated, saying "In Canada, you are balancing individual rights vs. collective rights, and (this) document... has none of that. By signing on, you default to this document by saying that the only rights in play here are the rights of the First Nations. And, of course, in Canada, that's inconsistent with our constitution." He gave an example: "In Canada... you negotiate on this... because (native rights) don't trump all other rights in the country. You need also to consider the people who have sometimes also lived on those lands for two or three hundred years, and have hunted and fished alongside the First Nations."

The Assembly of First Nations passed a resolution in December 2007 to invite Presidents Hugo Chávez and Evo Morales to Canada to put pressure on the government to sign the Declaration on the Rights of Indigenous Peoples, calling the two heads of state "visionary leaders" and demanding Canada resign its membership on the United Nations Human Rights Council.

On 3 March 2010, in the Speech From the Throne, the Governor General of Canada announced that the government was moving to endorse the declaration. "We are a country with an Aboriginal heritage. A growing number of states have given qualified recognition to the United Nations Declaration on the Rights of Indigenous Peoples. Our Government will take steps to endorse this aspirational document in a manner fully consistent with Canada's Constitution and laws." On 12 November 2010, Canada officially endorsed the declaration.

New Zealand

In 2007 New Zealand's Minister of Mâori Affairs Parekura Horomia described the Declaration as "toothless", and said, "There are four provisions we have problems with, which make the declaration fundamentally incompatible with New Zealand's constitutional and legal arrangements." Article 26 in particular, he said, "appears to require recognition of rights to lands now lawfully owned by other citizens, both indigenous and non-indigenous. This ignores contemporary reality and would be impossible to implement."

In response, Mâori Party leader Pita Sharples said it was "shameful to the extreme that New Zealand voted against the outlawing of discrimination against indigenous people; voted against justice, dignity and fundamental freedoms for all".

On 7 July 2009, the New Zealand government announced that it would support the Declaration; this, however, appeared to be a premature announcement by Pita Sharples, the current Minister of Mâori Affairs, as the New Zealand government cautiously backtracked on Sharples' July announcement. However, in April 2010 Pita Sharples announced New Zealand's support of the declaration at a speech in New York. On 19 April 2010, Sharples announced that New Zealand endorsed the UN declaration.

United States

Speaking for the United States mission to the UN, spokesman Benjamin Chang said, "What was done today is not clear. The way it stands now is subject to multiple interpretations and doesn't establish a clear universal principle." The U.S. mission also issued a floor document, "Observations of the United States with respect to the Declaration on the Rights of Indigenous Peoples", setting out its objections to the Declaration. Most of these are based on the same points as the three other countries' rejections but, in addition, the United States drew attention to the Declaration's failure to provide a clear definition of exactly whom the term "indigenous peoples" is intended to cover.

On 16 December 2010, President Obama declared that the United States is going to sign the declaration. The decision was announced during the second White House Tribal Conference, where he said he is "working hard to live up to" the name that was given to him by the Crow Nation: "One Who Helps People Throughout the Land." Obama has told Native American leaders that he wants to improve the "nation-to-nation" relationship between the United States and the tribes and repair broken promises. Today, there are more than 560 Indian tribes in the United States. Many had representatives at the White House conference and applauded Obama's announcement.

United Kingdom

Speaking on behalf of the United Kingdom government, UK Ambassador and Deputy Permanent Representative to the United Nations, Karen Pierce, "emphasized that the Declaration was non-legally binding and did not propose to have any retroactive application on historical episodes. National minority groups and other ethnic groups within the territory of the United Kingdom and its overseas territories did not fall within the scope of the indigenous peoples to which the Declaration applied."

Finland

Finland signed the International Declaration on the Rights of Indigenous Peoples when it was originally put forward. However the reindeer owners and Forest Administration (Metsähallitus) have a long dispute in the area of the forests. The UN Human Rights Committee ordered the Finnish State to stop logging in some of the disputed areas.

LGBT RIGHTS AT THE UNITED NATIONS

Discussions of LGBT rights at the United Nations have mainly centered around resolutions in the General Assembly and the United Nations Human Rights Council regarding the topic. In the General Assembly, a proposed resolution supporting LGBT rights originally submitted in its first form in 2008 by French/Dutch representatives, backed by the European Union, remains open for signature, with ninety-four countries having signed thus far. In the

United Nations Human Rights Council another resolution supporting LGBT rights, proposed by South Africa, was passed in 2011.

Since its founding in 1945, the United Nations had not discussed LGBT rights (regarding equality regardless of sexual orientation or gender identity) until December 2008, when a Dutch/French-initiated, European Union-backed statement was presented to the United Nations General Assembly. The statement, originally intended to be adopted as resolution, prompted an Arab League-backed statement opposing it. Both statements remain open for signature and neither of them has been officially adopted by the United Nations General Assembly.

The proposed declaration includes a condemnation of violence, harassment, discrimination, exclusion, stigmatization, and prejudice based on sexual orientation and gender identity that undermine personal integrity and dignity. It also includes condemnation of killings and executions, torture, arbitrary arrest, and deprivation of economic, social, and cultural rights on those grounds. In the declaration text, para 7 that "we recall *the statement* in 2006 before the Human Rights Council by fifty four countries requesting the President of the Council to provide an opportunity, at an appropriate future session of the Council, for discussing these violations." and para 8 that "we commend *the attention* paid to those issues by special procedures of the Human Rights Council and treaty bodies and encourage them to continue to integrate consideration of human rights violations based on sexual orientation and gender identity within their relevant mandate.", indicate The Yogyakarta Principles which provide definitions in detail on sexual orientation and on gender identity as a document on international human rights law.

The Declaration been praised as a breakthrough for human rights, breaking the previous taboo against speaking about LGBT rights in the United Nations.

On June 17, 2011, South Africa initiated a resolution in the United Nations Human Rights Council requesting the United Nations High Commissioner for Human Rights to draft a report detailing the situation of LGBT citizens worldwide to follow up and implementation of the Vienna Declaration and Programme of Action. The resolution passed 23 to 19 with the three abstentions being Burkina Faso, China, and Zambia. It was the first such resolution and was hailed as "historic."

The report, which came out in December 2011, documented violations of the rights of LGBT people, including hate crime, criminalization of homosexuality, and discrimination. High Commissioner Navi Pillay called for the repeal of laws criminalizing homosexuality; equitable ages of consent; comprehensive laws against discrimination based on sexual orientation; prompt investigation and recording of hate crime incidents; and other measures to ensure the protection of LGBT rights. The text of the report from the Human Rights Commission is dated on 17 November 2011.

BACKGROUND

Same-sex relationships are currently illegal in 76 countries and punishable by death in five. In the 1980s, early United Nations reports on the AIDS-HIV pandemic made some reference to homosexuality, and the 1986 Human Freedom Index did include a specific question, in judging the human rights record of each nation, with regards to the existence of criminal laws against homosexuality.

In its 1994 decision in *Toonen v. Australia*, The UN Human Rights Committee, which is responsible for the International Covenant on Civil and Political Rights (ICCPR), declared that such laws are in violation of human rights law. In 2003 a number of predominantly European countries put forward the Brazilian Resolution at the UN Human Rights Commission stating the intention that lesbian and gay rights be considered as fundamental as the rights of all human beings.

In 2006, with the effort of its founder, Louis George Tin, International Day Against Homophobia (IDAHO) launched a worldwide campaign to end the criminalisation of same-sex relationships. The campaign was supported by dozens of international public figures including Nobel laureates, academics, clergy and celebrities. In 2008, the 34 member countries of the Organization of American States unanimously approved a declaration affirming that human rights protections extend to sexual orientation and gender identity.

Following meetings between Tin and French Minister of Human Rights and Foreign Affairs Rama Yade in early 2008, Yade announced that she would appeal at the UN for the universal decriminalization of homosexuality; the appeal was quickly taken up as an international concern.

Co-sponsored by France, which then held the rotating presidency of the European Union, and The Netherlands on behalf of the European Union, the declaration had been intended as a resolution; it was decided to use the format of a declaration of a limited group of States because there was not enough support for the adoption of an official resolution by the General Assembly as a whole. The declaration was read out by Ambassador Jorge Argüello of Argentina on 18 December 2008, and was the first declaration concerning gay rights read in the General Assembly.

GENERAL ASSEMBLY RESOLUTION AND DECLARATION

Support

Several speakers addressing a conference on the declaration noted that in many countries laws against homosexuality stemmed as much from the British colonial past as from alleged religious or tradition reasons.

Voicing France's support for the draft declaration, Rama Yade asked: "How can we tolerate the fact that people are stoned, hanged, decapitated and tortured only because of their sexual orientation?"

UK-based activist Peter Tatchell said of the declaration:

- "This was history in the making... Securing this statement at the UN is the result of an inspiring collective global effort by many LGBT and human rights organisations. Our collaboration, unity and solidarity have won us this success. As well as IDAHO, I pay tribute to the contribution and lobbying of Amnesty International; ARC International; Center for Women's Global Leadership; COC Netherlands; Global Rights; Human Rights Watch; International Committee for IDAHO (the International Day Against Homophobia); International Gay and Lesbian Human Rights Commission (IGLHRC); International Lesbian and Gay Association (ILGA); International Service for Human Rights; Pan Africa ILGA; and Public Services International."

Opposition

Among the first to voice opposition for the declaration, in early December 2008, was the Holy See's Permanent Observer at the United Nations, Archbishop Celestino Migliore, who claimed that the declaration could be used to force countries to recognise same-sex marriage:

- "If adopted, they would create new and implacable discriminations. For example, states which do not recognise same-sex unions as 'matrimony' will be pilloried and made an object of pressure."

A key part of the Vatican opposition to the draft Declaration relates to the concept of gender identity. In a statement on 19 December, Archbishop Migliore noted:

- "In particular, the categories 'sexual orientation' and 'gender identity', used in the text, find no recognition or clear and agreed definition in international law. If they had to be taken into consideration in the proclaiming and implementing of fundamental rights, these would create serious uncertainty in the law as well as undermine the ability of States to enter into and enforce new and existing human rights conventions and standards."

However, Archbishop Migliore also made clear the Vatican's opposition to legal discrimination against homosexuals: "The Holy See continues to advocate that every sign of unjust discrimination towards homosexual persons should be avoided and urges States to do away with criminal penalties against them." In an editorial response, Italy's La Stampa newspaper called the Vatican's reasoning "grotesque", claiming that the Vatican feared a "chain reaction in favour of legally recognised homosexual unions in countries, like Italy, where there is currently no legislation."

The United States, citing conflicts with US law, originally opposed the adoption of the nonbinding measure, as did Russia, China, the Holy See, and members of the Organisation of Islamic Cooperation. The Holy See's

Permanent Observer Mission issued a statement saying that the draft declaration "challenges existing human rights norms." The Obama administration changed the US position to support the measure in February 2009.

An alternative statement, supported by 57 member nations, was read by the Syrian representative in the General Assembly. The statement, led by the Organization of the Islamic Conference, rejected the idea that sexual orientation is a matter of genetic coding and claimed that the declaration threatened to undermine the international framework of human rights, adding that the statement "delves into matters which fall essentially within the domestic jurisdiction of states" and could lead to "the social normalization, and possibly the legitimization, of many deplorable acts including paedophilia."(although scientific research has shown that neither heterosexuals nor homosexuals are any more likely to inflict child abuse) The Organization failed in a related attempt to delete the phrase "sexual orientation" from a Swedish-backed formal resolution condemning summary executions, although recently the phrase was removed with 79 votes to 70, and then subsequently restored by a vote of 93 to 55.

Signatories

57 UN member nations had initially co-sponsored the opposing statement in 2008:

Some of these countries later switched their position to support the original resolution backing LGBT rights in 2011, leaving 54 countries as continued sponsors of the statement opposing LGBT rights. The countries which removed themselves as co-sponsors of the statement opposing LGBT who all subsequently switched to sponsoring the statement supporting LGBT rights.

UN HUMAN RIGHTS COUNCIL RESOLUTION AND DISCUSSION

A resolution submitted by South Africa requesting a study on discrimination and sexual orientation (A/HRC/17/L.9/Rev.1) passed, 23 to 19 with 3 abstentions, in the Human Rights Council on June 17, 2011. This is the first time that any United Nations body approved a resolution affirming the rights of LGBT people. The resolution called on the office of United Nations High Commissioner for Human Rights Navi Pillay to draw up the first U.N. report on challenges faced by gay people worldwide.

The High Commissioner's report, released December 2011, found that violence against LGBT persons remains common, and confirmed that "Seventy-six countries retain laws that are used to criminalize people on the basis of sexual orientation or gender identity", and that "In at least five countries the death penalty may be applied to those found guilty of offences relating to consensual, adult homosexual conduct".

The High Commissioner's report led to a panel discussion by the Human Rights Council in March 2012. The divided nature of the UN, and the Council members in particular, was again evident. Secretary-General Ban Ki-moon described violence and discrimination based on sexual orientation as "a monumental tragedy for those affected and a stain on the collective consciousness", and many others voiced similar concerns. However, "A number of states had signaled their opposition to any discussion of sexual orientation and gender identity by leaving the Council chamber at the start of the meeting," and "A number voiced their opposition on cultural or religious grounds, or argued that sexual orientation and gender identity were new concepts that lay outside the framework of international human rights law"

7

International Human Rights Conventions

INTERNATIONAL COVENANT ON CIVIL AND POLITICAL RIGHTS

The International Covenant on Civil and Political Rights (ICCPR) is a multilateral treaty adopted by the United Nations General Assembly on 16 December 1966, and in force from 23 March 1976. It commits its parties to respect the civil and political rights of individuals, including the right to life, freedom of religion, freedom of speech, freedom of assembly, electoral rights and rights to due process and a fair trial. As of May 2013, the Covenant had 74 signatories and 167 parties.

The ICCPR is part of the International Bill of Human Rights, along with the International Covenant on Economic, Social and Cultural Rights (ICESCR) and the Universal Declaration of Human Rights (UDHR).

The ICCPR is monitored by the United Nations Human Rights Committee (a separate body to the United Nations Human Rights Council), which reviews regular reports of States parties on how the rights are being implemented. States must report initially one year after acceding to the Covenant and then whenever the Committee requests (usually every four years). The Committee normally meets in Geneva and normally holds three sessions per year.

GENESIS

The ICCPR has its roots in the same process that led to the Universal Declaration of Human Rights. A "Declaration on the Essential Rights of Man" had been proposed at the 1945 San Francisco Conference which led to the founding of the United Nations, and the Economic and Social Council was given the task of drafting it. Early on in the process, the document was split into a declaration setting forth general principles of human rights, and a convention or covenant containing binding commitments. The former evolved into the UDHR and was adopted on 10 December 1948.

Drafting continued on the convention, but there remained significant differences between UN members on the relative importance of negative Civil and Political versus positive Economic, Social and Cultural rights. These eventually caused the convention to be split into two separate covenants, "one to contain civil and political rights and the other to contain economic, social and cultural rights." The two covenants were to contain as many similar provisions as possible, and be opened for signature simultaneously. Each would also contain an article on the right of all peoples to self-determination.

The first document became the International Covenant on Economic, Social and Cultural Rights and the second the International Covenant on Civil and Political Rights. The drafts were presented to the UN General Assembly for discussion in 1954, and adopted in 1966. As a result of diplomatic negotiations the International Covenant on Economic, Social and Cultural Rights was adopted shortly before the International Covenant on Civil and Political Rights.

SUMMARY

The Covenant follows the structure of the UDHR and ICESCR, with a preamble and fifty-three articles, divided into six parts.

Part 1 (Article 1) recognises the right of all peoples to self-determination, including the right to "freely determine their political status", pursue their economic, social and cultural goals, and manage and dispose of their own resources. It recognises a negative right of a people not to be deprived of its means of subsistence, and imposes an obligation on those parties still responsible for non-self governing and trust territories (colonies) to encourage and respect their self-determination.

Part 2 (Articles 2 – 5) obliges parties to legislate where necessary to give effect to the rights recognised in the Covenant, and to provide an effective legal remedy for any violation of those rights. It also requires the rights be recognised "without distinction of any kind, such as race, colour, sex, language, religion, political or other opinion, national or social origin, property, birth or other status," and to ensure that they are enjoyed equally by women. The rights can only be limited "in time of public emergency which threatens the life of the nation," and even then no derogation is permitted from the rights to life, freedom from torture and slavery, the freedom from retrospective law, the right to personhood, and freedom of thought, conscience and religion.

Part 3 (Articles 6 – 27) lists the rights themselves. These include rights to

- Physical integrity, in the form of the right to life and freedom from torture and slavery (Articles 6, 7, and 8);
- Liberty and security of the person, in the form of freedom from arbitrary arrest and detention and the right to *habeas corpus* (Articles 9 – 11);
- Procedural fairness in law, in the form of rights to due process, a fair and impartial trial, the presumption of innocence, and recognition as a person before the law (Articles 14, 15, and 16);

- Individual liberty, in the form of the freedoms of movement, thought, conscience and religion, speech, association and assembly, family rights, the right to a nationality, and the right to privacy (Articles 12, 13, 17 – 24);
- Prohibition of any propaganda for war as well as any advocacy of national or religious hatred that constitutes incitement to discrimination, hostility or violence by law (Article 20);
- Political participation, including the right to join a political party and the right to vote (Article 25);
- Non-discrimination, minority rights and equality before the law (Articles 26 and 27).

Many of these rights include specific actions which must be undertaken to realise them.

Part 4 (Articles 28 – 45) governs the establishment and operation of the Human Rights Committee and the reporting and monitoring of the Covenant. It also allows parties to recognise the competence of the Committee to resolve disputes between parties on the implementation of the Covenant (Articles 41 and 42). Part 5 (Articles 46 – 47) clarifies that the Covenant shall not be interpreted as interfering with the operation of the United Nations or "the inherent right of all peoples to enjoy and utilize fully and freely their natural wealth and resources".

Part 6 (Articles 48 – 53) governs ratification, entry into force, and amendment of the Covenant.

CORE PROVISIONS

Rights to physical integrity

Article 6 of the Covenant recognises the individual's "inherent right to life" and requires it to be protected by law. It is a "supreme right" from which no derogation can be permitted, and must be interpreted widely. It therefore requires parties to take positive measures to reduce infant mortality and increase life expectancy, as well as forbidding arbitrary killings by security forces.

While Article 6 does not prohibit the death penalty, it restricts its application to the "most serious crimes" and forbids it to be used on children and pregnant women or in a manner contrary to the Convention on the Prevention and Punishment of the Crime of Genocide. The UN Human Rights Committee interprets the Article as "strongly suggest[ing] that abolition is desirable", and regards any progress towards abolition of the death penalty as advancing this right. The Second Optional Protocol commits its signatories to the abolition of the death penalty within their borders.

Article 7 prohibits torture and cruel, inhuman or degrading punishment. As with Article 6, it cannot be derogated from under any circumstances. The article is now interpreted to impose similar obligations to those required by the United Nations Convention Against Torture, including not just prohibition of torture, but active measures to prevent its use and a prohibition on refoulement. In response to Nazi human experimentation during WW2 this article explicitly includes a prohibition on medical and scientific experimentation without consent.

Article 8 prohibits slavery and enforced servitude in all situations. The article also prohibits forced labour, with exceptions for criminal punishment, military service and civil obligations.

Liberty and security of person

Article 9 recognises the rights to liberty and security of the person. It prohibits arbitrary arrest and detention, requires any deprivation of liberty to be according to law, and obliges parties to allow those deprived of their liberty to challenge their imprisonment through the courts. These provisions apply not just to those imprisoned as part of the criminal process, but also to those detained due to mental illness, drug addiction, or for educational or immigration purposes.

Articles 9.3 and 9.4 impose procedural safeguards around arrest, requiring anyone arrested to be promptly informed of the charges against them, and to be brought promptly before a judge. It also restricts the use of pre-trial detention, requiring it to be imposed only in exceptional circumstances and for as short a period of time as possible.

Article 10 requires anyone deprived of liberty to be treated with dignity and humanity. This applies not just to prisoners, but also to those detained for immigration purposes or psychiatric care. The right complements the Article 7 prohibition on torture and cruel, inhuman or degrading treatment. The article also imposes specific obligations around criminal justice, requiring prisoners in pretrial detention to be separated from convicted prisoners, and children to be separated from adults. It requires prisons to be focused on reform and rehabilitation rather than punishment.

Article 11 prohibits the use of imprisonment as a punishment for breach of contract.

Procedural fairness and rights of the accused

Article 14 recognizes and protects a right to justice and a fair trial. Article 14.1 establishes the ground rules: everyone must be equal before the courts, and any hearing must take place in open court before a competent, independent and impartial tribunal, with any judgment or ruling made public. Closed hearings are only permitted for reasons of privacy, justice, or national security, and judgments may only be suppressed in divorce cases or to protect the interests of children. These obligations apply to both criminal and civil hearings, and to all courts and tribunals.

The rest of the article imposes specific and detailed obligations around the process of criminal trials in order to protect the rights of the accused and the right to a fair trial. It establishes the Presumption of innocence and forbids double jeopardy. It requires that those convicted of a crime be allowed to appeal to a higher tribunal, and requires victims of a Miscarriage of justice to be compensated. It establishes rights to a speedy trial, to counsel, against self-incrimination, and for the accused to be present and call and examine witnesses.

Article 15 prohibits prosecutions under Ex post facto law and the imposition of retrospective criminal penalties, and requires the imposition of the lesser penalty where criminal sentences have changed between the offence and conviction. Article 16 requires states to recognize everyone as a person before the law.

Individual liberties

Article 12 guarantees freedom of movement, including the right of persons to choose their residence and to leave a country. These rights apply to legal aliens as well as citizens of a state, and can be restricted only where necessary to protect national security, public order or health, and the rights and freedoms of others. The article also recognises a right of people to enter their own country. The Human Rights Committee interprets this right broadly as applying not just to citizens, but also to those stripped of or denied their nationality. They also regard it as near-absolute; "there are few, if any, circumstances in which deprivation of the right to enter one's own country could be reasonable".

Article 13 forbids the arbitrary expulsion of resident aliens and requires such decisions to be able to be appealed and reviewed.

Article 17 mandates the right of privacy. This provision, specifically article 17(1), protects private adult consensual sexual activity, thereby nullifying prohibitions on homosexual behaviour, however, the wording of this covenant's marriage right (Article 23) excludes the extrapolation of a same-sex marriage right from this provision. Article 17 also protects people against unlawful attacks to their honor and reputation. Article 17 (2) grants the protection of the Law against such attacks

- Article 18 mandates freedom of religion.
- Article 19 mandates freedom of expression.
- Article 20 mandates sanctions against inciting hatred.
- Articles 21 and 22 mandate freedom of association. These provisions guarantee the right to freedom of association, the right to trade unions and also defines the International Labour Organisation.
- Article 23 mandates the right of marriage. The wording of this provision neither requires nor prohibits same-sex marriage.
- Article 24 mandates the right to a nationality.

- Article 27 mandates the rights of ethnic, religious and linguistic minority to enjoy their own culture, to profess their own religion, and to use their own language.

Political rights

Article 3 provides an accessory non-discrimination principle. Accessory in the way that it cannot be used independently and can only be relied upon in relation to another right protected by the ICCPR.

In contrast, Article 26 contains a revolutionary norm by providing an autonomous equality principle which is not dependant upon another right under the convention being infringed. This has the effect of widening the scope of the non-discrimination principle beyond the scope of ICCPR.

OPTIONAL PROTOCOLS

There are two Optional Protocols to the Covenant. The First Optional Protocol establishes an individual complaints mechanism, allowing individuals to complain to the Human Rights Committee about violations of the Covenant. This has led to the creation of a complex jurisprudence on the interpretation and implementation of the Covenant. As of July 2013, the First Optional Protocol has 114 parties.

The Second Optional Protocol abolishes the death penalty; however, countries were permitted to make a reservation allowing for use of death penalty for the most serious crimes of a military nature, committed during wartime. As of July 2013, the Second Optional Protocol had 77 parties.

RESERVATIONS

A number of parties have made reservations and interpretative declarations to their application of the Covenant.

Argentina will apply the fair trial rights guaranteed in its constitution to the prosecution of those accused of violating the general law of nations.

Australia reserves the right to progressively implement the prison standards of Article 10, to compensate for miscarriages of justice by administrative means rather than through the courts, and interprets the prohibition on racial incitement as being subject to the freedoms of expression, association and assembly. It also declares that its implementation will be effected at each level of its federal system.

Austria reserves the right to continue to exile members of the House of Habsburg, and limits the rights of the accused and the right to a fair trial to those already existing in its legal system.

Bahamas, due to problems with implementation, reserves the right not to compensate for miscarriages of justice.

Bahrain interprets Articles 3 (no sexual discrimination), 18 (freedom of religion) and 23 (family rights) within the context of Islamic Sharia law.

Bangladesh reserves the right to try people *in absentia* where they are fugitives from justice and declares that resource constraints mean that it cannot necessarily segregate prisons or provide counsel for accused persons.

Barbados reserves the right not to provide free counsel for accused persons due to resource constraints. Belgium interprets the freedoms of speech, assembly and association in a manner consistent with the European Convention on Human Rights. It does not consider itself obliged to ban war propaganda as required by Article 20, and interprets that article in light of the freedom of expression in the UDHR. Belize reserves the right not to compensate for miscarriages of justice, due to problems with implementation, and does not plan to provide free legal counsel for the same reasons as above. It also refuses to ensure the right to free travel at any time, due to a law requiring those travelling abroad to provide tax clearance certificates.

Congo, as per the Congolese Code of Civil, Commercial, Administrative and Financial Procedure, in matters of private law, decisions or orders emanating from conciliation proceedings may be enforced through imprisonment for debt. Denmark reserves the right to exclude the press and the public from trials as per its own laws. Reservation is further made to Article 20, paragraph 1. This reservation is in accordance with the vote cast by Denmark in the XVI General Assembly of the United Nations in 1961 when the Danish Delegation, referring to the preceding article concerning freedom of expression, voted against the prohibition against propaganda for war.

Gambia, as per its constitution, will provide free legal assistance for accused persons charged with capital offences only.

The United States has made reservations that none of the articles should restrict the right of free speech and association; that the US government may impose capital punishment on any person other than a pregnant woman, including persons below the age of 18; that "cruel, inhuman and degrading treatment or punishment" refers to those treatments or punishments prohibited by the Fifth, Eighth and/or Fourteenth Amendments to the US Constitution; that Paragraph 1, Article 15 will not apply; and that, notwithstanding paragraphs 2(b) and 3 of Article 10 and paragraph 4 of Article 14, the US government may treat juveniles as adults, and accept volunteers to the military prior to the age of 18. The United States also submitted five "understandings", and four "declarations".

NATIONAL IMPLEMENTATION AND EFFECTS

The International Covenant on Civil and Political Rights has 167 states parties, 67 by signature and ratification, and the remainder by accession or succession. Another five states have signed but have yet to ratify the treaty.

Australia

The covenant is not enforceable in Australia, however, AHRC legislation allows the Australian Human Rights Commission (AHRC) to examine enacted legislation (to suggest remedial enactments), its administration (to suggest avoidance of practices) and general compliance with the covenant which is schedule to the AHRC legislation.

Ireland

Ireland's use of Special Criminal Courts where juries are replaced by judges and other special procedures apply has been found to violate the treaty.

New Zealand

While New Zealand has not incorporated the ICCPR into law, it took measures to give effect to many of the rights contained within it by passing the New Zealand Bill of Rights Act in 1990.

United States

Reservations, understandings, and declarations

The United States Senate ratified the ICCPR in 1992, with five reservations, five understandings, and four declarations. Some have noted that with so many reservations, its implementation has little domestic effect. Included in the Senate's ratification was the declaration that "the provisions of Article 1 through 27 of the Covenant are not self-executing", and in a Senate Executive Report stated that the declaration was meant to "clarify that the Covenant will not create a private cause of action in U.S. Courts."

Where a treaty or covenant is not self-executing, and where Congress has not acted to implement the agreement with legislation, no private right of action within the U.S. judicial system is created by ratification. Thus while the ICCPR is binding upon the United States *as a matter of international law*, it does not form part of the domestic law of the nation.

As a reservation that is "incompatible with the object and purpose" of a treaty is void as a matter of the Vienna Convention on the Law of Treaties and international law, there is some issue as to whether the non-self-execution declaration is even legal under domestic law. Taking the opposing view, it is argued by many U.S. Senators and legal scholars that, since for any treaty to be enforceable in the United States, it must strictly conform to the terms of ratification issued by the Senate; and, that no term of any treaty which is subject to the Senate's reservation(s) can be interpreted to have been confirmed, lawful or enforceable in the United States, according to the sovereign operation of the Constitution.

Prominent critics in the human rights community, such as Prof. Louis Henkin (non-self-execution declaration incompatible with the Supremacy Clause) and Prof. Jordan Paust ("Rarely has a treaty been so abused") have denounced the United States' ratification subject to the non-self-execution declaration as a blatant fraud upon the international community, especially in light of its subsequent failure to conform domestic law to the minimum human rights standards as established in the Covenant and in the Universal Declaration of Human Rights over the last thirty years.

Constitutionality

It has been argued that Article 20(2) of the ICCPR, as well as Article 4 of the ICERD, may be unconstitutional according to Supreme Court precedent, which is the reason behind the Senate reservations.

Non-compliance

In 1994, the United Nations' Human Rights Committee expressed concerns with compliance:

- Of particular concern are widely formulated reservations which essentially render ineffective all Covenant rights which would require any change in national law to ensure compliance with Covenant obligations. No real international rights or obligations have thus been accepted. And when there is an absence of provisions to ensure that Covenant rights may be sued on in domestic courts, and, further, a failure to allow individual complaints to be brought to the Committee under the first Optional Protocol, all the essential elements of the Covenant guarantees have been removed.

Indeed, the United States has not accepted a single international obligation required under the Covenant. It has not changed its domestic law to conform with the strictures of the Covenant. Its citizens are not permitted to sue to enforce their basic human rights under the Covenant. It has not ratified the Optional Protocol to the Convention against Torture (OPCAT). As such, the Covenant has been rendered ineffective, with the bone of contention being United States officials' insistence upon preserving a vast web of sovereign, judicial, prosecutorial, and executive branch immunities that often deprives its citizens of the "effective remedy" under law the Covenant is intended to guarantee. In 2006, the Human Rights Committee expressed concern over what it interprets as material non-compliance, exhorting the United States to take immediate corrective action:

The *Principal subjects of concern and recommendations* portion of the of the report spans section 10 through 39 of the report. Section 10 reads as follows:

- The Committee notes with concern the restrictive interpretation made by the State party of its obligations under the Covenant, as a result in particular of (a) its position that the Covenant does not apply with respect to individuals under its jurisdiction but outside its territory, nor in time of war, despite the contrary opinions and established jurisprudence of the Committee and the International Court of Justice; (b) its failure to take fully into consideration its obligation under the Covenant not only to respect, but also to ensure the rights prescribed by the Covenant; and (c) its restrictive approach to some substantive provisions of the Covenant, which is not in conformity with the interpretation made by the Committee before and after the State party's ratification of the Covenant.

- The State party should review its approach and interpret the Covenant in good faith, in accordance with the ordinary meaning to be given to its terms in their context, including subsequent practice, and in the light of its object and purpose. The State party should in particular (a) acknowledge the applicability of the Covenant with respect to individuals under its jurisdiction but outside its territory, as well as its applicability in time of war; (b) take positive steps, when necessary, to ensure the full implementation of all rights prescribed by the Covenant; and (c) consider in good faith the interpretation of the Covenant provided by the Committee pursuant to its mandate.

As of February 2013, the United States is among States scheduled for examination in the 107th (11–28 March 2013) and 109th (14 October – 1 November 2013) sessions of the Committee.

WITHDRAWAL

On 23 August 1997 the Democratic People's Republic of Korea drafted a notification of withdrawal from the Covenant. On 23 September the Secretary-General forwarded an aide-mémoire to the government of the DPRK and the other signatories stating that, since the covenant did not contain a mechanism for withdrawal it would not be possible for the DPRK to leave the covenant except with the agreement of all other state parties.

CRIME OF APARTHEID

The crime of Apartheid is defined by the 2002 Rome Statute of the International Criminal Court as inhumane acts of a character similar to other crimes against humanity "committed in the context of an institutionalized regime of systematic oppression and domination by one racial group over any other racial group or groups and committed with the intention of maintaining that regime." On November 30, 1973, the United Nations General Assembly opened for signature and ratification the International Convention on the Suppression and Punishment of the Crime of Apartheid. It defined the crime of apartheid as "inhuman acts committed for the purpose of establishing and maintaining domination by one racial group of persons over any other racial group of persons and systematically oppressing them."

HISTORY

The term *apartheid*, from Afrikaans for "apartness," was the official name of the South African system of racial segregation which existed after 1948. Complaints about the system were brought to the United Nations as early as 12 July 1948 when Dr. Padmanabha Pillai, the representative of India to the United Nations, circulated a letter to the Secretary-General expressing his concerns over treatment of ethnic Indians within the Union of South Africa. As it became more widely known, South African apartheid was condemned internationally as unjust and racist and many decided that a formal legal framework was needed in order to apply international pressure on the South African government.

In 1971, the USSR and Guinea together submitted early drafts of a convention to deal with the suppression and punishment of apartheid. In 1973, the General Assembly of the United Nations agreed on the text of the International Convention on the Suppression and Punishment of the Crime of Apartheid (ICSPCA). The Convention has 31 signatories and 107 parties.

"As such, apartheid was declared to be a crime against humanity, with a scope that went far beyond South Africa. While the crime of apartheid is most often associated with the racist policies of South Africa after 1948, the term more generally refers to racially based policies in any state."

Seventy-six other countries subsequently signed on, but a number of nations have neither signed nor ratified the ICSPCA, including Canada, France, Germany, Israel, Italy, the Netherlands, the United Kingdom, Australia, New Zealand and the United States. In explanation of the US vote against the convention, Ambassador Clarence Clyde Ferguson Jr. said: "[W]e cannot...accept that apartheid can in this manner be made a crime against humanity. Crimes against humanity are so grave in nature that they must be meticulously elaborated and strictly construed under existing international law..."

In 1977, Addition Protocol 1 to the Geneva Conventions designated apartheid as a grave breach of the Protocol and a war crime. There are 169 parties to the Protocol. The International Criminal Court provides for individual criminal responsibility for crimes against humanity, including the crime of apartheid.

The International Criminal Court (ICC) came into being on 1 July 2002, and can only prosecute crimes committed on or after that date. The Court can generally only exercise jurisdiction in cases where the accused is a national of a state party, the alleged crime took place on the territory of a state party, or a situation is referred to the Court by the United Nations Security Council. The ICC exercises complimentary jurisdiction. Many of the member states have provided their own national courts with universal jurisdiction over the same offenses and do not recognize any statute of limitations for crimes against humanity. As of July 2008, 106 countries are states parties (with Suriname and Cook Islands set to join in October 2008), and a further 40 countries have signed but not yet ratified the treaty. However, many of the world's most populous nations, including China, India, the United States, Indonesia, and Pakistan are not parties to the Court and therefore are not subject to its jurisdiction, except by Security Council referral.

ICSPCA DEFINITION OF THE CRIME OF APARTHEID

Article II of the ICSPCA defines the crime of apartheid as below:

International Convention on the Suppression and Punishment of the Crime of Apartheid, Article II:

For the purpose of the present Convention, the term 'the crime of apartheid', which shall include similar policies and practices of racial segregation and discrimination as practiced in southern Africa, shall apply to the following inhumane acts committed for the purpose of establishing and maintaining domination by one racial group of persons over any other racial group of persons and systematically oppressing them:

- Denial to a member or members of a racial group or groups of the right to life and liberty of person
  - By murder of members of a racial group or groups;
  - By the infliction upon the members of a racial group or groups of serious bodily or mental harm, by the infringement of their freedom or dignity, or by subjecting them to torture or to cruel, inhuman or degrading treatment or punishment;
  - By arbitrary arrest and illegal imprisonment of the members of a racial group or groups;
- Deliberate imposition on a racial group or groups of living conditions calculated to cause its or their physical destruction in whole or in part;
- Any legislative measures and other measures calculated to prevent a racial group or groups from participation in the political, social, economic and cultural life of the country and the deliberate creation of conditions preventing the full development of such a group or groups, in particular by denying to members of a racial group or groups basic human rights and freedoms, including the right to work, the right to form recognised trade unions, the right to education, the right to leave and to return to their country, the right to a nationality, the right to freedom of movement and residence, the right to freedom of opinion and expression, and the right to freedom of peaceful assembly and association;
- Any measures including legislative measures, designed to divide the population along racial lines by the creation of separate reserves and ghettos for the members of a racial group or groups, the prohibition of mixed marriages among members of various racial groups, the expropriation of landed property belonging to a racial group or groups or to members thereof;

- Exploitation of the labour of the members of a racial group or groups, in particular by submitting them to forced labour;
- Persecution of organizations and persons, by depriving them of fundamental rights and freedoms, because they oppose apartheid.

Definition of racial discrimination

According to the United Nations Convention on the Elimination of All Forms of Racial Discrimination,

- The term "racial discrimination" shall mean any distinction, exclusion, restriction or preference based on race, colour, descent, or national or ethnic origin which has the purpose or effect of nullifying or impairing the recognition, enjoyment or exercise, on an equal footing, of human rights and fundamental freedoms in the political, economic, social, cultural or any other field of public life.

This definition does not make any difference between discrimination based on ethnicity and race, in part because the distinction between the two remains debatable among anthropologists. Similarly, in British law the phrase *racial group* means "any group of people who are defined by reference to their race, colour, nationality (including citizenship) or ethnic or national origin".

ICC DEFINITION OF THE CRIME OF APARTHEID

Article 7 of the Rome Statute of the International Criminal Court defines crimes against humanity as:

Article 7: Crimes against humanity:

1. For the purpose of this Statute, 'crime against humanity' means any of the following acts when committed as part of a widespread or systematic attack directed against any civilian population, with knowledge of the attack:
   - Murder;
   - Extermination;
   - Enslavement;
   - Deportation or forcible transfer of population;
   - Imprisonment or other severe deprivation of physical liberty in violation of fundamental rules of international law;
   - Torture;
   - Rape, sexual slavery, enforced prostitution, forced pregnancy, enforced sterilization, or any other form of sexual violence of comparable gravity;
   - Persecution against any identifiable group or collectivity on political, racial, national, ethnic, cultural, religious, gender as defined in paragraph 3, or other grounds that are universally recognized as impermissible under international law, in connection with any act referred to in this paragraph or any crime within the jurisdiction of the Court;

- Enforced disappearance of persons;
- The crime of apartheid;
- Other inhumane acts of a similar character intentionally causing great suffering, or serious injury to body or to mental or physical health.

Later in Article 7, the crime of apartheid is defined as:

The 'crime of apartheid' means inhumane acts of a character similar to those referred to in paragraph 1, committed in the context of an institutionalised regime of systematic oppression and domination by one racial group over any other racial group or groups and committed with the intention of maintaining that regime.

ISRAEL

Critics have accused Israel of committing the crime of apartheid; In a 2007 report, United Nations Special Rapporteur for Palestine John Dugard stated that "elements of the [state of Israel's] occupation constitute forms of colonialism and of apartheid, which are contrary to international law." and suggested that the "legal consequences of a prolonged occupation with features of colonialism and apartheid" be put to the International Court of Justice.

The UN Special Rapporteur concludes that this "general structure of apartheid that exists in the Occupied Palestinian Territories... makes the allegation increasingly credible despite the differences between the specific characteristics of South African apartheid and that of the Occupied Palestinian Territories regime".

South African Judge Richard Goldstone, head of the Report of the United Nations Fact Finding Mission on the Gaza Conflict, also known as the Goldstone Report, writing in The New York Times in October 2011, said that "in Israel, there is no apartheid. Nothing there comes close to the definition of apartheid under the 1998 Rome Statute." Goldstone noted that Arab citizens of Israel are allowed to vote, have political parties, and hold seats in the Knesset and other positions, including one on the Israeli Supreme Court. Goldstone wrote that the situation in the West Bank was more complex, but that there is no attempt to maintain "an institutionalized regime of systematic oppression and domination by one racial group", and claimed that the seemingly oppressive measures taken by Israel were taken to protect its own citizens from attacks by Palestinian militants.

However the Goldstone Report does not contain any reference to charges of apartheid, whether supported or not. With regard to associated issue of positive findings of Israeli war crimes in the report, Goldstone has argued for a redaction. However the other three authors of the Goldstone Report have publicly rejected this arguing Goldstone has "misrepresented facts in an attempt to delegitimise the [Goldstone Report's] findings and to cast doubts on its credibility".

Israeli journalist Yonatan Silverman wrote in *Ynetnews* that while inequality and injustice existed in the West Bank, Israel was not an apartheid state. Silverman wrote that while South Africa was a legally segretated society, Israel's actions in the West Bank are not rooted in legislation and stem from security concerns rather than racial bias. Contrary to these, the Russell Tribunal on Palestine tends to judge in favor of the apartheid allegations. Amongst a large list of violations of international law, by both the US and Israel, the Tribunal judges "Violation of the prohibition of discrimination based on national origin through Israeli policies and practices akin to Apartheid (2011 Capetown findings of this Tribunal). Final conclusions of this Tribunal are expected in February 2013. The Russell Tribunal on Palestine has been criticised as biased against Israel by judge Richard Goldstone, and South African journalist and human rights activist Benjamin Pogrund, described the Cape Town Session of the Russell Tribunal on Palestine "theatre". The Tribunal has on the other hand been endorsed by the Center for Constitutional Rights, Jewish Voice for Peace, Israeli Committee Against House Demolitions and other organizations.

INTERNATIONAL COVENANT ON ECONOMIC, SOCIAL AND CULTURAL RIGHTS

The International Covenant on Economic, Social and Cultural Rights (ICESCR) is a multilateral treaty adopted by the United Nations General Assembly on 16 December 1966, and in force from 3 January 1976. It commits its parties to work toward the granting of economic, social, and cultural rights (ESCR) to individuals, including labour rights and the right to health, the right to education, and the right to an adequate standard of living. As of 2013, the Covenant had 160 parties. A further seven countries, including the United States of America, had signed but not yet ratified the Covenant.

The ICESCR is part of the International Bill of Human Rights, along with the Universal Declaration of Human Rights (UDHR) and the International Covenant on Civil and Political Rights (ICCPR), including the latter's first and second Optional Protocols. The Covenant is monitored by the UN Committee on Economic, Social and Cultural Rights.

CONVENTION RELATING TO THE STATUS OF REFUGEES

The Convention relating to the Status of Refugees (CRSR) is a United Nations multilateral treaty that defines who is a refugee, and sets out the rights of individuals who are granted asylum and the responsibilities of nations that grant asylum. The Convention also sets out which people do *not* qualify as refugees, such as war criminals. The Convention also provides for some visa-free travel for holders of travel Documents issued under the convention.

HISTORY

The Convention was approved at a special United Nations conference on 28 July 1951. It entered into force on 22 April 1954. It was initially limited to protecting European refugees from before 1 January 1951 (after World War II), though states could make a declaration that the provisions would apply to refugees from other places. A 1967 Protocol removed the time limits and applied to refugees "without any geographic limitation", but declarations previously made by parties to the Convention on geographic scope were grandfathered in. (Although, like many international treaties, the Refugee Convention was agreed in Geneva, it is incorrect to refer to it as "the Geneva Convention," because there are four treaties regulating armed conflict known as the Geneva Conventions.) Denmark was the first state to ratify the treaty on 4 December 1952. As of July 2013 there were 145 parties to the Convention, and 146 to the protocol. Most recently, the President of Nauru, Marcus Stephen, signed both the Convention and the Protocol on 17 June 2011 and acceded on 28 June 2011. Madagascar and Saint Kitts and Nevis are parties only to the Convention, while Cape Verde, the United States of America and Venezuela are parties only to the Protocol.

DEFINITION OF A REFUGEE

Article 1 of the Convention as amended by the 1967 Protocol provides the definition of a refugee:

- "A person who owing to a well-founded fear of being persecuted for reasons of race, religion, nationality, membership of a particular social group or political opinion, is outside the country of his nationality and is unable or, owing to such fear, is unwilling to avail himself of the protection of that country; or who, not having a nationality and being outside the country of his former habitual residence as a result of such events, is unable or, owing to such fear, is unwilling to return to it.."

Additional definitions based on the Convention

Several groups have built upon the 1951 Convention and attempted to create a more objective definition. While their terms differ to that of the 1951 Convention, the Convention has significantly shaped these new, more objective definitions.

The Organisation of African Unity (OAU) Convention Governing the Specific Aspects of Refugee Problems in Africa adopted a regional treaty based on the Convention, adding to the definition that a refugee is

- Any person compelled to leave his/her country owing to external aggression, occupation, foreign domination or events seriously disturbing public order in either part or the whole of his country of origin or nationality

In 1984, a group of Latin American governments adopted the Cartagena Declaration, which like the OAU Convention, added more objectivity based on significant consideration to the 1951 Convention. The Cartegena Declaration determine that a 'refugee' includes:

- Persons who flee their countries because their lives, safety or freedom have been threatened by generalised violence, foreign aggression, internal conflicts, massive violation of human rights or other circumstances which have seriously disturbed public order.

RESPONSIBILITIES OF STATES PARTIES TO THE REFUGEE CONVENTION

In the general principle of international law, treaties in force are binding upon the parties to it and must be performed in good faith. Countries that have ratified the Refugee Convention are obliged to protect refugees that are on their territory, in accordance with its terms.

There are a number of provisions that States who are parties of the Refugee Convention and 1967 Protocol must adhere to. Among them are:

- Cooperation With the UNHCR: Under Article 35 of the Refugee Convention and Article II of the 1967 Protocol, states agree to cooperate with United Nations High Commissioner for Refugees (UNHCR) in the exercise of its functions and to help UNHCR supervise the implementation of the provisions in the Convention.
- Information on National Legislation: parties to the Convention agree to inform the United Nations Secretary-General about the laws and regulations they may adopt to ensure the application of the Convention.
- Exemption from Reciprocity: The notion of reciprocity- where, according to a country's law, the granting of a right to an alien is subject to the granting of similar treatment by the alien's country of nationality- does not apply to refugees. This notion does not apply to refugees because refugees do not enjoy the protection of their home state.

INNOCENCE OF REFUGEES UNLAWFULLY ENTERING THE COUNTRY OF REFUGE

A refugee has the right to be free from penalties pertaining to the illegality of their entry to or presence within a country, if it can be shown that they acted in good faith- that is, if the refugee believes that there was ample cause for their illegal entry/presence, i.e. to escape threats upon their life or freedom, and if they swiftly declare their presence. This right is protected in Article 31:

- "The Contracting States shall not impose penalties, on account of their illegal entry or presence, on refugees who, coming directly from a territory where their life or freedom was threatened in the sense of article 1, enter or are present in their territory without authorization, provided they present themselves without delay to the authorities and show good cause for their illegal entry or presence. (Article 31, (1))

THE PRINCIPLE OF NON-REFOULEMENT

A refugee's right to be protected against forcible return, or refoulement, is set out in the 1951 Convention relating to the Status of Refugees:

- "No Contracting State shall expel or return ('refouler') a refugee in any manner whatsoever to the frontiers of territories where his life or freedom would be threatened on account of his race, religion, nationality, membership of a particular social or political opinion" (Article 33(1)).

It is widely accepted that the prohibition of forcible return is part of customary international law. This means that even States that are not party to the 1951 Refugee Convention must respect the principle of non-refoulement. Therefore, States are obligated under the Convention and under customary international law to respect the principle of non-refoulement. If and when this principle is threatened, UNHCR can respond by intervening with relevant authorities, and if it deems necessary, will inform the public.

CONVENTION ON THE RIGHTS OF THE CHILD

The United Nations Convention on the Rights of the Child (commonly abbreviated as the CRC, CROC, or UNCRC) is a human rights treaty setting out the civil, political, economic, social, health and cultural rights of children. The Convention defines a child as any human being under the age of eighteen, unless the age of majority is attained earlier under a state's own domestic legislation.

Nations that ratify this convention are bound to it by international law. Compliance is monitored by the UN Committee on the Rights of the Child, which is composed of members from countries around the world. Once a year, the Committee submits a report to the Third Committee of the United Nations General Assembly, which also hears a statement from the CRC Chair, and the Assembly adopts a Resolution on the Rights of the Child.

Governments of countries that have ratified the Convention are required to report to, and appear before, the United Nations Committee on the Rights of the Child periodically to be examined on their progress with regards to the advancement of the implementation of the Convention and the status of child rights in their country. Their reports and the committee's written views and concerns are available on the committee's website.

The UN General Assembly adopted the Convention and opened it for signature on 20 November 1989 (the 30th anniversary of its Declaration of the Rights of the Child). It came into force on 2 September 1990, after it was ratified by the required number of nations. Currently, 193 countries are party to it, including every member of the United Nations except Somalia, South

Sudan and the United States. Somalia's cabinet ministers had announced plans in late 2009 to ratify the treaty. Two optional protocols were adopted on 25 May 2000. The First Optional Protocol restricts the involvement of children in military conflicts, and the Second Optional Protocol prohibits the sale of children, child prostitution and child pornography. Both protocols have been ratified by more than 150 states.

A third optional protocol relating to communication of complaints was adopted in December 2011 and opened for signature on 28 February 2012.

The Convention deals with the child-specific needs and rights. It requires that states act in the best interests of the child. This approach is different from the common law approach found in many countries that had previously treated children as possessions or chattels, ownership of which was sometimes argued over in family disputes. In many jurisdictions, properly implementing the Convention requires an overhaul of child custody and guardianship laws, or, at the very least, a creative approach within the existing laws. The Convention acknowledges that every child has certain basic rights, including the right to life, his or her own name and identity, to be raised by his or her parents within a family or cultural grouping, and to have a relationship with both parents, even if they are separated.

The Convention obliges states to allow parents to exercise their parental responsibilities. The Convention also acknowledges that children have the right to express their opinions and to have those opinions heard and acted upon when appropriate, to be protected from abuse or exploitation, and to have their privacy protected, and it requires that their lives not be subject to excessive interference. The Convention also obliges signatory states to provide separate legal representation for a child in any judicial dispute concerning their care and asks that the child's viewpoint be heard in such cases. The Convention forbids capital punishment for children.

In its General Comment 8 (2006) the Committee on the Rights of the Child stated that there was an "obligation of all States parties to move quickly to prohibit and eliminate all corporal punishment and all other cruel or degrading forms of punishment of children". Article 19 of the Convention states that State Parties must "take all appropriate legislative, administrative, social and educational measures to protect the child from all forms of physical or mental violence", but it makes no reference to corporal punishment. The Committee's interpretation on this point has also been explicitly rejected by several States Party to the Convention, including Australia, Canada and the United Kingdom.

The European Court of Human Rights has made reference to the Convention when interpreting the European Convention on Human Rights.

STATES PARTY AND SIGNATORIES

Currently 193 countries have ratified, accepted, or acceded to it (some with stated reservations or interpretations) including every member of the United Nations except Somalia, South Sudan and the United States. Both Somalia and the United States have signed the document but have not ratified it. Somalia had announced in late 2009 that it would eventually do so.

Canada

Canada became a signatory to the Convention on 28 May 1990 and ratified in 1991. Prior to ratifying the treaty, Canada's laws were either largely or entirely in conformity with the treaty. Youth criminal laws in Canada underwent major changes resulting in the Youth Criminal Justice Act (YCJA) which went into effect on 1 April 2003. The Act specifically references Canada's different commitments under the Convention.

The convention was influential in the following administrative Law decision of *Baker v. Canada (Minister of Citizenship and Immigration).*

India

In India there is law that children under the age of 18 should not work but, there is no outright ban on child labor, and the practice is generally permitted in most industries except those deemed "hazardous". Although a law in October 2006 banned child labor in hotels, restaurants, and as domestic servants, there continues to be high demand for children as hired help in the home. Current estimates as to the number of child laborers in the country range from the government's conservative estimate of 12 million children under 13 years of age to the much higher estimates of children's rights activists, which hover around 60 million. Little is being done to address the problem since the economy is booming and the nuclear family is spreading, thereby increasing demand for child laborers.In India many people are still suffering from non-nutritious food, many parents are still leaving their children on riverside,in trains etc. Under the auspices of the Unicef financed Odisha initiative the Government of India is specifying the outline of a means of change and improvement in child care, and many trusts such as childLine, plannindia and savethechildren too are taking efforts to outdate child labour from India

Iran

Islamic Republic of Iran has adhered to the convention on 1991 and ratified it in the Parliament in 1994. Iran, however, has made the following reservation: "If the text of the Convention is or becomes incompatible with the domestic laws and Islamic standards at any time or in any case, the Government of the Islamic Republic shall not abide by it." Iran has also signed the both optional protocols which relate to the special protection of children against involvement in armed conflict and the sale of children and sexual exploitation.

Although the Islamic Republic of Iran is a state party to the Convention on the Rights of the Child, international human rights organisations and foreign governments routinely denounced executions of Iranian child offenders as a violation of the treaty. But on 10 February 2012 Iran's parliament changed the controversial law of executing juveniles. In the new law, the age of 18 (solar year) would be for both genders considered and juvenile offenders will be sentenced on a separate law than of adults." Based on the Islamic law which now seems to have been revised, girls at the age of 9 and boys at 15 of lunar year (11 days shorter than a solar year) were fully responsible for their crimes.

Ireland

The Republic of Ireland signed the Convention on the Rights of the Child on 30 September 1990 and ratified it, without reservation, on 28 September 1992. In response to criticisms expressed in the 1998 review by the UN Committee on the Rights of the Child in Geneva, the Irish government established the office of Ombudsman for Children and drew up a national children's strategy. In 2006, following concerns expressed by the committee that the wording of the Irish Constitution does not allow the State to intervene in cases of abuse other than in very exceptional cases, the Irish government undertook to amend the constitution to make a more explicit commitment to children's rights.

Israel

Israel ratified the Convention on the Rights of the Child in 1991. In 2010 UNICEF criticized Israel for its failure to create a government-appointed commission on children's rights or to adopt a national children's rights strategy or program in order to implement various Israeli laws addressing children's rights. The report criticizes Israel for holding that the Convention does not apply in the West Bank and for defining as Palestinians under the age of 16 in the occupied territories as children, even though Israeli law defines a child as being under 18, in line with the Convention. A contemporaneous report by the Organization for Economic Cooperation and Development found that Israel's investment in children is below the international average and the actual investment had fallen between 1995 and 2006. In 2012 the United Nations Committee on the Rights of the Child criticized Israel for its bombing attacks on Palestinians in the Gaza Strip, stating "Destruction of homes and damage to schools, streets and other public facilities gravely affect children" and called them "gross violations of the Convention on the Rights of the Child, its Optional Protocol on the involvement of children in armed conflict and international humanitarian law." It also criticized Palestinian rocket attacks from Gaza on southern Israel which traumatized Israeli children, calling on all parties to protect children.

New Zealand

New Zealand ratified the Convention on 6 April 1993 with reservations concerning the right to distinguish between persons according to the nature of their authority to be in New Zealand, the need for legislative action on economic exploitation - which it argued was adequately protected by existing law, and the provisions for the separation of juvenile offenders from adult offenders. In 1994, the Court of Appeal dismissed the suggestion that the Minister for Immigration and his department were at liberty to ignore the convention, arguing that this would imply that the country's adherence was 'at least partly window-dressing'.

The Children's Commissioner Act 2003 enhanced the office of Children's Commissioner, giving them significantly stronger investigative powers. In May 2007, New Zealand passed the Crimes (Substituted Section 59) Amendment Act 2007, which removed the defence of "reasonable force" for the purpose of correction. In its third and final vote parliament votes 113 to eight in favour of the legislation.

Saudi Arabia

Saudi Arabia ratified the Convention in 1996, with a reservation 'with respect to all such articles as are in conflict with the provisions of Islamic law' and considers it to be a valid source of domestic law. The Committee on the Rights of the Child, which reviewed Saudi Arabia's treatment of children under the Convention in January 2005, strongly condemned the government for its practice of imposing the death penalty on juveniles, calling it "a serious violation of the fundamental rights". The committee said it was "deeply alarmed" over the discretionary power judges hold to treat juveniles as adults: In its 2004 report the Saudi Arabia government had stated that it "never imposes capital punishment on persons... below the age of 18". The government delegation later acknowledged that a judge could impose the death penalty whenever he decided that the convicted person had reached his or her majority, regardless of the person's actual age at the time of the crime or at the time of the scheduled execution.

United Kingdom

The United Kingdom ratified the Convention on 16 December 1991, with several declarations and reservations, and made its first report to the Committee on the Rights of the Child in January 1995. Concerns raised by the Committee included the growth in child poverty and inequality, the extent of violence towards children, the use of custody for young offenders, the low age of criminal responsibility, and the lack of opportunities for children and young people to express views. The 2002 report of the Committee expressed similar concerns, including the welfare of children in custody, unequal treatment of asylum seekers, and the negative impact of poverty on children's rights. In September 2008 the UK government decided to give up its reservations and agree to the Convention in these respects.

The 2002 report's criticism of the legal defence of 'reasonable chastisement' of children by parents, which the Committee described as 'a serious violation of the dignity of the child', was rejected by the UK Government. The Minister for Children, Young People and Families commented that while fewer parents are using smacking as a form of discipline, the majority said they would not support a ban.

In evidence to the Parliamentary Joint Committee on Human Rights, the Committee was criticised by the Family Education Trust for "adopting radical interpretations of the UN Convention on the Rights of the Child in its pursuit of an agenda". The Joint Committee's report recommended that "the time has come for the Government to act upon the recommendations of the UN Committee on the Rights of the Child concerning the corporal punishment of children and the incompatibility of the defence of reasonable chastisement with its obligations under the Convention." The UK Government responded that "the use of physical punishment is a matter for individual parents to decide".

United States

The United States government played an active role in the drafting of the Convention and signed it on 16 February 1995, but has not ratified it, and will not be able in the near future because the Convention forbids both death sentences and life imprisonment for children. Along with Somalia and South Sudan (the most recent independent country), the United States is one of only three countries in the world which have not ratified the Convention. It has been claimed that opposition to the Convention stems primarily from political and religious conservatives. For example, the Heritage Foundation sees it as threatening national control over domestic policy and the Home School Legal Defense Association (HSLDA) argues that the CRC threatens homeschooling. President Barack Obama has described the failure to ratify the Convention as 'embarrassing' and had promised to review this.

The United States has signed and ratified two of the optional protocols to the Convention, the Optional Protocol on the Involvement of Children in Armed Conflict, and the Optional Protocol on the Sale of Children, Child Prostitution and Child Pornography.

Optional protocols

Two optional protocols were adopted by the UN General Assembly on 25 May 2000. The first, the Optional Protocol on the Involvement of Children in Armed Conflict, requires governments to ensure that children under the age of eighteen are not recruited compulsorily into their armed forces, and calls on governments to do everything feasible to ensure that members of their armed forces who are under eighteen years of age do not take part in hostilities. This protocol entered into force on 12 July 2002; currently, 151 states are party to the protocol and another 20 states have signed but not ratified it.

The second, the Optional Protocol on the Sale of Children, Child Prostitution and Child Pornography, requires states to prohibit the sale of children, child prostitution and child pornography. It entered into force on 18 January 2002; currently, 163 states are party to the protocol and another 13 states have signed but not ratified it.

A third, the Optional Protocol to the Convention on the Rights of the Child on a Communications Procedure, which would allow children or their representatives to file individual complaints for violation of the rights of children, was adopted in December 2011 and opened for signature on 28 February 2012. The protocol currently has 42 signatures and 8 ratifications: it will enter into force following the tenth ratification.

UNITED NATIONS CONVENTION AGAINST TORTURE

The Convention against Torture and Other Cruel, Inhuman or Degrading Treatment or Punishment (United Nations Convention against Torture) is an international human rights instrument, under the review of the United Nations, that aims to prevent torture and cruel, inhuman degrading treatment or punishment around the world.

The Convention requires states to take effective measures to prevent torture within their borders, and forbids states to transport people to any country where there is reason to believe they will be tortured.

The text of the Convention was adopted by the United Nations General Assembly on 10 December 1984 and, following ratification by the 20th state party, it came into force on 26 June 1987. 26 June is now recognised as the International Day in Support of Victims of Torture, in honour of the Convention. As of September 2013, the Convention has 154 state parties.

The Covenant follows the structure of the Universal Declaration of Human Rights (UDHR), International Covenant on Civil and Political Rights (ICCPR) and the International Covenant on Economic, Social and Cultural Rights (ICESCR), with a preamble and 33 articles, divided into three parts:

- Part I (Articles 1–16) defines torture (Article 1), and commits parties to taking effective measures to prevent any act of torture in any territory under their jurisdiction (Article 2). These include ensuring that torture is a criminal offense (Article 4), establishing jurisdiction over acts of torture committed by or against a party's citizens (Article 5), ensuring that torture is an extraditable offense (Article 8), and establishing universal jurisdiction to try cases of torture where an alleged torturer cannot be extradited (Article 5). Parties must promptly investigate any allegation of torture (Articles 12 and 13), and victims of torture must have an enforceable right to compensation (Article 14). Parties must also ban the use of evidence produced by torture in their courts (Article 15), and are barred from deporting, extraditing or refouling people where there are substantial grounds for believing they will be tortured (Article 3). Parties are also obliged to prevent other acts of cruel, inhuman or degrading treatment or punishment, and to investigate any allegation of such treatment within their jurisdiction (Article 16).

- Part II (articles 17 – 24) governs reporting and monitoring of the Convention and the steps taken by the parties to implement it. It establishes the Committee against Torture (Article 17), and empowers it to investigate allegations of systematic torture (Article 20). It also establishes an optional dispute-resolution mechanism between parties (Articles 21) and allows parties to recognize the competence of the Committee to hear complaints from individuals about violations of the Convention by a party (Article 22).
- Part III (Articles 25 – 33) governs ratification, entry into force, and amendment of the Convention. It also includes an optional arbitration mechanism for disputes between parties (Article 30).

MAIN PROVISIONS

Definition of torture

Article 1 of the Convention defines torture as:

- Any act by which severe pain or suffering, whether physical or mental, is intentionally inflicted on a person for such purposes as obtaining from him or a third person, information or a confession, punishing him for an act he or a third person has committed or is suspected of having committed, or intimidating or coercing him or a third person, or for any reason based on discrimination of any kind, when such pain or suffering is inflicted by or at the instigation of or with the consent or acquiescence of a public official or other person acting in an official capacity. It does not include pain or suffering arising only from, inherent in or incidental to lawful sanctions.— Convention Against Torture, Article 1.1

Actions which fall short of torture may still constitute cruel, inhuman or degrading treatment under Article 16.

Ban on torture and cruel and degrading treatment

Article 2 of the convention prohibits torture, and requires parties to take effective measures to prevent it in any territory under its jurisdiction. This prohibition is absolute and non-derogable. "No exceptional circumstances whatsoever" may be invoked to justify torture, including war, threat of war, internal political instability, public emergency, terrorist acts, violent crime, or any form of armed conflict. Torture cannot be justified as a means to protect public safety or prevent emergencies. Neither can it be justified by orders from superior officers or public officials. The prohibition on torture applies to all territories under a party's effective jurisdiction, and protects all people under its effective control, regardless of citizenship or how that control is exercised. Since the convention's entry into force, this absolute prohibition has become accepted as a principle of customary international law.

Because it is often difficult to distinguish between cruel, inhuman or degrading treatment and torture, the Committee regards Article 16's prohibition of such treatment as similarly absolute and non-derogable.

The other articles of part I lay out specific obligations intended to implement this absolute prohibition by preventing, investigating and punishing acts of torture.

Ban on *refoulement*

Article 3 prohibits parties from returning, extraditing or *refouling* any person to a state "where there are substantial grounds for believing that he would be in danger of being subjected to torture". The Committee against Torture has held that this danger must be assessed not just for the initial receiving state, but also to states to which the person may be subsequently expelled, returned or extradited.

OPTIONAL PROTOCOL

The Optional Protocol to the Convention against Torture and other Cruel, Inhuman or Degrading Treatment or Punishment (OPCAT), adopted by the General Assembly on 18 December 2002 and in force since 22 June 2006, provides for the establishment of "a system of regular visits undertaken by independent international and national bodies to places where people are deprived of their liberty, in order to prevent torture and other cruel, inhuman or degrading treatment or punishment," to be overseen by a Subcommittee on Prevention of Torture and Other Cruel, Inhuman or Degrading Treatment or Punishment.

COMMITTEE AGAINST TORTURE

The Committee against Torture (CAT) is a body of human rights experts that monitors implementation of the Convention by State parties. The Committee is one of eight UN-linked human rights treaty bodies. All state parties are obliged under the Convention to submit regular reports to the CAT on how rights are being implemented. Upon ratifying the Convention, states must submit a report within one year, after which they are obliged to report every four years. The Committee examines each report and addresses its concerns and recommendations to the State party in the form of "concluding observations." Under certain circumstances, the CAT may consider complaints or communications from individuals claiming that their rights under the Convention have been violated. The CAT usually meets in April/May and November each year in Geneva. Members are elected to four-year terms by State parties and can be re-elected if nominated.

INTERNATIONAL CONVENTION ON THE ELIMINATION OF ALL FORMS OF RACIAL DISCRIMINATION

The International Convention on the Elimination of All Forms of Racial Discrimination (ICERD) is a United Nations convention. A third-generation human rights instrument, the Convention commits its members to the elimination of racial discrimination and the promotion of understanding among all races. Controversially, the Convention also requires its parties to outlaw hate speech and criminalize membership in racist organizations.

The Convention also includes an individual complaints mechanism, effectively making it enforceable against its parties. This has led to the development of a limited jurisprudence on the interpretation and implementation of the Convention.

The convention was adopted and opened for signature by the United Nations General Assembly on 21 December 1965, and entered into force on 4 January 1969. As of September 2013, it has 87 signatories and 176 parties. The Convention is monitored by the Committee on the Elimination of Racial Discrimination (CERD).

In December 1960, following incidents of antisemitism in several parts of the world, the United Nations General Assembly adopted a resolution condemning "all manifestations and practices of racial, religious and national hatred" as violations of the United Nations Charter and Universal Declaration of Human Rights and calling on the governments of all states to "take all necessary measures to prevent all manifestations of racial, religious and national hatred". The Economic and Social Council followed this up by drafting a resolution on "manifestations of racial prejudice and national and religious intolerance", calling on governments to educate the public against intolerance and rescind discriminatory laws. Lack of time prevented this from being considered by the General Assembly in 1961, but it was passed the next year.

During the early debate on this resolution, African nations led by the Central African Republic, Chad, Dahomey, Guinea, Côte d'Ivoire, Mali, Mauritania, and Upper Volta pushed for more concrete action on the issue, in the form of an international convention against racial discrimination. Some nations preferred a declaration rather than a binding convention, while others wanted to deal with racial and religious intolerance in a single instrument. The eventual compromise, forced by the Arab nations' political opposition to treating religious intolerance at the same time as racial intolerance plus other nations' opinion that religious intolerance was less urgent, was for two resolutions, one calling for a declaration and draft convention aimed at eliminating racial discrimination, the other doing the same for religious intolerance.

The draft Declaration on the Elimination of All Forms of Racial Discrimination was adopted by the General Assembly on 20 November 1963. The same day the General Assembly called for the Economic and Social Council and the Commission on Human Rights to make the drafting of a Convention on the subject an absolute priority. The draft was completed by mid-1964, but delays in the General Assembly meant that it could not be adopted that year. It was finally adopted on 21 December 1965.

CORE PROVISIONS

Definition of "racial discrimination"

Article 1 of the Convention defines "racial discrimination" as

- ...any distinction, exclusion, restriction or preference based on race, colour, descent, or national or ethnic origin which has the purpose or effect of nullifying or impairing the recognition, enjoyment or exercise, on an equal footing, of human rights and fundamental freedoms in the political, economic, social, cultural or any other field of public life.

Distinctions made on the basis of citizenship (that is, between citizens and non-citizens) are specifically excluded from the definition, as are affirmative action policies and other measures taken to redress imbalances and promote equality.

This definition does not distinguish between discrimination based on ethnicity and discrimination based on race, in part because the distinction between the ethnicity and race remains debatable among anthropologists. The inclusion of descent specifically covers discrimination on the basis of caste and other forms of inherited status.

Discrimination need not be strictly based on race or ethnicity for the Convention to apply. Rather, whether a particular action or policy discriminates is judged by its effects.

- In seeking to determine whether an action has an effect contrary to the Convention, it will look to see whether that action has an unjustifiable disparate impact upon a group distinguished by race, colour, descent, or national or ethnic origin.

The question of whether an individual belongs to a particular racial group is to be decided, in the absence of justification to the contrary, by self-identification.

Prevention of discrimination

Article 2 of the Convention condemns racial discrimination and obliges parties to "undertake to pursue by all appropriate means and without delay a policy of eliminating racial discrimination in all its forms". It also obliges parties to promote understanding among all races. To achieve this, the Convention requires that signatories:

- Not practice racial discrimination in public institutions
- Not "sponsor, defend, or support" racial discrimination
- Review existing policies, and amend or revoke those that cause or perpetuate racial discrimination
- Prohibit "by all appropriate means, including legislation," racial discrimination by individuals and organisations within their jurisdictions
- Encourage groups, movements, and other means that eliminate barriers between races, and discourage racial division

Parties are obliged "when the circumstances so warrant" to use affirmative action policies for specific racial groups to guarantee "the full and equal enjoyment of human rights and fundamental freedoms". However, these measures must be finite, and "shall in no case entail as a consequence the maintenance of unequal or separate rights for different racial groups after the objectives for which they were taken have been achieved".

Article 5 expands upon the general obligation of Article 2 and creates a specific obligation to guarantee the right of everyone to equality before the law regardless of "race, colour, or national or ethnic origin". It further lists specific rights this equality must apply to: equal treatment by courts and tribunals, security of the person and freedom from violence, the civil and political rights affirmed in the ICCPR, the economic, social and cultural rights affirmed in the ICESCR, and the right of access to any place or service used by the general public, "such as transport hotels, restaurants, cafes, theatres and parks." This list is not exhaustive, and the obligation extends to all human rights. Article 6 obliges parties to provide "effective protection and remedies" through the courts or other institutions for any act of racial discrimination. This includes a right to a legal remedy and damages for injury suffered due to discrimination.

Condemnation of apartheid

Article 3 condemns apartheid and racial segregation and obliges parties to "prevent, prohibit and eradicate" these practices in territories under their jurisdiction. This article has since been strengthened by the recognition of apartheid as a crime against humanity in the Rome Statute of the International Criminal Court.

The Committee on the Elimination of Racial Discrimination regards this article as also entailing an obligation to eradicate the consequences of past policies of segregation, and to prevent racial segregation arising from the actions of private individuals.

Prohibition of incitement

Article 4 of the Convention condemns propaganda and organizations that attempt to justify discrimination or are based on the idea of racial supremacism. It obliges parties, "with due regard to the principles embodied in the Universal Declaration of Human Rights", to adopt "immediate and positive measures" to eradicate these forms of incitement and discrimination. Specifically, it obliges parties to criminalize hate speech, hate crimes and the financing of racist activities, and to prohibit and criminalize membership in organizations that "promote and incite" racial discrimination. A number of parties have reservations on this article, and interpret it as not permitting or requiring measures that infringe on the freedoms of speech, association or assembly.

The Committee on the Elimination of Racial Discrimination regards this article as a mandatory obligation of parties to the Convention, and has repeatedly criticized parties for failing to abide by it. It regards the obligation as consistent with the freedoms of opinion and expression affirmed in the UNDHR and ICCPR and notes that the latter specifically outlaws inciting racial discrimination, hatred and violence. It views the provisions as necessary to prevent organised racial violence and the "political exploitation of ethnic difference."

Promotion of tolerance

Article 7 obliges parties to adopt "immediate and effective measures", particularly in education, to combat racial prejudice and encourage understanding and tolerance between different racial, ethnic and national groups.

Dispute resolution mechanism

Articles 11 through 13 of the Convention establish a dispute resolution mechanism between parties. A party that believes another party is not implementing the Convention may complain to the Committee on the Elimination of Racial Discrimination. The Committee will pass on the complaint, and if it is not resolved between the two parties, may establish an ad hoc Conciliation Commission to investigate and make recommendations on the matter. This procedure has never been used.

Article 22 further allows any dispute over the interpretation or application of the Convention to be referred to the International Court of Justice. This clause has been invoked only once, by Georgia against Russia.

Individual complaints mechanism

Article 14 of the Convention establishes an individual complaints mechanism similar to that of the First Optional Protocol to the International Covenant on Civil and Political Rights, Optional Protocol to the Convention on the Rights of Persons with Disabilities and Optional Protocol to the Convention on the Elimination of All Forms of Discrimination against Women. Parties may at any time recognise the competence of the Committee on the Elimination of Racial Discrimination to consider complaints from individuals or groups who claim their rights under the Convention have been violated. Such parties may establish local bodies to hear complaints before they are passed on. Complainants must have exhausted all domestic remedies, and anonymous complaints and complaints that refer to events that occurred before the country concerned joined the Optional Protocol are not permitted. The Committee can request information from and make recommendations to a party.

The individual complaints mechanism came into operation in 1982, after it had been accepted by ten states-parties. As of 2010, 58 states had recognised the competence of the Committee, and 54 cases have been dealt with by the Committee.

RESERVATIONS

A number of parties have made reservations and interpretative declarations to their application of the Convention. The Convention text forbids reservations "incompatible with the object and purpose of this Convention" or that would inhibit the operation of any body established by it. A reservation is considered incompatible or inhibitive if two-thirds of parties object to it.

Article 22

Afghanistan, Bahrain, China, Cuba, Egypt, Equatorial Guinea, India, Indonesia, Iraq, Israel, Kuwait, Lebanon, Libya, Madagascar, Morocco, Mozambique, Nepal, Saudi Arabia, Syria, Thailand, Turkey, Vietnam, and Yemen do not consider themselves bound by Article 22. Some interpret this article as allowing disputes to be referred to the International Court of Justice only with the consent of all involved parties.

Obligations beyond existing constitution

Antigua and Barbuda, the Bahamas, Barbados, Guyana, Jamaica, Nepal, Papua New Guinea, Thailand and United States interpret the Convention as not implying any obligations beyond the limits of their existing constitutions.

Hate speech

Austria, Belgium, France, Ireland, Italy, Japan, Malta, Monaco, Switzerland and Tonga all interpret Article 4 as not permitting or requiring measures that threaten the freedoms of speech, opinion, association, and assembly. Antigua and Barbuda, the Bahamas, Barbados, Fiji, Nepal, Papua New Guinea, Thailand and United Kingdom interpret the Convention as creating an obligation to enact measures against hate speech and hate crimes only when a need arises. The United States of America does not accept any obligation to enact measures under Article 4, which it views as incompatible with freedom of expression.

Immigration

Monaco and Switzerland reserve the right to apply their own legal principles on the entry of foreigners into their labour markets. The United Kingdom does not regard the Commonwealth Immigrants Act 1962 and Commonwealth Immigrants Act 1968 as constituting any form of racial discrimination.

Indigenous people

Tonga reserves the right not to apply the Convention to any restriction on the alienation of land held by indigenous Tongans. Fiji has significant reservations around Article 5, and reserves the right not to implement those provisions if they are incompatible with existing law on voting rights, the alienation of land by indigenous Fijians.

JURISPRUDENCE

The individual complaints mechanism has led to a limited jurisprudence on the interpretation and implementation of the Convention. So far 45 complaints have been registered with the Committee; 17 of these have been deemed inadmissible, 14 have led to a finding of no violation, and in 10 cases a party has been found to have violated the Convention. Four cases are still pending.

Several cases have dealt with the treatment of Romani people in Eastern Europe. In *Koptova v. Slovakia* the Committee found that resolutions by several villages in Slovakia forbidding the residence of Roma were discriminatory and restricted freedom of movement and residence, and recommended the Slovak government take steps to end such practices. In *L.R. v. Slovakia* the Committee found that the Slovak government had failed to provide an effective remedy for discrimination suffered by Roma after the cancellation of a housing project on ethnic grounds. In *Durmic v. Serbia and Montenegro* the Committee found a systemic failure by the Serbian government to investigate and prosecute discrimination against Roma in access to public places.

In several cases, notably *L.K. v. Netherlands* and *Gelle v. Denmark*, the Committee has criticized parties for their failure to adequately prosecute acts of racial discrimination or incitement. In both cases, the Committee refused to accept "any claim that the enactment of law making racial discrimination a criminal act in itself represents full compliance with the obligations of States parties under the Convention". Such laws "must also be effectively implemented by the competent national tribunals and other State institutions".

While the Committee accepts the discretion of prosecutors on whether or not to lay charges, this discretion "should be applied in each case of alleged racial discrimination in the light of the guarantees laid down in the Convention"

In The Jewish community of Oslo et al. v. Norway, the Committee found that the prohibition of hate speech was compatible with freedom of speech, and that the acquittal of a neo-Nazi leader by the Supreme Court of Norway on freedom of speech grounds was a violation of the Convention.

In *Hagan v. Australia,* the Committee ruled that, while not originally intended to demean anyone, the name of the "E. S. 'Nigger' Brown Stand" (named in honour of 1920s rugby league player Edward Stanley Brown) at a Toowoomba sports field was racially offensive and should be removed.

IMPACT

The impact of an international treaty can be measured in two ways: by its acceptance, and by its implementation. On the first measure, the Convention has gained near-universal acceptance by the international community, with fewer than twenty (mostly small) states yet to become parties. Most major states have also accepted the Convention's individual complaints mechanism, signaling a strong desire to be bound by the Convention's provisions.

On the second measure, the Convention has had a significant impact on national legislation, with many states adopting legislation outlawing racial discrimination by the state, in the workplace, or in the provision of services such as housing and education. Such legislation may be either civil or criminal. Examples of the former include the Race Relations Act 1971 (New Zealand), Racial Discrimination Act 1975 (Australia), Race Relations Act 1976 (UK), and Canadian Human Rights Act (Canada). Criminal provisions are used in Belgium, Denmark, France, Italy, Norway and Portugal. Despite reservations to the Convention, most western European nations have criminalized the incitement of racial hatred.

The Convention has faced persistent problems with reporting since its inception, with parties frequently failing to report fully, or even at all. As of 2008, twenty parties had failed to report for more than ten years, and thirty parties had failed to report for more than five. One party, Sierra Leone, had failed to report since 1976, while two more – Liberia and Saint Lucia had never met their reporting requirements under the Convention. The Committee has responded to this persistent failure to report by reviewing the late parties anyway – a strategy that has produced some success in gaining compliance with reporting requirements.

This lack of reporting is seen by some as a significant failure of the Convention. However the reporting system has also been praised as providing "a permanent stimulus inducing individual States to enact anti-racist legislation or amend the existing one when necessary."

COMMITTEE ON THE ELIMINATION OF RACIAL DISCRIMINATION

The Committee on the Elimination of Racial Discrimination is a body of human rights experts tasked with monitoring the implementation of the Convention. It consists of 18 independent human rights experts, elected for four-year terms, with half the members elected every two years. Members are elected by secret ballot of the parties, with each party allowed to nominate one of its nationals to the Committee.

All parties are required to submit regular reports to the Committee outlining the legislative, judicial, policy and other measures they have taken to give effect to the Convention. The first report is due within a year of the Convention entering into effect for that state; thereafter reports are due every two years or whenever the Committee requests. The Committee examines each report and addresses its concerns and recommendations to the state party in the form of "concluding observations". The Committee typically meets every March and August in Geneva.

CONVENTION ON THE ELIMINATION OF ALL FORMS OF DISCRIMINATION AGAINST WOMEN

The Convention on the Elimination of all Forms of Discrimination against Women (CEDAW) is an international treaty adopted in 1979 by the United Nations General Assembly. Described as an international bill of rights for women, it came into force on 3 September 1981. Over fifty countries that have ratified the Convention have done so subject to certain declarations, reservations, and objections, including 38 countries who rejected the enforcement article 29, which addresses means of settlement for disputes concerning the interpretation or application of the Convention. Australia's declaration noted the limitations on central government power resulting from its federal constitutional system. The United States and Palau have signed, but not yet ratified the treaty. The Holy See, Iran, Somalia, South Sudan, Sudan and Tonga are not signatories to CEDAW.

THE CONVENTION

The Convention defines discrimination against women in the following terms:

- Any distinction, exclusion or restriction made on the basis of sex which has the effect or purpose of impairing or nullifying the recognition, enjoyment or exercise by women, irrespective of their marital status, on a basis of equality of men and women, of human rights and fundamental freedoms in the political, economic, social, cultural, civil or any other field.

It also establishes an agenda of action for putting an end to sex-based discrimination: States must take measures to seek to eliminate prejudices and customs based on the idea of the inferiority or the superiority of one sex or on stereotyped role for men and women. States ratifying the Convention are required to enshrine gender equality into their domestic legislation, repeal all discriminatory provisions in their laws, and enact new provisions to guard against discrimination against women. However, special protection for maternity is not regarded as gender discrimination (Article 4). Appropriate measures, including legislation, to suppress all forms of trafficking in women and forced prostitution are also not regarded as gender discrimination (Article 6). Equal opportunity in education for female students is required, and coeducation is encouraged. (Article 10). States ratifying the Convention must also establish tribunals and public institutions to guarantee women effective protection against discrimination, and take steps to eliminate all forms of discrimination practiced against women by individuals, organizations, and enterprises (Article 2,(e)).

CEDAW WITH UNSCR 1325 AND 1820

Resolutions 1325 10th anniversary events highlight use of CEDAW mechanisms

- The 10th anniversary of Resolution 1325 in October 2010 highlighted the increasing demand for accountability to UN Security Council Resolution 1325 on Women, Peace and Security. Many expressed concern about the fact that only 22 Member States out of 192 have adopted national action plans. Women are still underrepresented if not totally absent in most official peace negotiations and sexual violence in conflict continue to increase.

These realities emphasized the need to use other legal mechanisms to strengthen the implementation of SCR 1325, particularly CEDAW. The well-established mechanisms of CEDAW – the Member States compliance report and the civil society shadow reporting process were cited as powerful instruments to ensure accountability.

Several regional and international meetings including the High Level Seminar "1325 in 2020: Looking Forward...Looking Back," organized by the African Center for the Constructive Resolution of Disputes, and the "Stockholm International Conference 10 years with 1325 – What now?" called for the use of CEDAW to improve 1325 implementation.

Intersection between SCR 1325 and CEDAW

- While CEDAW and UN Security Council Resolutions 1325 and 1820 on Women, Peace and Security are important international instruments on their own, there is also an intersection among the three standards that can be used to enhance their implementation and impact.

Resolutions 1325 and 1820 broaden the scope of CEDAW application by clarifying its relevance to all parties in conflict, whereas CEDAW provides concrete strategic guidance for actions to be taken on the broad commitments outlined in the two Resolutions (UNIFEM, 2006. CEDAW and SCR 1325: A Quick Guide). CEDAW is a global human rights treaty that should be incorporated into national law as the highest standard for women's rights. It requires UN Member States that have ratified it (185 to date) to set in place mechanisms to fully realize women's rights.

Resolution 1325 is an international law unanimously adopted by the Security Council that mandates UN Member States to engage women in all aspects of peace building including ensuring women's participation on all levels of decision–making on peace and security issues. Resolution 1820 links sexual violence as a tactic of war with the maintenance of international peace and security. It also demands a comprehensive report from the UN Secretary General on implementation and strategies for improving information flow to the Security Council; and adoption of concrete protection and prevention measures to end sexual violence. Resolutions 1325 and 1820, and CEDAW share the following agenda on women's human rights and gender equality:

- Demand women's participation in decision-making at all levels
- Rejection of violence against women as it impedes the advancement of women and maintains their subordinate status
- Equality of women and men under the law; protection of women and girls through the rule of law
- Demand security forces and systems to protect women and girls from gender-based violence
- Recognition of the fact that distinct experiences and burdens of women and girls come from systemic discrimination
- Ensure that women's experiences, needs and perspectives are incorporated into the political, legal and social decisions that determine the achievement of just and lasting peace

A General Comment from the CEDAW committee could strengthen women's advocacy for the full implementation of Resolutions 1325 and 1820 at the country and community levels. Conversely, CEDAW's relevance to conflict-affected areas will be underscored further by the two Resolutions. In other words, all three international instruments will reinforce each other and be much more effective if used together in leveraging women's human rights.

MEMBERS AND RATIFICATION

The seven UN member states that have not ratified or acceded to the convention are Iran, Palau, Somalia, South Sudan, Sudan, Tonga, and the United States. The one UN non-member state that had not acceded to the convention is the Holy See/Vatican City. The Republic of China (Taiwan) in 2007 has also ratified the treaty in its legislature, but is unrecognized by the United Nations and is a party to the treaty only unofficially. The latest state to have acceded the convention was Nauru on 23 June 2011.

COMMITTEE ON THE ELIMINATION OF DISCRIMINATION AGAINST WOMEN

The Committee on the Elimination of Discrimination Against Women is the United Nations (U.N.) treaty body that oversees the Convention on the Elimination of All Forms of Discrimination Against Women (CEDAW). The formation of this committee was outlined in Article 17 of the CEDAW, which also established the rules, purpose, and operating procedures of the committee. Throughout its years of operation the committee has held multiple sessions to ensure the rules outlined in the CEDAW are being followed. Over time the practices of the committee have evolved due to an increased focus on women's rights issues.

History of the committee

The Committee on the Elimination of Discrimination Against Women was formed on 3 September 1981 after the CEDAW received the 20 ratifications required for it to enter into force. Article 17 of the CEDAW established the committee in order to ensure that the provisions of the CEDAW were followed by the countries that had signed and agreed to be bound by it. The first regular session of the committee was held from 18–22 October 1982. In this session the first officers of the committee were elected by simple majority, with Ms. L. Ider of Mongolia becoming chairperson. Other officers elected were three vice chairpersons: Ms. M. Caron of Canada, Ms. Z. Ilic of Yugoslavia and Ms. L. Mukayiranga of Rwanda. The final officer elected was Ms. D. P. Bernard of Guyana as rapporteur of the committee. During this session the committee also unanimously approved to adopt its rules of procedure.

Sessions

The rules regarding where and when the committee can hold sessions are laid out in their rules of procedure.

The committee is allowed to hold as many meetings as are required to perform their duties effectively, with the states party to the CEDAW and the Secretary-General of the United Nations authorizing the number of regular sessions held. In addition, special sessions can be held at the request of either a state party to the convention or the majority of the members serving on the committee. Fifty-three sessions have been held to date, with the most recent taking place from 1 October 2012 to 19 October 2012. The first thirty-nine sessions were held at the United Nations headquarters building in New York City, with the fortieth session and alternating sessions following it held in the Palais des Nations in Geneva. During each of its regular sessions the committee hears reports from states party to the CEDAW on their progress in adhering to CEDAW and implementing its ideas in their countries. The committee also holds pre-sessional work groups to discuss the issues and questions that the committee should deal with during the following session.

Reports

Under article 18 of the CEDAW states must report to the committee on the progress they have made in implementing the CEDAW within their state. As most of the information the committee works with comes from these reports, guidelines have been developed to help states prepare accurate and useful reports. Initial reports discussing the current picture of discrimination against women in the reporting states are required to specifically deal with each article of the CEDAW, and consist of no more than one-hundred pages. States are required to prepare and present these initial reports within one year of ratifying the CEDAW. Periodic reports detailing the state's progress in adhering to the articles of the CEDAW should be no more than seventy-five pages in length and should focus on the specific period of time since the state's last report. States party to the CEDAW are typically required to provide periodic reports every four years, but if the committee is concerned about the situation in that state they can request a report at any time.

The committee chooses which reports to address by considering factors such as the amount of time the report has been pending, whether the report is initial or periodic (with more priority given to initial reports), and from which region the report originates. Eight states are invited to give their reports during each session and it is required a representative from the state is in attendance when the report is presented. The committee focuses on constructive dialogue when a report is presented, and appreciates careful time management on the part of the state presenting its report. Due to the high backlog of overdue reports the committee has encouraged states to combine all of their outstanding reports into one document, and sends reminders to states who have reports five years overdue. The CEDAW also requires that the committee provide an annual report that includes its activities, comments relating to the reports provided by states, information relating to the Optional Protocol of the CEDAW, and any other general suggestions or recommendations the committee has made. This report is given to the United Nations General Assembly through the Economic and Social Council. All reports, agendas and other official documents pertaining to the committee, including the reports provided by the states, are provided to the public unless otherwise decided by the committee.

General Recommendations

Along with issuing its annual report and offering advice to reporting states, the committee has the ability to issue general recommendations that elaborate on its views of the obligations imposed by CEDAW. To date, the committee has issued twenty-five general recommendations, the latest dealing with the committee's interpretation of the CEDAW's obligations relating to women's role in public life, and women's access to healthcare. The recommendations issued by the committee in its first decade were short and dealt mainly with the content of states' reports and reservations to the convention. Since 1991, however, recommendations have been focused on guiding states' application of the CEDAW in specific situations. The formulation of a general recommendation begins with dialogue between the committee on the topic in the recommendation with various non-governmental organizations and other U.N. bodies. The recommendation is then drafted by a member of the committee and discussed and revised in the next session, and finally adopted in the following session.

Changes in the committee

For the first ten years it operated the committee operated significantly differently than it does now. The only form of censure given to the committee by the CEDAW was their general recommendations and concluding comments following a report. Due to the emergence of the Global Campaign for Women's Human Rights in 1991 more attention was given to the CEDAW, reviving the committee. The committee made changes to the CEDAW that allowed it to meet more than once a year, and have taken advantage of this by meeting at least twice a year since 1997. The committee originally only met for two weeks in its annual sessions, but that has now been changed to meeting multiple times a year in eighteen day sessions. CEDAW also gained new complaint and inquiry proceedings allowing the committee to initiate inquiry proceedings if it believes a state is in severe violation of the articles of the CEDAW.

Recommendations for improvement

Despite evolving since the committee was first formed, members believe there are ways in which the committee can better meet the goals outlined in the CEDAW. One of the committee's main goals moving forward is expanding its information base, allowing it to more effectively deal with issues that arise concerning the CEDAW. The committee is authorized in Article 22 of the CEDAW to invite specialized U.N. agencies such as the United Nations Development Programme to deliver reports discussing women's rights issues in the state under discussion. Another method for gathering information is requesting reports from non-governmental organizations dealing with discrimination against women that are operating in the country under discussion. This is recommended to insure that the committee is receiving the full, unbiased picture of affairs within the reporting state.

Another recommendation for improvement involves interpreting and clarifying the language used in the CEDAW in order to make the document as useful as it can be. A third improvement that has been suggested is improving the efficiency of the committee. Due to the backlog in reports faced by the committee it has been suggested that the government officials who prepare reports presented to the committee should be trained, in order to make all reports uniform and more easily processed. A final suggestion for improvement is the implementation of a right of petition in the CEDAW, allowing the committee to hear complaints from citizens of a state against the state, increasing the committee's strength and direct impact on the problem of discrimination against women.

Languages

The official languages of the committee are English, Arabic, French, Russian, and Spanish, with any statement made in one of the official languages translated into the other four. A speaker who does not speak one of the official languages provides a translator. All formal decisions and documents issued by the committee are provided in each of the official languages. The original rules of procedure adopted by the committee did not include Arabic as an official language, but the rule was amended in the committees second session to include Arabic.

Members and Officers of the Committee

Twenty-three members serve on the committee, described as experts for their experience and expertise in women's issues. The members are nominated by their national governments and elected through a secret ballot by states party to the convention. Upon winning the election and taking up their responsibilities the members of the committee recite the following statement, known as the solemn declaration, "I solemnly declare that I shall perform my duties and exercise powers as a member of the Committee on the Elimination of Discrimination against Women honourably, faithfully, impartially and conscientiously".

The members come from a wide range of occupations including doctors, lawyers, diplomats and educators, providing various viewpoints to the committee due to their diversity. Many members continue to hold full-time jobs outside of the committee and receive little monetary payment for their work on the committee.

To insure that the nationality of members encompasses all the diverse states who have signed the CEDAW, members are elected according to regions divided into Latin America and the Caribbean, Africa, Asia, Western Europe, and Eastern Europe. The members of the committee differ from those of other treaty bodies of the United Nations in that they have all been women with only one exception.

In the event a member of the committee is unable to continue serving on the committee before her term is up the state that had nominated the resigning member shall nominate another expert from their country to fill in her seat. Committee members and experts also attend an annual luncheon, hosted by the NGO Committee on the Status of Women, NY (NGO CSW/NY), where key issues are discusses and the efforts of the committee are honored.

Officers of the Committee

The officers of the committee are composed of a chairperson, three vice-chairpersons and a rapporteur. Officers of the committee are nominated by another member of the committee, as opposed to a government which nominates members for the committee. All officers are elected by majority vote to a two-year term of office, and remain eligible for re-election after their term expires. The chairperson's duties include declaring a meeting to be open or closed, directing the discussion in a session, announcing decisions made by the committee, preparing agendas in consultation with the secretary-general, designating the members of pre-sessional working groups and representing the committee at United Nations meetings which the committee is invited to participate in. In the case the chairperson is unable to perform any her duties she designates one of the three vice-chairpersons to take over her role. If the chairperson fails to designate a vice-chairperson prior to her absence then the vice-chairperson with the first name in English alphabetical order takes over. In the event an officer is unable to continue serving on the committee before her term expires a new officer from the same region as the original officer shall be nominated, elected and will take over the vacated office.

OPTIONAL PROTOCOL

The Optional Protocol to the Convention on the Elimination of All Forms of Discrimination against Women is a side-agreement to the Convention which allows its parties to recognise the competence of the Committee on the Elimination of Discrimination against Women to consider complaints from individuals. The Optional Protocol was adopted by the UN General Assembly on 6 October 1999 and entered into force on 22 December 2000. Currently it has 80 signatories and 104 parties.

CONTROVERSY

In an article in *Moment* magazine in February 2011, Paula Kweskin, in discussing so-called "honor" killings taking place in the Palestinian Authority, writes that two-thirds of all murders in the Palestinian Authority and Gaza are "honor" killings. These crimes go unpunished and laws grant impunity to those who kill based on "family honor." In interviews and press releases on their websites, many NGOs, including Badil, the Palestinian Center for Human Rights, and the Women's Center for Legal Aid and Counseling, have decried "honor" killings and the lack of legal protection for Palestinian women; yet these NGOs are silent when given a forum at CEDAW to address these problems.

The CEDAW has been controversial for statements that have been made by some of its members which were seen by a number of states and NGOs as promoting Western-style feminism. Often referenced is a 2000 report which said that in Belarus, "the Committee is concerned by the continuing prevalence of sex-role stereotypes and by the reintroduction of such symbols as a Mothers' Day and a Mothers' Award, which it sees as encouraging women's traditional roles." Other controversial positions of CEDAW include supporting the decriminalization of prostitution in specific countries, criticizing Slovenia because only 30 per cent of children are in daycare, and pressuring numerous states to decriminalize abortion. Other requests are seen by groups as a backdoor to forcing states parties to adopt an Equal Rights Amendment or comparable national legislation, which is seen as a violation of the CEDAW treaty mandate and the sovereignty of states parties.

More recently, the controversy concerning CEDAW has centered around the question of easy access to abortion and contraception. According to C-FAM (the Catholic Family and Human Rights Institute), at UN meetings officials pressed the delegation from Slovakia to liberalize its abortion laws and to inaugurate campaigns encouraging contraceptive use and "reproductive health awareness".

UNITED NATIONS CONVENTION ON THE PROTECTION OF THE RIGHTS OF ALL MIGRANT WORKERS AND MEMBERS OF THEIR FAMILIES

The United Nations International Convention on the Protection of the Rights of All Migrant Workers and Members of Their Families is an international agreement governing the protection of migrant workers and families. Signed on 18 December 1990, it entered into force on 1 July 2003 after the threshold of 20 ratifying States was reached in March 2003. The Committee on Migrant Workers (CMW) monitors implementation of the convention, and is one of the seven UN-linked human rights treaty bodies.

In 2005, the number of international migrants was between 185 and 192 million. This represents approximately three per cent of the world population, comparable to the population of Brazil. Nearly all countries are concerned by migration, whether as sending, transit, or receiving countries, or as a combination of these. International migration has become an intrinsic feature of globalization.

"It is time to take a more comprehensive look at the various dimensions of the migration issue, which now involves hundreds of millions of people, and affects countries of origin, transit and destination. We need to understand better the causes of international flows of people and their complex interrelationship with development." United Nations Secretary General, Kofi Annan, from his report on strengthening the Organization, 9 November 2002.

The United Nations Convention constitutes a comprehensive international treaty regarding the protection of migrant workers' rights. It emphasizes the connection between migration and human rights, which is increasingly becoming a crucial policy topic worldwide. The Convention aims at protecting migrant workers and members of their families; its existence sets a moral standard, and serves as a guide and stimulus for the promotion of migrant rights in each country.

In the *Preamble,* the Convention recalls conventions by International Labour Organisation on migrant workers: Migration for Employment Convention (Revised), 1949, Migrant Workers (Supplementary Provisions) Convention, 1975 and on forced labour; Forced Labour Convention and Abolition of Forced Labour Convention as well as international human rights treaties including Convention against Discrimination in Education.

The primary objective of the Convention is to foster respect for migrants' human rights. Migrants are not only workers, they are also human beings. The Convention does not create new rights for migrants but aims at guaranteeing equality of treatment, and the same working conditions for migrants and nationals. The Convention innovates because it relies on the fundamental notion that all migrants should have access to a minimum degree of protection. The Convention recognizes that legal migrants have the legitimacy to claim more rights than undocumented migrants, but it stresses that undocumented migrants must see their fundamental human rights respected, like all human beings.

In the meantime, the Convention proposes that actions be taken to eradicate clandestine movements, notably through the fight against misleading information inciting people to migrate irregularly, and through sanctions against traffickers and employers of undocumented migrants.

Article 7 of this Convention protects the rights of migrant workers and their families regardless of "sex, race, colour, language, religion or conviction, political or other opinion, national, ethnic or social origin, nationality, age, economic position, property, marital status, birth, or other status". This Convention is also recalled by the Convention on the Rights of Persons with Disabilities at the Preamble.

STATE OF RATIFICATIONS AND SIGNATURES

The Convention required a minimum of 20 ratifications before it could enter into force. When El Salvador and Guatemala ratified it on 14 March 2003, this threshold was reached.

The following 47 states have ratified the Convention as of September 2013: Albania, Argentina, Algeria, Azerbaijan, Bangladesh, Belize, Bolivia, Bosnia and Herzegovina, Burkina Faso, Cape Verde, Chile, Colombia, East Timor, Ecuador, Egypt, El Salvador, Ghana, Guatemala, Guyana, Guinea, Honduras, Indonesia, Jamaica, Kyrgyzstan, Lesotho, Libya, Mali, Mauritania, Mexico, Morocco, Mozambique, Nicaragua, Niger, Nigeria, Paraguay, Peru, Philippines, Rwanda, Senegal, Seychelles, Sri Lanka, Saint Vincent and the Grenadines, Syria, Tajikistan, Turkey, Uganda and Uruguay. In addition, several countries have signed the Convention but not yet ratified it. (This means that their government has expressed the intention of adhering to the Convention but is not yet bound to do so at international law.) These countries are: Armenia, Benin, Cambodia, Cameroon, Chad Comoros, Republic of the Congo, Gabon, Guinea-Bissau, Liberia, Palau, São Tomé and Príncipe, Serbia and Montenegro (now applies to Serbia and Montenegro), Sierra Leone, Togo, and Venezuela.

So far, countries that have ratified the Convention are primarily countries of origin of migrants (such as Mexico, Morocco and the Philippines). For these countries, the Convention is an important vehicle to protect their citizens living abroad. In the Philippines, for example, ratification of the Convention took place in a context characterized by several cases of Filipino workers being mistreated abroad: such cases hurt the Filipino population and prompted the ratification of the Convention. However, these countries are also transit and destination countries, and the Convention delineates their responsibility to protect the rights of migrants on their territory.

No migrant-receiving State in Western Europe or North America has ratified the Convention. Other important receiving countries, such as Australia, Arab states of the Persian Gulf, India and South Africa have not ratified the Convention.

GENOCIDE CONVENTION

The Convention on the Prevention and Punishment of the Crime of Genocide was adopted by the United Nations General Assembly on 9 December 1948 as General Assembly Resolution 260. The Convention entered into force on 12 January 1951. It defines genocide in legal terms, and is the culmination of years of campaigning by lawyer Raphael Lemkin. Yair Auron writes "When Raphael Lemkin coined the word genocide in 1944 he cited the 1915 annihilation of Armenians as a seminal example of genocide." All participating countries are advised to prevent and punish actions of genocide in war and in peacetime. The number of states that have ratified the convention is currently 143.

DEFINITION OF GENOCIDE

Article 2 of the Convention defines genocide as:

- ...any of the following acts committed with intent to destroy, in whole or in part, a national, ethnical, racial or religious group, as such:
  - Killing members of the group;
  - Causing serious bodily or mental harm to members of the group;
  - Deliberately inflicting on the group conditions of life calculated to bring about its physical destruction in whole or in part;
  - Imposing measures intended to prevent births within the group;
  - Forcibly transferring children of the group to another group.

Article 3 defines the crimes that can be punished under the convention:

- Genocide;
- Conspiracy to commit genocide;
- Direct and public incitement to commit genocide;
- Attempt to commit genocide;
- Complicity in genocide.

The convention was passed to outlaw actions similar to the Holocaust by Nazi Germany during World War II. The first draft of the Convention included political killings, but the USSR along with some other nations would not accept that actions against groups identified as holding similar political opinions or social status would constitute genocide, so these stipulations were subsequently removed in a political and diplomatic compromise.

PARTIES

Provisos granting immunity from prosecution for genocide without its consent were made by Bahrain, Bangladesh, India, Malaysia, the Philippines, Singapore, the United States, Vietnam, Yemen, and Yugoslavia. Prior to its ratification of the convention, the United States Senate was treated to a speech by Senator William Proxmire in favor of this treaty every day that the Senate was in session between 1967 and 1986.

Reservations

Immunity from prosecutions

- Persons charged with genocide or any of the other acts enumerated in article III shall be tried by a competent tribunal of the State in the territory of which the act was committed, or by such international penal tribunal as may have jurisdiction with respect to those Contracting Parties which shall have accepted its jurisdiction.— Convention on the Prevention and Punishment of the Crime of Genocide, Article 6
- Any Contracting Party may call upon the competent organs of the United Nations to take such action under the Charter of the United Nations as they consider appropriate for the prevention and suppression of acts of genocide or any of the other acts enumerated in article III.— Convention on the Prevention and Punishment of the Crime of Genocide, Article 8
- Disputes between the Contracting Parties relating to the interpretation, application or fulfilment of the present Convention, including those relating to the responsibility of a State for genocide or for any of the other acts enumerated in article III, shall be submitted to the International Court of Justice at the request of any of the parties to the dispute.— Convention on the Prevention and Punishment of the Crime of Genocide, Article 9

BREACHES

Rwanda

The first time that the 1948 law was enforced occurred on 2 September 1998 when the International Criminal Tribunal for Rwanda found Jean-Paul Akayesu, the former mayor of a small town in Rwanda, guilty of nine counts of genocide. The lead prosecutor in this case was Pierre-Richard Prosper. Two days later, Jean Kambanda became the first head of government to be convicted of genocide.

Yugoslavia

The first state to be found in breach of the Genocide convention was Serbia. In the *Bosnia and Herzegovina v. Serbia and Montenegro* case the International Court of Justice presented its judgment on 26 February 2007. It cleared Serbia of direct involvement in genocide during the Bosnian war, but ruled that Belgrade did breach international law by failing to prevent the 1995 Srebrenica genocide, and for failing to try or transfer the persons accused of genocide to the ICTY, in order to comply with its obligations under Articles I and VI of the Genocide Convention, in particular in respect of General Ratko Mladiæ.

UNITED STATES

One of the first accusations of genocide submitted to the UN after the Convention entered into force concerned treatment of Black people in the United States. The Civil Rights Congress drafted a 237-page petition arguing that even after 1945, the United States had been responsible for hundreds of wrongful deaths, both legal and extra-legal, as well as numerous other genocidal abuses. Leaders from the Black community, including William Patterson, Paul Robeson, and W. E. B. DuBois presented this petition to the UN in December 1951.

CONVENTION ON THE RIGHTS OF PERSONS WITH DISABILITIES

The Convention on the Rights of Persons with Disabilities is an international human rights treaty of the United Nations intended to protect the rights and dignity of persons with disabilities. Parties to the Convention are required to promote, protect, and ensure the full enjoyment of human rights by persons with disabilities and ensure that they enjoy full equality under the law. The Convention has served as the major catalyst in the global movement from viewing persons with disabilities as objects of charity, medical treatment and social protection towards viewing them as full and equal members of society, with human rights. It is also the only UN human rights instrument with an explicit sustainable development dimension. The

Convention was the first human rights treaty of the third millennium. Mexico initiated negotiations, with active support from the GRULAC (the Latin American regional group, see United Nations Regional Groups). When support for a Convention was foundering in 2002 due to WEOG opposition, New Zealand played a pivotal role in achieving cross-regional momentum. Acting as facilitator from 2002–03, New Zealand eventually assumed the formal role of Chair of Ad Hoc Committee and led negotiations to a consensus agreement in August 2006, working closely with other Bureau members Jordan, Costa Rica, the Czech Republic, and South Africa, as well as Korea and Mexico. The Convention became one of the most quickly supported human rights instrument in history, with strong support from all regional groups. 155 States signed the Convention upon its opening in 2007 and 126 States ratified the Convention within its first five years. In recognition of its role in creating the Convention, as well as the quality of New Zealand's landmark national Disability Strategy, the New Zealand Head of State was honoured with the World Disability Award in 2008.

The text was adopted by the United Nations General Assembly on 13 December 2006, and opened for signature on 30 March 2007. Following ratification by the 20th party, it came into force on 3 May 2008. As of October 2013, it has 158 signatories and 138 parties, including the European Union (which ratified it on 23 December 2010 to the extent responsibilities of the member states were transferred to the European Union). The United States Senate failed to ratify the Convention on December 3, 2012, as ratification received just 61 of the 67 votes (2/3 of the Senate) required for ratification. The Convention is monitored by the Committee on the Rights of Persons with Disabilities.

GENESIS

1981 to 1992 was the UN "Decade of Disabled Persons". In 1987, a global meeting of experts to review progress recommended that the UN General Assembly should draft an international convention on the elimination of discrimination against persons with disabilities. Draft convention outlines were proposed by Italy and subsequently Sweden, but no consensus was reached. Many government representatives argued that existing human rights documents were sufficient. Instead, non-compulsory "Standard Rules on the Equalisation of Opportunities for Persons with Disabilities" were adopted by the General Assembly in 1993. In 2000, leaders of five international disability NGOs issued a declaration, calling on all governments to support a Convention. In 2001, the General Assembly, following a proposal by Mexico, established an Ad Hoc Committee to consider proposals for a comprehensive and integral convention to promote and protect the rights and dignity of persons with disabilities, based on a holistic approach. Disability rights organisations, including the International Disability Alliance as coordinator of an ad hoc International Disability Caucus, participated actively in the drafting process, in particular seeking a role for disabled people and their organisations in the implementation and monitoring of what became the Convention.

SUMMARY

The Convention follows the civil law tradition, with a preamble, in which the principle that "all human rights are universal, indivisible, interdependent and interrelated " of Vienna Declaration and Programme of Action is cited, followed by 50 articles. Unlike many UN covenants and conventions, it is not formally divided into parts.

Article 1 defines the purpose of the Convention:

- To promote, protect and ensure the full and equal enjoyment of all human rights and fundamental freedoms by all persons with disabilities, and to promote respect for their inherent dignity

Articles 2 and 3 provide definitions and general principles including communication, reasonable accommodation and universal design.

Articles 4–32 define the rights of persons with disabilities and the obligations of states parties towards them. Many of these mirror rights affirmed in other UN conventions such as the International Covenant on Civil and Political Rights, International Covenant on Economic, Social and Cultural Rights or the Convention Against Torture, but with specific obligations ensuring that they can be fully realised by persons with disabilities.

Rights specific to this convention include the rights to accessibility including the information technology, the rights to live independently and be included in the community (Article 19), to personal mobility (article 20), habilitation and rehabilitation (Article 26), and to participation in political and public life, and cultural life, recreation and sport (Articles 29 and 30). In addition, parties to the Convention must raise awareness of the human rights of persons with disabilities (Article 8), and ensure access to roads, buildings, and information (Article 9).

Articles 33–39 govern reporting and monitoring of the convention by national human rights institutions (Article 33) and Committee on the Rights of Persons with Disabilities (Article 34). Articles 40–50 govern ratification, entry into force, and amendment of the Convention. Article 49 also requires that the Convention be available in accessible formats.

CORE PROVISIONS

Guiding principles of the Convention

There are eight guiding principles that underlie the Convention:

1. Respect for inherent dignity, individual autonomy including the freedom to make one's own choices, and independence of persons

2. Non-discrimination
3. Full and effective participation and inclusion in society
4. Respect for difference and acceptance of persons with disabilities as part of human diversity and humanity
5. Equality of opportunity
6. Accessibility
7. Equality between men and women
8. Respect for the evolving capacities of children with disabilities and respect for the right of children with disabilities to preserve their identities

Definition of disability

The Convention adopts a social model of disability, and defines disability as including

- Those who have long-term physical, mental, intellectual or sensory *impairments* which in interaction with various barriers may hinder their full and effective participation in society on an equal basis with others.

Principle of "reasonable accommodation"

The Convention defines "reasonable accommodation" to be "necessary and appropriate modification and adjustments not imposing a disproportionate or undue burden, where needed in a particular case, to ensure to persons with disabilities the enjoyment or exercise on an equal basis with others of all human rights and fundamental freedoms" at the Article 2 and demands this all aspects of life including inclusive education.

Prevention of discrimination

The Article 8 of Convention stresses the awareness raising to foster respect for the rights and dignity against discrimination:

- To raise awareness throughout society, including at the family level, regarding persons with disabilities, and to foster respect for the rights and dignity of persons with disabilities.
- To combat stereotypes, prejudices and harmful practices relating to persons with disabilities, including those based on sex and age, in all areas of life.
- To promote awareness of the capacities and contributions of persons with disabilities.
- Initiating and maintaining effective public awareness campaigns designed:
  - To nurture receptiveness to the rights of persons with disabilities.
  - To promote positive perceptions and greater social awareness towards persons with disabilities.

- To promote recognition of the skills, merits and abilities of persons with disabilities, and of their contributions to workplace and the labour market.
- Encouraging all organs of the mass media to portray persons with disabilities in a manner consistent with the purpose of the present Convention.
- Promoting awareness-training programmes regarding persons with disabilities and the rights of persons with disabilities.

Accessibility

The Convention stresses that persons with disabilities should be able to live independently and participate fully in all aspects of life. To this end, States Parties should take appropriate measures to ensure that persons with disabilities have access, to the physical environment, to transportation, to information and communications technology, and to other facilities and services open or provided to the public.

Situations of risk and humanitarian emergency

Article 11 of the Convention affirms that States Parties shall take, in accordance with their obligations under international law, including international humanitarian law and international human rights law, all necessary measures to ensure the protection and safety of persons with disabilities in situations of armed conflict, humanitarian emergencies and the occurrence of natural disaster.

Recognition before the law and legal capacity

Article 12 of the Convention affirms the equal recognition before law and legal capacity of the persons with disabilities.

States Parties should:

- Reaffirm that persons with disabilities have the right to recognition everywhere as a person before the law.
- Recognize that persons with disabilities enjoy legal capacity on an equal basis with others in all aspects of life.
- Take appropriate measures to provide access by persons with disabilities to the support they may require in exercising their legal capacity.
- Ensure that all measures that relate to the exercise of legal capacity provide for appropriate and effective safeguards to prevent abuse in accordance with international human rights law. Such safeguards shall ensure that measures relating to the exercise of legal capacity respect the rights, will and preferences of the person, are free of conflict of interest and undue influence, are proportional and tailored to the person's circumstance, apply for the shortest time possible

and are subject to regular review by a competent, independent and impartial authority or judicial body. The safeguards shall be proportional to the degree to which such measures affect the person's rights and interests.

Access to justice

Article 13 of the Convention affirms the effective access to justice for persons with disabilities, stating that:

- States parties shall ensure effective access to justice for persons with disabilities on an equal basis with others, including through the provision of procedural and age-appropriate accommodations, in order to facilitate their effective role as a direct and indirect participants, including as witnesses, in all legal proceeding, including at investigative and other preliminary stages.
- In order to help to ensure effective access to justice for persons with disabilities, states Parties shall promote appropriate training for those working in the field of administration of justice, including police and prison staff. This Article together with the Article 12 are cited by the "Handbook on prisoners with special needs" by United Nations Office on Drugs and Crime.

Right to education

The Convention states that persons with disabilities should be guaranteed the right to inclusive education at all levels, regardless of age, without discrimination and on the basis of equal opportunity.

States Parties should ensure that:

- Children with disabilities are not excluded from free and compulsory primary education, or from secondary education;
- Adults with disabilities have access to general tertiary education, vocational training, adult education and lifelong learning;
- Persons with disabilities receive the necessary support, within the general education system, to facilitate their effective education; and
- Effective individualized support measures are put in place to maximize academic and social development.

States Parties should take appropriate measures, such as:

- Endorsing the learning of Braille, alternative script, augmentative and alternative modes, means and formats of communication and orientation and mobility skills, and facilitating peer support and mentoring;
- Supporting the learning of sign language and promoting the linguistic identity of the deaf community;
- Advocating that education of persons, particularly children, who are blind and/or deaf, is delivered in the most appropriate languages and means of communication for the individual; and

- Employing teachers, including teachers with disabilities, who are qualified in sign language and/or Braille, and to train education professionals and staff about disability awareness, use of augmentative and alternative modes and formats of communication, and educational techniques and materials to support persons with disabilities.

Right to health

Article 25 specifies that "persons with disabilities have the right to the enjoyment of the highest attainable standard of health without discrimination on the basis of disability."

Protecting the integrity of the person

Article 17 of the Convention states that every person with disabilities has a right to respect for his or her physical and mental integrity on an equal basis with others.

Respect for the family

Article 23 of the Convention prohibits compulsory sterilization of disabled persons and guarantees their right to adopt children.

Habilitation and rehabilitation

Article 26 of the Convention affirms that "States Parties shall take effective and appropriate measures, including through peer support, to enable persons with disabilities to attain and maintain maximum independence, full physical, mental, social and vocational ability, and full inclusion and participation in all aspects of life. To that end, States Parties shall organize, strengthen and extend comprehensive habilitation and rehabilitation services and programmes, particularly in the areas of health, employment, education and social services, in such a way that these services and programmes:

- Begin at the earliest possible stage, and are based on the multidisciplinary assessment of individual needs and strengths;
- Support participation and inclusion in the community and all aspects of society, are voluntary, and are available to persons with disabilities as close as possible to their own communities, including in rural areas.
- States Parties shall promote the development of initial and continuing training for professionals and staff working in habilitation and rehabilitation service.
- States Parties shall promote the availability, knowledge and use of assistive devices and technologies, designed for persons with disabilities, as they relate to habilitation and rehabilitation.

Participation rights

The Convention on the Right of Persons with Disabilities recognised that "that disability results from the interaction between persons with impairments and attitudinal and environmental barriers that hinders their full and effective participation in society on an equal basis with others" and that "persons with disabilities continue to face barriers in their participation as equal members of society."

The Convention makes participation of the disabled one of its principles, stating "The principles of the present Convention shall be:...Full and effective participation and inclusion in society", subsequently enshrining the right of disabled to participate fully and equally in the community, education, all aspect of life (in the context of habilitation and rehabilitation), political and public life, cultural life, leisure and sports.

States Parties should take appropriate measure such as:

- To enables persons with disabilities to have the opportunity to develop and utilize their creative, artistic and intellectual potential, not only for their own benefit, but also for the enrichment of society.
- In accordance with international law, to ensure that law protecting intellectual property rights do not constitute an unreasonable or discriminatory barrier to access by persons with disabilities to cultural materials.
- So that persons with disabilities should be entitled, on an equal basis with others, to recognition and support of their specific cultural and linguistic identity, including sign languages and deaf culture.

Work and employment

Article 27 requires that States Parties recognize the right of persons with disabilities to work, on an equal basis of others; this includes the right to the opportunity to gain a living by work freely chosen or accepted in a labour market and work environment that is open, inclusive and accessible to persons with disabilities. And that States Parties shall safeguard and promote the realization of the right to work, including for those who acquire a disability during the course of employment, by taking appropriate steps, including through legislation, to inter alia:

- Prohibit discrimination on the basis of disability with regard to all matters concerning all forms of employment, continuance of employment, career advancement and safe and healthy working conditions;
- Protect the rights of persons with disabilities, on an equal basis with others, to just and favourable conditions of work, including equal opportunities and equal remuneration for work of equal value, safe and healthy working conditions, including protection from harassment, and the redress of grievances;
- Ensure that persons with disabilities are able to exercise their labour and trade union rights on an equal basis with others;
- Enable persons with disabilities to have effective access to general

technical and vocational guidance programmes, placement services and vocational and continuing training;

- Promote employment opportunities and career advancement for persons with disabilities in the labour market, as well as assistance in finding, obtaining, maintaining and returning to employment;
- Promote opportunities for self-employment, entrepreneurship, the development of cooperative and starting one's own business.
- Ensure that reasonable accommodation is provided to persons with disabilities in the workplace.
- Promote the acquisition by persons with disabilities of work experience in the open labour market.
- Promote vocational and professional rehabilitation, job retention and return-to-work programmes for persons with disabilities.

States Parties shall ensure that persons with disabilities are not held in slavery or in servitude, and are protected, on an equal basis with others, from forces or compulsory labour.

Adequate standard of living and social protection

Article 28 requires that States Parties recognize the right of persons with disabilities to an adequate standard of living for themselves and their families, including adequate food, clothing and housing, and to the continuous improvement of living conditions, and shall take appropriate steps to safeguard and promote the realization of this rights without discrimination on the basis of disability. States Parties recognize the right of persons with disabilities to social protection and to the enjoyment of that rights without discrimination on the basis of disability, and shall take appropriate steps to safegurad and promote the realization of the rights, including measures;

- To ensure equal access by persons with disabilities to clean water service, and to ensure access to appropriate and affordable service, device and other assistance for disability-related needs.
- To ensure access by persons with disabilities, in particular women and girls with disabilities and older persons with disabilities, to social protection programmes and poverty reduction programmes.
- To ensure access by persons with disabilities and their families living in situations of poverty to assistance from the State with disability-related expenses, including adequate training, counselling, financial assictance and respite care.
- To ensure access by persons with disabilities to public housing programmes.
- To ensure equal access by persons with disabilities to retirement benefits and programmes.

Right to vote

Article 29 requires that all Contracting States protect "the right of persons with disabilities to vote by secret ballot in elections and public referendums". According to this provision, each Contracting State should provide for voting equipment which would enable disabled voters to vote independently and secretly. Some democracies, e.g., the US, Japan, Netherlands, Slovenia, Albania or India allow disabled voters to use electronic voting machines or electronic aides which help disabled voters to fill the paper ballot. In others, among them Azerbaijan, Kosovo, Canada, Ghana, United Kingdom, and most of African and Asian countries, visually impaired voters can use ballots in Braille or paper ballot templates. Many of these and also some other democracies, Chile for example, use adjustable desks so that voters on wheelchairs can approach them. Some democracies only allow another person to cast a ballot for the blind or disabled voter. Such arrangement, however, does not assure secrecy of the ballot. Article 29 also requires that Contracting States ensure "that voting procedures, facilities and materials are appropriate, accessible and easy to understand and use." In some democracies, i.e. Sweden and the US, all the polling places already are fully accessible for disabled voters.

RESERVATIONS

A number of parties have made reservations and interpretative declarations to their application of the Convention.

- Australia does not consider itself bound to stop forcibly medicating those labeled mentally ill.
- El Salvador accepts the Convention to the extent that it is compatible with its constitution.
- Malta interprets the right to health in Article 25 of the Convention as not implying any right to abortion. It also reserves the right to continue to apply its own election laws around accessibility and assistance.
- Mauritius does not consider itself bound by the Article 11 obligation to take all necessary measures to protect people with disabilities during natural disasters, armed conflict or humanitarian emergencies, unless permitted by domestic legislation.
- The Netherlands interprets the right to life in Article 10 within the framework of its domestic laws. It also interprets Article 25(f), which bars the discriminatory denial of health care, as permitting a person to refuse medical treatment, including food or fluids.
- Poland interprets Articles 23 and 25 as not conferring any right to abortion.
- The United Kingdom has reservations relating to the right to education, immigration, service in the armed forces and an aspect of social security law.

OPTIONAL PROTOCOL

The Optional Protocol to the Convention on the Rights of Persons with

Disabilities is a side-agreement to the Convention which allows its parties to recognise the competence of the Committee on the Rights of Persons with Disabilities to consider complaints from individuals. The text is based heavily on the Optional Protocol to the Convention on the Elimination of All Forms of Discrimination against Women.

The Optional Protocol entered into force with the Convention on 3 May 2008. As of September 2012, it has 92 signatories and 78 parties.

COMMITTEE ON THE RIGHTS OF PERSONS WITH DISABILITIES

The Committee on the Rights of Persons with Disabilities is a body of human rights experts tasked with monitoring the implementation of the Convention. It initially consisted of 12 independent human rights experts, with half elected for a two-year term and half elected for four-years. Thereafter members will be elected for four-year terms, with half the members elected every two years.

As the Convention has achieved 80 ratifications, the Committee will be expanded to 18 members.

INTERNATIONAL CONVENTION FOR THE PROTECTION OF ALL PERSONS FROM ENFORCED DISAPPEARANCE

The International Convention for the Protection of All Persons from Enforced Disappearance (ICCPED) is an international human rights instrument of the United Nations and intended to prevent forced disappearance defined in international law, crimes against humanity. The text was adopted by the United Nations General Assembly on 20 December 2006 and opened for signature on 6 February 2007. It entered into force on 23 December 2010. As of September 2013, 93 states have signed the convention and 40 have ratified it.

Following a General Assembly resolution in 1992 containing a 21 article declaration about enforced disappearance, and its resolution of 1978 requesting that recommendations be made, the Commission on Human Rights established an "inter-sessional open-ended working group to elaborate a draft legally binding normative instrument for the protection of all persons from enforced disappearance" in 2001.

The Group concluded its work in 2006 and its draft international convention was adopted by the Human Rights Council on 29 June 2006, and welcomed the offer by France to host the signing ceremony.

On 20 December 2006, the General Assembly adopted without a vote the text of the Convention and opened it for signature at the signing ceremony in Paris. The convention is modelled heavily on the United Nations Convention Against Torture.

"Enforced disappearance" is defined in Article 2 of the Convention as

- The arrest, detention, *abduction* or any other form of deprivation of liberty by agents of the State or by persons or groups of persons acting with the authorization, support or acquiescence of the State, followed by a refusal to acknowledge the deprivation of liberty or by concealment of the fate or whereabouts of the disappeared person, which place such a person outside the protection of the law.

Article 1 of the Convention further states that

- No exceptional circumstances whatsoever, whether a state of war or a threat of war, internal political instability or any other public emergency, may be invoked as a justification for enforced disappearance.

The widespread or systematic use of enforced disappearance is further defined as a crime against humanity in Article 6.

Parties to the convention undertake to:

- Investigate acts of enforced disappearance and bring those responsible to justice;
- Ensure that enforced disappearance constitutes an offence under its criminal law;
- Establish jurisdiction over the offence of enforced disappearance when the alleged offender is within its territory, even if they are not a citizen or resident;
- Cooperate with other states in ensuring that offenders are prosecuted or extradited, and to assist the victims of enforced disappearance or locate and return their remains;
- Respect minimum legal standards around the deprivation of liberty, including the right for imprisonment to be challenged before the courts;
- Establish a register of those currently imprisoned, and allow it to be inspected by relatives and counsel;
- Ensure that victims of enforced disappearance or those directly affected by it have a right to obtain reparation and compensation. (Article 24. 4)
- The right to obtain reparation covers material and dangers and, where appropriate, other forms of reparation such as; a) Restitution. b) Rehabilitation. c) Satisfication, including restoration of dignity and reparation. d) Guarantee of non-repetition. (Article 24. 5)

The Convention will be governed by a Committee on Enforced Disappearances elected by its parties. Parties are obliged to report to this committee on the steps they have taken to implement it within two years of becoming subject to it.

The Convention includes an optional complaints system whereby citizens of parties may appeal to the Committee for assistance in locating a disappeared person. Parties may join this system at any time, but may only opt out of it upon signature.

RESERVATIONS

New Zealand

While the New Zealand government supports the Convention and joined the consensus leading to its adoption, it retains significant concerns around inconsistencies between the convention and established international law. These include the definition of enforced disappearance as a crime against humanity in Article 5, and the Article 6 provisions relating to command responsibility. According to an MFAT spokesperson, New Zealand "has no immediate plans" to sign or ratify the Convention

United Kingdom

The United Kingdom stated its position during the discussion that followed the adoption of the General Assembly resolution on several technical points about the Convention. For example, on Article 18, which sets out the minimum information that a lawyer or relative of a person deprived of liberty should have access to (such as when the arrest took place, who gave the order, and the health of the person), the ambassador explained that if the deprivation of liberty of a person was done legally according to the laws of the country, and was not an "enforced disappearance", then such information could be withheld from the relatives and legal counsel.

A question asked in Parliament about whether there was any intention to sign the Convention, resulted in the answer that the Government needed "to conduct a detailed analysis of the provisions of the treaty and their implications for implementation in order to determine the UK's position towards ratification".

United States

A question during the daily State Department Press briefing that coincided with the date of the signing ceremony resulted in the following exchange:

- *QUESTION:* Did you notice that 57 countries signed a treaty today that would basically bar governments from holding secret detainees and the U.S. did not join?
- *MR. MCCORMACK:* Yeah. This is — I understand that there is a Convention for the Protection of All Persons and Enforced Disappearances. And I know — I have some information on it here, George. I confess I don't have all the details. I do know that we participated in all the meetings that produced the draft. Beyond that, I can't give you specific reasons here from the podium as to why we didn't sign on to it. We've put out a public document that I can give you the citation for afterwards and it explains our reasons for not participating in the draft. But I think just as a general comment,

clearly the draft that was put up for a vote or put for signature was not one that met our needs and expectations.

SIGNATORIES AND RATIFICATIONS

The Convention attracted 57 signatures when opened for signature in Paris. Controversially, the United States refused to sign, saying that "did not meet our expectations". A number of European countries also refused to become parties. These included the United Kingdom, Spain, Italy, Germany, and the Netherlands.

The initial signatories were France, Albania, Algeria, Argentina, Austria, Brazil, Burkina Faso, Burundi, Congo, Croatia, Ghana, Guatemala, Haiti, Japan, Lithuania, Maldives, Moldavia, Morocco, Uganda, Senegal, Serbia, Sierra Leone, Macedonia, Chad, Tunisia, Vanuatu, Belgium, Bolivia, Bosnia Herzegovina, Cameroon, Cape Verde, Chile, Comoros, Costa Rica, Cuba, Cyprus, Finland, Grenada, Honduras, India, Kenya, Lebanon, Luxembourg, Madagascar, Malta, Mexico, Monaco, Mongolia, Montenegro, Niger, Paraguay, Portugal, Samoa, Sweden, Uruguay, Mali, and Azerbaijan

The Republic of Ireland signed the Convention on 29 March 2007. Armenia signed on 10 April 2007, Ecuador on 24 May 2007 and Italy on 3 July 2007. Colombia, Denmark, Gabon, Germany, Liechtenstein, Norway, Panama, Slovakia, Slovenia, Spain and Swasiland signed the Convention between September and December 2007. The Netherlands signed in 2008, while Indonesia, Lesotho, Togo and Zambia signed in 2010 and Switzerland in 2011. As of January 2011, Albania, Argentina, Armenia, Bolivia, Burkina Faso, Chile, Ecuador, Gabon, Germany Mexico, Nigeria, Honduras, France, Senegal, Spain, Cuba, Kazakhstan, Uruguay, Mali, Paraguay, Japan and Iraq had ratified the Convention, Iraq being the twentieth. Lithuania became the 40th state to ratify in August 2013.

INTERNATIONAL CAMPAIGN FOR THE CONVENTION

The International Coalition against Enforced Disappearances (ICAED) is a global network of organisations of families of disappeared and NGO's campaigning in a nonviolent manner against the practice of enforced disappearances at the local, national and international level. The ICAED was founded in 2007 as a result from the 25 year long struggle of families of disappeared and human rights defenders for an international legally binding instrument against enforced disappearances. The primary purpose of the ICAED is working together towards early ratification and effective implementation of the International Convention for the Protection of all Persons from Enforced Disappearances.

Amnesty International is campaigning for Costa Rica, Pakistan, East Timor, Burundi, Portugal, Morocco, Lebanon, Cape Verde, Serbia, and Paraguay to ratify the convention.

INDIGENOUS AND TRIBAL PEOPLES CONVENTION, 1989

Indigenous and Tribal Peoples Convention, 1989 is an International Labour Organization Convention, also known as ILO-convention 169, or C169. It is the major binding international convention concerning indigenous peoples, and a forerunner of the Declaration on the Rights of Indigenous Peoples.

It was established in 1989, with the preamble stating:

- Noting the international standards contained in the Indigenous and Tribal Populations Convention and Recommendation, 1957, and
- Recalling the terms of the Universal Declaration of Human Rights, the International Covenant on Economic, Social and Cultural Rights, the International Covenant on Civil and Political Rights, and the many international instruments on the prevention of discrimination, and
- Considering that the developments which have taken place in international law since 1957, as well as developments in the situation of indigenous and tribal peoples in all regions of the world, have made it appropriate to adopt new international standards on the subject with a view to removing the assimilationist orientation of the earlier standards, and
- Recognising the aspirations of these peoples to exercise control over their own institutions, ways of life and economic development and to maintain and develop their identities, languages and religions, within the framework of the States in which they live, and
- Noting that in many parts of the world these peoples are unable to enjoy their fundamental human rights to the same degree as the rest of the population of the States within which they live, and that their laws, values, customs and perspectives have often been eroded.

Index